THE PARKING LOT RAPIST

A DETECTIVE'S ACCOUNT OF HOW A POLICE DEPARTMENT BROUGHT DOWN A KILLER

LEE DEVORE

Genius
Book Publishing

Published by: Genius Book Publishing, PO Box 250380 Milwaukee Wisconsin 53225

https://GeniusBookPublishing.com

Cover Art by Rich Wickliffe

ISBN: 978-1-958727-39-3

240721 LH Digest

CONTENTS

PROLOGUE

Friday, January 2, 1976

THE LAST DAY of nineteen-year-old Gina Marie Tisher's life started out well. Gina slept in that morning because she had the day off. She planned to meet her mom Betty later that afternoon. Recently, they'd had a misunderstanding about something so small she couldn't even remember exactly why they had been arguing. Gina was anxious to mend their relationship and spend some quality time with her mom. After her mom's divorce, Betty had been living in an apartment in a nearby city in Orange County, California. Gina had been upset by the divorce as Donald Maloney was more like a real father than a stepfather. She had been raised by Donald, and he was the only father she really knew. Even after the divorce, Gina maintained a good relationship with him.

At thirty-two degrees, the day was a little on the cold side, especially for Southern California. However, it was expected to be almost sixty by the time Gina would leave her home in Whittier, a community southeast of Los Angeles, for her mom's apartment in Anaheim, a couple of miles from Disneyland. You could see the Disney Matterhorn replica from her mom's neighborhood, a fact that had always fascinated Gina. Sometimes, when the sun hit it just right, it looked like the real thing, with glistening snowcapped sides. She was looking forward to having a fun day with her mom—doing some shopping and having a chance to talk.

Gina was content and elated with her life. She had just turned nineteen two weeks earlier and couldn't help but be excited by how well everything was turning out for her. At five-two and a hundred-and-two pounds, she was a beautiful young woman with short brown hair and striking blue eyes. Her happy nature made her popular with everyone. She had recently married Charles Tisher, age twenty-five, the love of her life, and they were beginning their new future together. Both had good jobs, they even worked together at Board Ford in Whittier. They were happy with their jobs, with their new apartment, and with each other. Charles was tall, good looking, full of fun, and well liked. Life was very good for the young couple, and they were looking forward to their future together.

Gina arrived at her mom's at approximately two o'clock, the drive from Whittier to Anaheim having taken longer than expected. She had forgotten it was Friday, and the beginning of the weekend "exodus" from the Southern California basin. Gina picked up her mother, and they headed for Don Burns Volkswagen, Gina's previous employer in Garden Grove, to get a paycheck that was waiting for her. After visiting for a few minutes with her former colleagues, Gina and her mom decided to go to the West Anaheim Shopping Center. Gina bought a small item for her new apartment from Country Kitchen and a sweater at Robinson's department store for her friend's birthday. Just before five, Gina drove her mom back to her apartment then left to do some errands before going home. As she was leaving, Gina said, "I love you, Mama."

Gina was happy with how the day had gone. She and her mom had been able to talk out the issues that stood between them and reach a mutual understanding. Looking at her watch,

Gina remembered she needed to hurry to the dry cleaners in Whittier to pick up some clothing before they closed. Traffic at that hour could be unbearable, especially on a Friday, and there was no painless way to get back to Whittier from West Anaheim. She decided it would be easier to take surface streets all the way and avoid the gridlock of the freeway.

At nine o'clock, his quitting time, Charles Tisher waited for Gina to pick him up. It had been a long day, and he was anxious to spend the rest of the evening with his new wife. When she didn't show up, Charles started to get worried. It wasn't like Gina to be late. What Charles didn't realize as he waited was that he would never see his beautiful young wife again.

Gina Marie Tisher in her wedding Dress 1976

CHAPTER 1
THE MURDER OF GINA MARIE TISHER

Friday, January 2, 1976
Whittier, California

THE RAPIST KNEW EXACTLY what he was looking for. He always knew when he had found the right one. Until he found her, he continued to walk aimlessly through the Whittier shopping center. He followed one young woman, but she never left the security of the crowded center. He followed another younger girl and thought she might be the one, but she kept looking back at him nervously. He would stop and look in the shop windows pretending to be interested in the merchandise. Finally, he gave up on her and went back into the parking lot to look for another.

He knew he should be at work. He had just gotten the job at the Chevron Station and had promised his common-law wife Mollye he would stay with it this time and not lose this job as he had the others. But when the urge came over him to follow a girl, he could not seem to help himself. He had to do it again, as he had many times before. He couldn't remember exactly when it started, but it had been going on for a while now. He couldn't stop. It used to be he could go for weeks before the impulse came over him, but lately, it seemed to happen more often. He couldn't explain why.

From the transcribed confession of the killer:

I was supposed to be at work, but that urge came over me, and something was driving me to go look for a girl. I was talking to myself. I drove around for a long time, and then I was at the Whitwood Shopping Center in Whittier. I was hanging around there a long time also. I was about to give up and go home, and I was walking through a rear exit or something. There was a dry cleaner by a Vons or an Albertsons. It's a shopping center, and there was a grocery store there, and there are a couple of little businesses there, and there's a dry cleaner. And she was putting her clothes in [the car] from the dry cleaners, and I walked on by her, and I started to go around her car, and I looked back and she was having a hard time. And I turned around, and I looked, and there wasn't anybody watching. She had long dark hair. She was wearing a dress, and I think a sweater, nylons, and shoes. She was pretty, young, and I think she was about twenty or twenty-two years old. She was sophisticated looking, but not the kind of sophisticated where they have an air about them. She was driving a newer gold or brown-colored Granada.

So, anyway, she was putting the clothes in, and I turned around, and I walked back around her and walked right up to her, and by then she had gotten into the car. I was standing there, and then I turned around, and I walked back behind the car, and just as I got behind it, I turned, and I looked into the back window, and she was just about started up, and she reached around and messed with the clothes again or something and she saw me. I pointed to her left rear tire and said, "Ah, you aren't gonna get far with that tire like that." Or something, and she said, "OK." So, I started to walk away, and I turned around, and I looked at her, and I said, "Did you hear what I said?" And she said, "What?" I was yelling at her or something. I walked back around to the driver's side of the car, and I reached down, and I kicked the tire or something, and I said, "You've got a flat tire here." She said, "I do?" And she cracked the door open.

As soon as she got the door open, I pulled the gun out and stuck it in her face. I said, "Scoot over." She said, "What?" I said, "Scoot over, right now, quick. Don't give me no shit, just scoot over, scoot your ass over." And I pulled the door open, and I jumped in, and half pushed her over, and she slid over. I said, "Give me the keys." She said something like, "What the hell is going on?" I told her, "Just shut up and give me the keys. Put the keys in the ignition." She put the keys in the ignition, and I started the car up. I think it was about five-thirty or six. Yeah, because the banks were still open until six. I drove out of the parking lot across into a tract of homes due east of Whitwood Center, and I pulled around the corner, and I said, "OK, take all the money out of your purse. You haven't got any weapons or anything? Knives or guns or anything like that?" She said, "No, I never had one." "What's in the back seat?" I asked her. She said, "Laundry." And I think she had a present or something for someone. I'm not sure. Anyway, she told me what was in the back seat, and she gave me the money she had. I told her it wasn't enough, and she said they were newlyweds, and they just had a vacation and spent most of their money on vacation or something or other. And I said, "Well, what about a bank account?" She said the car was a rental from the place where her husband works because her car was being worked on or something and that they really didn't have any money. They spent it on their honeymoon. The only thing she had was ten or twenty bucks that she gave me and her paycheck, her paycheck that she had to cash.

She showed the paycheck to me, and I jumped on it, and I said, "OK, we're going to go cash it." Anyway, she told me what bank she banked at, and I said, "Well, where is one of those?" And she said, "Well, where are we?" And I pulled back out to the main street. I don't know the name of it, but anyway I saw the name of it, and I told her, and she said, "OK, well, we've got to go that way." And she named the place. I was going to go to a drive-up window or a walk-up window without going inside the bank, and I told her that. She said, "Well, the only one I know like that is my bank. It is on the other side of town or something. It's a quarter to six now and closes in fifteen minutes so we'll have to hurry."

So, I said, "OK, in the meantime, climb over into the back seat and get on the floor." And it had bucket seats. She got on the floor, and I took off. I was driving with my left hand. I had my gun stuck in the back seat pointed at her in my right hand. I had it stuck between her legs. I took off. I said, "OK, we're coming to (so-and-so) street, which way?" She said the bank was on Imperial. So, I took what I thought I knew was a shortcut or something. Somehow, we got off on a side street and went all over the goddamn place and didn't ever come out. We just kept getting deeper and deeper.

Finally, I told her to get up in the front and show me the way out, and she didn't know where we were. It was about five minutes to six. She said if we go back to Whitwood Shopping Center the bank there was open. I told her that was no go—that there had to be somewhere, a store or some grocery store or somebody that knew her that would cash it. She said she knew of a place or two that had cashed her checks. I said, "For how much?" "Well, for ten or twenty dollars or for the amount of purchase only," and that she didn't know of any place that would take, I think it was a two-hundred-and-forty-dollar check, or something like that, a payroll check. We drove around trying to find a place for a half hour or an hour where she could cash the check, but we never stopped anywhere. And so finally I got pissed off and told her.

Well, she was in the back all that time. She got back in the back from Whitwood before we took off. So, we took off and drove around and looked at these places. Nothing. I got pissed off. I kept sticking … I had the gun between her legs up her skirt, and I kept sticking it into her, poking her, and poking her with it. I drove off up Hacienda Boulevard up over the hills somewhere. I drove back, and I turned off a side road and went halfway back up it—parked underneath this bank that there was a house up on. I told her to get back up in the front seat. I started asking her questions about her family, and when her husband got home from work, where did her parents live. They live in Anaheim; I think—Anaheim or Santa Ana. Did they have any money to buy her back? No, they didn't have much money, but her mom had a turquoise necklace that was worth a thousand dollars or something. I told her, "Well, I could only get ten percent on that. That's only a hundred bucks, and I need five hundred dollars." She said, well, she thought they had a hundred or a hundred and fifty dollars in cash. I told her that was still two hundred dollars short.

I turned back north on Hacienda and got going up over the hill, and she said she didn't know where she could get the money. And so, we got up over the hill, and we started coming down the hill, and I turned right off into the tract of homes again and was driving around in those homes and telling her she had to come up with more money, she had to come up with more money. And she couldn't do it. I said, "Well, you've got to come up with some collateral or something to make up for the money." "Well, you can have the car," she told me. I said, "Well, I already planned to take the car. I can get five hundred bucks for it, but I need a thousand. We're still two hundred and fifty short. You gotta come up with two hundred and fifty dollars' worth of something."

So, we went around and around and around for a while, and finally, I drove up to the City of Industry. I think that is where we ended up, back there in some factories or something. In the meantime, I had convinced her that she could give me two hundred and fifty dollars' worth of sex, and I'd call it even. I had her unbutton her clothes while I was driving, and somewhere along the line I undid my fly, and I'm beating off while she was undressing, I mean while she was undressing, and I was driving.

I went down in front of this factory and pulled behind it. There was a whole row of factories, and I went down to the last one, and I went behind it and parked. I told her just to open up her dress. I think it was a one-piece dress. I told her to open it up and to just climb in the back seat, and she said the seats recline. I told her to show me how to recline the seat, and she did. I told her to take off her shoes. She took off her shoes. Then she took off her nylons. I know she took off her underclothes anyway, and so I started screwing her in her seat. Her back was on the seat. I kept telling her, "Faster! Faster!" She kept going faster and harder. "I want my money's worth; I want my money's worth." She kept working harder and harder. I was playing with her all the while we were doing that, and she started panting and getting in rhythm. She started liking it. I said, "You really like this, don't you? Have you ever been screwed in the ass?" She said, "No." She said, "I think it will hurt." I said, "No it won't. Come on." So, I pulled it out, and she turned over, and she laid across the seat. And I rammed her really hard, and she jerked away, and she said it hurt too much—do it the other way.

So, I said, "OK," and she turned back over. She started going again. I was playing with her tits. We went for about five minutes, and she started coming, and I was chewing on her neck or something. She was saying, "Yeah, yeah," and I was saying, "Yeah, yeah." Tighter and tighter. I started squeezing my muscles tighter and tighter, and I kept squeezing my hands tighter and tighter. I just kept squeezing, and she kept squeezing, and it felt good. She kept squeezing harder and harder and harder, and I come. As soon as I come, she stopped. I took my hands off her, and she just lay there. I felt her neck, and she didn't have any pulse. I felt her wrist, and she didn't have any pulse. I yanked her off me, and I jumped back over in the driver's seat. I started the car back up. I tried to get my pants on, but I couldn't get them on. I jumped out of the car and got dressed, and I got back in the car, and I just kept looking at her, and she was dead, but I couldn't believe she was dead. I just kept expecting her to do something. But she didn't do shit, she just laid there.[1]

So, I put the car in gear and started to drive away, and she fell over against me. I pushed her off me, and I just stopped the car, and I picked her up, and threw her over in the back seat, threw her down on the floor, and I was looking at her, and she didn't do nothing. I took off, and I drove somewhere. I don't know. I drove for a while. I drove, and I drove, and I kept looking at her and driving and looking at her and driving, and nothing happened. I finally ended up on some freeway somewhere. I ended up on the Pomona Freeway. Yeah, the Pomona Freeway going east. I had all the windows pulled down, and I was going about eighty-five or ninety. I was sweating and going faster, and I had the tape deck turned up full blast. She just lay there. I saw this sign saying the Orange Freeway, or the 57 Freeway or whatever it is, and I turned onto it, and I thought home, I gotta get home. Oh man, I must have done ninety or a hundred down that freeway all the way home.

I got to what I think was Imperial. No, maybe it was Lambert Road. I pulled off, and I stopped. I tried to collect myself. What was I going to do? I reached back, and she was cold. I was sure she was dead then, and I had to get rid of her.

I pulled off on Lambert Road, on the off-ramp, and I just sat there for a second. I turned the tape deck down. I thought, "I gotta wipe my prints off and get out of here." I was really pissed because she was dead. I was really pissed! I reached back, and I

---

1. Even in his confession of this cold-blooded murder, Hulbert attempts to minimize his acts by saying that the victim was "starting to enjoy it" and she kept squeezing, when in fact he was strangling her to death. He also fails to mention the fact he bit her breast so severely the criminalist was able to cast the bite after her death. Throughout these interviews, he never showed any remorse or compassion for his victims or their families.

hit her. I hit her hard on the chest. I hit her right in the sternum because I remember she, ah, gasped or something, and I thought, oh wow, maybe she's going to come back alive. I remember that I got back on the freeway, and I got to Yorba Linda Boulevard, and I got off there. I turned left, and I went over to K-mart. You know the K-mart on Yorba Linda Boulevard and Placentia?

And I drove around the K-mart parking lot for a while, and I parked in there. I just sat for a while, and I smoked a cigarette. Then I tore all the clothes down and the clothes hanger and covered her up. I got out of the car, and I locked it up, and I went into the K-mart, and I bought—what did I buy? Oh yeah, I forgot about the jewelry. I took the jewelry from her when we were parked in Hacienda Heights. She told me it wasn't worth much, and I told her, "I could get something for it." It was a wedding ring set. She told me she didn't know how much her husband had paid for it. I told her it looked like it was worth something. She said there was a green class ring or something. She told me it was jade or an emerald or something and was valuable. So, I took it, and I think she had a watch. I think she had post earrings or something. I took all of that back in Hacienda Heights somewhere.

I went in the K-mart, and I bought something. Shit, I don't know what the hell it was, and I went back to the auto supply section, and I bought some brake fluid. I remember the brake fluid was something somebody told me about, that brake fluid was good for cleaning things. I thought, well, I'll clean up the car with the brake fluid. I bought a can of brake fluid, and I know I got something for, I think I bought a toy for Unity, my daughter, a little mouse, or something.

I went back out to the car, I got in the car, and I was going to wipe it down right there. Then somebody drove into the parking lot that I knew that I thought I knew or that they thought they knew me, or I don't know, and they were driving around and looked at me weird. I thought, "I think I know those people.

That must be why they're driving around me wondering what I'm doing in this nice car."

I started the car up, and I hauled ass out of there and went over to Gemco. It was kind of catty-corner. I drove around the Gemco parking lot for a couple of minutes, and I forgot about what I was doing, and then I followed this girl out to her car, and I was going to get out of the car and go rob her or something, but then I remembered that I had to clean that car up.

So, I drove over by the cleaners and parked in front of a liquor store. The cleaners and the liquor store are by each other in the Gemco parking lot. And I parked there, and I took some kind of rag and dumped brake fluid on it. I spent about five or ten minutes wiping the car down. And I started the car up, and I drove across the parking lot towards Yorba Linda Boulevard, and I stopped again and got the check. I wiped the dash down a couple of times and the steering wheel and a couple of other things down.

Then I drove around, and I got out of the car again in a garage area of some apartments. I poured some of the brake fluid on a rag. I then tried to stuff the can into her vagina, but when I found it wouldn't go, I think I stuffed the rag in. I think I wiped down the outside of the car. I know I locked the car up though, and I walked back up the alley towards State College, and I took the can of brake fluid and chucked it up on the roof of one of the carports, and I got to the end of the carports, back to the parking lot where the taco and pizza places are. I had the car keys, and I threw the keys in the trash. Then I thought, I might want them, so I took 'em back out of the trash, and I chucked 'em up on the corner of the roof.

Well, I walked out of there around Shakey's [pizza restaurant] and started walking. I had cut between the Tic Toc, the gas station, and the pizza place, right through Nutwood, and turned right around the Emporium. I turned right on Nutwood, and I walked along the north side of Nutwood under the underpass, and then I cut across a field or a parking lot. There's a field and a

parking lot there or something, and I cut across it into a fraternity house or whatever that is there. I cut across there and then
over to Commonwealth up off of Nutwood Street, then across
Commonwealth through some more fraternity houses or something, and came out almost across the street from some type of
camping store or, there's a ski shop there and the Sav-On
parking lot, cut across the street behind it, that is on Chapman,
then I went behind it, came back around it, went around the
front, walked in the Sav-On, and was eating an ice cream or
something when I saw Winchell's over on the corner. I decided
to go to Winchell's instead, so I walked over to Winchell's.

I called Ruby[2] on the phone from there. I told her that I'd
been kidnapped. I said I'd been kidnapped by four black guys
that morning, and they dragged me around in the trunk all day
and dumped me out in Irvine, and I'd just gotten this far, and
that I needed a ride the rest of the way home. I think it was
either nine-thirty or ten-thirty. She asked me, "Well, what do you
need, an alibi?" I said, "No, I'm telling you what happened."
She said, "What have you been drinking?" I said, "Forget it,
Ruby, I'm telling you the truth. Just get in touch with Mollye and
tell her I'm on my way home and that I'm OK. I'll walk from
here, and it'll be a little while till I get home. Tell her not to
worry." She said, "OK," she'd get in touch with her.

So, then I called up a Yellow Cab from Winchell's. Then I
went over, and I sat and had a jelly donut and a cup of coffee.
While I was drinking the coffee, the taxi pulled up. We went up
to Commonwealth. I told him I had three or four bucks or something, and he took me as far as Gilbert and Commonwealth to a
McMahan's gas station and let me off there. It was twenty cents
under what I told him I had. That wasn't what I had, but that's
what I told him. And I got out from there, and I walked home.

---

2. Ruby Rose Patterson, the owner of the home the suspect was renting in southwest Fullerton, and the woman who had cared for him when he was a child, after
the death of his mother.

CHAPTER 2
INITIAL INVESTIGATION

Friday, April 23, 2004
Twin Falls, Idaho

THE DAY STARTED PRETTY ROUTINELY. I was the Chief of Police in Twin Falls, a city of about 40,000 in south-central Idaho and I had been there since retiring from the Fullerton Police Department in Orange County, California, in December of 1994.

On that day, I was working at my desk, looking over the activity of the last twenty-four hours, when my secretary, Alice DeLeon, told me about a telephone call I'd received while out of the office the previous afternoon. It was from a young man named David Lee. He had told her I had worked a murder case in 1976 involving a father trying to locate a little boy in California. He said he was that little boy. Now thirty-six years old, he wanted to thank me for helping him and discuss another issue which had to do with his case. Alice did not know what the issue was, but I knew exactly who she was talking about and remembered David well, even after twenty-eight years.

I called him immediately, and we spoke for a few minutes about the past and his life now, before he brought up the other purpose for his call. He said he wanted to discuss a murder that had occurred in June of 1974, in Jones County, Mississippi. That would have been during the time David and his mother Mollye Selfies had been living with a young man at Mollye's parents' home in Jones County, Mississippi. Two years later, in 1976, we had arrested that same young man for murder and rape when I worked for the Fullerton Police Department. This Mississippi incident had occurred when they lived in Jones County, and the case, which was strikingly like the later cases in Orange and Los Angeles Counties, California, was never solved.

The victim, Beverly Ann Moore, nineteen, had been reported missing in early June of 1974, and her badly decomposed body was found in a swampy area outside of town on June 16. I vaguely remembered we had been contacted by investigators from Mississippi when we were working the Hulbert case in 1976.

This case had been bothering David for years as he believed Hulbert had killed Beverly Moore, and he hoped I could talk to Jones County authorities about the possibility Hulbert may have been responsible. Over the next couple of months, I communicated with detectives in Jones County, Mississippi, and sent them information on Hulbert, including fingerprints and photos, but they were not able to put together enough evidence to solve their homicide. For one thing, back in 1974, they had not been able to establish the exact cause of death due to the advanced decomposition of the body from the heat and humidity in that part of the country. The Mississippi police suspected strangulation but were not certain. Also, given how old the case was, they didn't have any DNA evidence that could be compared with that of Ken Hulbert, as the crime preceded its use in police investigations. After hearing the circumstances surrounding their crime, I also became convinced Hulbert was responsible for the murder as there were too many similarities between the California cases and this one to be a coincidence. Unfortunately, there would be no way to prove it.

Speaking with him again after all these years, I thought back to the day when I first met David on January 30, 1976, during the investigation of a series of high-profile kidnappings and rapes. He was a scared eight-year-old boy who looked younger with long, scraggly hair and a sallow complexion. He was very thin, quiet, and subdued. He had a disconnected look often seen in kids who come from troubled families.

David was sitting quietly on a wooden bench on the porch of the Fullerton Police Department, waiting for his mother, who was being interviewed by detectives. He had been living for some time with his mother and her common-law husband, Kenneth Richard Hulbert, who we had just arrested as a suspect in a series of rapes and kidnappings and for killing at least one of his victims. I bought David a candy bar out of the machine downstairs and brought it up to him. He thanked me but didn't say anything else. He opened the candy bar but just continued to look out at the traffic going by on Commonwealth. I would never see David again, although I would hear a lot about him from his father over the years.

Monday, January 5, 1976

That call from David on that Friday in 2004 also took me back to that crisp January morning in 1976 when the body of Gina Marie Tisher, a nineteen-year-old newlywed, was discovered in the carport of an apartment complex in Fullerton, Califocrrnia. At the time, I was a thirty-three-year-old detective sergeant assigned as the supervisor of the Crimes Person Detail at the Fullerton Police Department. I was responsible for supervising all homicide investigations in the city. This investigation started on Monday, January 5, 1976, at approximately eight-thirty, when the desk officer received a call requesting we respond to the Moonraker Apartments, one of the many large east-side apartment complexes located near California State University at

Fullerton. The call was about a suspicious car parked in the carport, a routine call for that area.

Ken Head, a young and very competent patrol officer, was the first officer to arrive. He contacted the manager, Betty Walker. Walker said one of her tenants, Jefferson Grisham, had told her about a suspicious car parked in the carport on the south side of the complex. He said there was either the body of a female or a mannequin in the back seat of the car. He believed we should check it out.

Officer Head talked to Jefferson Grisham who said he'd first noticed the car, which he described as a late model Ford Granada, parked in Space D of his building sometime on Friday. Grisham couldn't remember what time he had first seen it. When he came out to the garage area on Sunday, January 4, in the late afternoon, the same car was still there. Curious because he knew it was not usually parked there, he approached it and looked inside. He noticed what appeared to be the nylon-clad legs of a female extending upward from the floorboard area of the back seat. Initially thinking they were the legs of a mannequin, he didn't take any further action. However, Grisham said when he left his apartment that morning for work, he was still troubled by what he had seen the previous afternoon. Seeing the car was still there, he reported it to the manager, Betty Walker.

After the conversation in the apartment office, the officer drove Walker and Grisham to the location of the car, still parked in space D. Officer Head identified it as a light tan 1975 Ford Granada with a California dealer plate, number 393-18A.

Approaching the rear passenger side of the car, Officer Head peered into it without touching anything and saw the legs of a female extending upward, just as Grisham had described. He could certainly understand why the witness thought it was a mannequin. He, too, was uncertain as to what exactly he was seeing, although his gut instinct was telling him this was the body of a young woman. The officer noticed there were several items of clothing covering the rest of the body, as though to deliberately conceal it. Looking into the front passenger area, he saw several small items on the floor, including a driver's license in the name of Gina Marie Tisher. This discovery led him to be almost certain what he was looking at was probably a deceased young woman.

Gina Tisher's car in the carport where she was found on January 5, 1976

Officer Head immediately requested a supervisor to respond to the location along with a crime scene investigator. Police radio logs show this request was made at eight fifty-five that morning. While waiting for them to arrive, he was informed by Walker that the tenant assigned to parking space D was Anna Williams and she might be home.

When the uniformed crime scene investigator Officer John

Milligan arrived, he looked into the car and noticed a blue high-heel shoe lying on the floor in the front passenger area. Near the shoe, he saw a purse as well as a credit card with the name Gina M. Maloney. At approximately nine o'clock, the on-duty field sergeant, Ed Baca, arrived at the scene and was briefed on the situation by Ken Head.

Meanwhile, Officer Head contacted Anna Williams. Anna was a schoolteacher who had been on vacation and had not returned home until around two a.m. that morning. She said the Granada was already in her assigned space, so she merely parked one space to the left (south) and went to her apartment. She said she'd been too tired to worry about it then, and besides, it was a common occurrence for visitors to park in her spot. Williams said she had never seen the car in the area before and didn't know who owned it. She had not looked inside the car and had no information on the contents.

Before returning to the carport, Officer Head contacted those in the surrounding apartments but was unable to locate anyone who had seen or heard anything or who had any further information about the car left in space D. During his absence, Sergeant Baca had radioed a request to the police dispatcher for a tow truck to be sent to the scene so they could enter the car and determine for sure if this was the victim of a crime. A few minutes later, a tow truck arrived, and the driver used a thin metal device commonly known as a "Slim Jim" to open the passenger door of the Granada.

It was instantly clear they were looking at the body of a young female victim of a murder. Through identification found in the car, they confirmed her identity her as Gina Marie Tisher, maiden name Maloney, a nineteen-year-old newlywed from Whittier, California. This initial identification was confirmed by her husband later that day. The car was registered to Board Ford in Whittier, a Los Angeles County community only a few miles from the East Fullerton location where they found Tisher's body.

As the homicide investigation supervisor, the dispatcher

called to brief me on the circumstances at the scene. I left the station for the east side and arrived just before Detective Leon Schauperl, who would be the lead investigator. We arrived at approximately nine-thirty that morning.

Schauperl was forty-two years old, tall, physically fit, soft-spoken, and could evaluate a crime scene very quickly. As an experienced detective, he had successfully investigated several major crimes, including homicides. Because of his experience, I was glad he was available for this one. His reputation was that of an outstanding investigator who paid attention to detail, who had legendary interview skills, and possessed the ability to testify in court professionally and in a way that could be easily understood by a jury. When he was interviewing a suspect, you had the impression he was not going to quit until he acquired all their information. His persistence resulted in many confessions from those he interviewed. I had personally seen him convince suspects to talk about their crimes just by getting very close to them and not letting up until they told the truth.

Part of Leon's responsibility as the lead investigator would be to maintain the murder book that was a part of every homicide investigation conducted by the department. The book usually consisted of one or more two-inch-wide black three-ring binders and contained all the documents associated with the investigation. They would continue to fill up as the case progressed. The book was divided into sections, and the information was maintained chronologically in each section. There could be multiple sections in the book, depending on the case, but there were always sections containing the original case reports, crime scene reports, and follow-up reports. A chronological log at the front of the book would guide you to any report, interview, or other information you wanted to review.

Detective Schauperl immediately removed everyone from the crime scene area and had it cordoned off. He also notified the coroner of the crime scene and the location of the murder victim. Next, he assigned a uniformed officer to record the names and the time of the entry of anyone who came to the crime scene area or who had already entered the area so a permanent record would be available for court purposes. Schauperl told the police dispatcher to check with the NCIC (National Crime Information Center) and the California Crime Information Center to see if the victim had been reported missing. That search resulted in their locating a report of a female named Gina Marie Tisher, reported missing on Sunday, January 4, 1976, but who had been missing since Friday evening, January 2nd. It was common practice in those days for police agencies to refuse to take missing reports on adults who had been missing less than twenty-four hours, since most of them returned home with no criminal activity involved. It was a bad idea, and this policy has long since been changed for the safety of those involved and because critical physical evidence could be destroyed by the delay in the event a crime was involved.

Tisher was last known to be driving a tan Granada with dealer plates. She was described as a white, female, adult, nineteen years of age, five-foot-two, and one-hundred five pounds, with brown hair, blue eyes, and wearing a blue dress. Tisher was said to have two moles on her neck. This detailed description fit the body of the female victim in the Ford Granada that Monday morning. Detective Schauperl requested Fullerton's Identification Technician Jim Babcock to assist with the scene. The ID technician was a recent civilian position within the department. Jim Babcock was a fingerprint identification expert, a photographer, and a crime-scene investigator. He was also the supervisor of the department's evidence and one of the uniformed investigators assigned to each shift who performed basic crime scene investigations in more routine cases. He was the first person to occupy that position in Fullerton.

Upon Babcock's arrival, he began to dust the interior and exterior of the vehicle for prints but soon found it had been wiped clean, probably with an oily substance. This was later identified as brake fluid. They never were able to obtain prints from Tisher's car.

Detective Schauperl again interviewed Jefferson Grisham, who had first reported the suspicious vehicle. Grisham repeated the same story he had given to Officer Head but in more detail. Schauperl then contacted Mrs. Walker, who confirmed her conversation with Grisham. Next, he obtained the names of the tenants who occupied the parking stalls next to space D. This information was given to Detectives Chuck Collins and Jerry Storey so they could locate and interview each of them.

It was during this time Captain Davis, the Commander of the Investigation Division, got to the scene. Schauperl and I briefed him on what we knew at that time and on what investigators had completed at the crime scene. Schauperl radioed the dispatcher and requested the Orange County Crime Lab and their identification technicians be called to the scene to help with the search for physical evidence

In the event of major cases, such as homicides and other critical incidents, it was the policy of the Fullerton Police Department to request the assistance of the Orange County Sheriff's Office. The Sheriff's Office identification technicians were full-time civilian employees. They were very well trained and specialized in major crime scene investigations. Because the County had trained criminalists and a complete crime laboratory at their disposal, the office offered their services to all local law enforcement agencies in the County.

The Orange County Crime Lab had an outstanding reputation for quality work, and their state-of-the-art equipment. They were capable of excellent, precise photography of crime scenes; footprint, shoe print, and fingerprint analysis; blood typing and analysis; and firearms identification in addition to many other procedures critical to a homicide investigation.

At around eleven that morning, Identification Technicians Robert Wagner and James Boyles, along with Crime Lab Criminalists James White and Mary Graves, arrived and were briefed by Schauperl. Technician Wagner made another attempt to lift fingerprints but only confirmed Babcock's findings. His report read in part, "Virtually all surfaces of the vehicle that would be suitable for latent fingerprints, including the gear shift, radio and air conditioning knobs, rear view mirrors, instrument panel, doors, the steering wheel, seat release catches, glove compartment door and turn signal lever, had been smeared with a sticky, oily substance, therefore, latent examination proved futile." The killer had made sure his fingerprints would not be found on Tisher's car.

At approximately ten minutes past eleven, Deputy Coroner Harold Minnick arrived. After the crime scene technicians had completed their work, Detective Schauperl was able to get a closer look at the car and the victim. He was able to see that the victim's body was partially covered by a man's maroon sports coat and a black and white plaid sports coat. He also saw a man's shirt and some trousers on a hanger lying near the victim's head.

The victim was wearing a blue dress, open down the front; pantyhose, which had been torn at the waist; then a bra, which was still on but ripped apart in the middle. There was a scarf around her neck that appeared as though it could have been used to strangle her. The only pieces of jewelry she was wearing were two necklaces and a yellow-colored ring with a red setting on her right ring finger. She was not wearing underwear, and there was a cloth stuffed into her vagina.

One of the County criminalists, James White, assisted Schauperl in attempting to locate evidence that might provide leads to what the victim was doing just before her death, or that might lead to the identity of the suspect. They searched the rear seat area and around the body of the victim. They noticed some of the clothing in the car still bore the tags from a cleaning establishment called Our Cleaners, and the hanger labels indicated the business had two locations: the City of Whittier and the unincorporated area of Los Angeles County.

After further searching, they located a State of California tax booklet for the year 1975, addressed to G. M. Maloney, which was the last name of Gina's stepfather and Tisher's maiden name, with an address in Anaheim, CA. In the left backseat was a woman's turtleneck sweater purchased at Robinson's, confirmed by a receipt found in her purse.

Deputy Coroner Minnick then removed Gina from the car. He noted marks on the front of her neck, in the area of the scarf. On the palm of her right hand, there was a mark in the shape of a V and on her right breast was what appeared to be a human bite. On the inside bottom of Gina's dress, they located a red stain. There was a similar stain on the back of the right front seat.

Criminalist White also checked the contents of the victim's purse and wallet for possible leads or any other evidence. He located a check made out to Gina Tisher from Don Burns Volkswagen, located in Garden Grove, California, dated Thursday, January 1, 1976. In the wallet, he found a birth certificate for Gina Marie Gavin from the State of Arizona with a date of birth of December 22, 1956, which was later confirmed to be the birth name of Gina Marie Tisher. In her checkbook, Schauperl noted the check record was complete to the last check written to Our Cleaners on Friday, January 2, 1976.

Apartment Complex where Gina Tisher's Body Was Found

After completing the search, Deputy Coroner Minnick sealed the Tisher car and had it towed to the Orange County Sheriff's Crime Lab garage for further examination. To preserve the chain of evidence, Detective Chuck Collins followed the car to the garage so anything discovered in the car could be used in court. Evidence not carefully handled in this way could end up being inadmissible. Any break in the "chain of evidence" could be a crack big enough to let a killer wiggle free. The deceased, who we were now sure was nineteen-year-old Gina Marie Tisher, was tagged by Deputy Coroner Minnick and transported to the Orange County Medical Center morgue.[1]

While they removed Gina from the car, Sergeant H. B. Saint of the L. A. Sheriff's Office homicide detail arrived at our location with a copy of the missing person report they had taken. Sergeant Saint confirmed the report had been made by the victim's husband, Charles Robert Tisher, to the Norwalk Substation on Sunday, January 4, but the victim had been missing since late Friday afternoon, January 2, 1976. According to the report, the last time she had been seen was approximately five-thirty on Friday evening when she picked up some cleaning from Our Cleaners in the Whitwood Mall.

Sergeant Saint said he had talked with Don Maloney, the stepfather of the victim, after they had taken the missing report on Sunday. Maloney had advised him that a David Carpenter, who had been employed by McClure Lincoln Mercury, had called the victim before Christmas, and insisted Gina go shopping with him, but she refused. Maloney told Sergeant Saint that Gina considered Carpenter to have a "mental problem" but couldn't elaborate further. Sergeant Saint had also learned from Maloney that David Carpenter worked at Santa Ana Lincoln-

---

1. It was the practice of the Coroner's Office to put a small informational tag on each body that contained the case number, date, and time, and any details known about the individual.

Mercury and lived at 1126 West Glenwood in Santa Ana. Here was a lead we would need to follow up on and soon.

From the facts of this case, we worried Gina Tisher would not be the only victim of this killer. Too many things pointed to the work of a violent, compulsory killer who would rape and kill again if he hadn't already. As I looked down on this beautiful young girl whose life was taken from her so violently, I wondered how many families would be shattered and how many lives would be altered forever by this vicious killer.

Later that day, we began the search for more victims. Some of our detectives recalled receiving teletypes from other police agencies describing similar crimes, which they were able to go back and find information about. Detective Schauperl had already sent out teletypes to all Southern California law enforcement agencies requesting any information on similar crimes. It didn't take long before the teletypes paid off, and we identified matching cases. Unfortunately, as it turned out, we didn't have long to wait to find the next victim, and this one would again be a Fullerton case.

Any experienced homicide investigator knows the first forty-eight hours of a case are the most critical, as leads and evidence can be quickly lost if not worked right away. The longer a case goes, the less chance it will be solved. We had a long way to go on this first day and a lot of evidence to find if we were to solve this one successfully. Nobody went home that night, and we would get very little sleep for the next week.

All the cases that looked like ours listed a suspect that was generally described as a white male adult in his early twenties, between five-foot-nine and six-foot-tall, slim build with light brown hair. His MO (method of operation) in these cases usually followed this pattern: He would watch for young females in shopping center parking lots and approach them as they returned to their car. In some cases, he would tell the victim her car had a flat tire. When she was distracted by this, he would display a small handgun and order her to get inside of her car, forcing her over to the passenger side.

Next, he would get into the driver's seat and drive the victim's car away from the area. Most often, the suspect would rob the victim of money from her purse, dumping the contents on the front passenger floor area, then take any jewelry she might be wearing, such as rings, wedding sets, and watches. On occasion, he would have her write a check and take her to a drive-through window at her bank to cash it or call her parents and extort money from them for the victim's release. As a last act of violence, he would commit a sexual assault on her, usually forcing her to orally copulate him or he would rape or sodomize the victim, and in some cases, he would do all three. He would strangle some of them during the sexual acts and leave them in their car, or he would take the victim's car and abandon it at another location. All the women were attractive, young, white females.

The ten cases we located from other agencies listed here are in chronological order. These are the cases we knew about at that time, but there were more to come.

- Attempted rape in West Covina on October 14, 1975
- Assault and battery in West Covina on October 22, 1975
- Homicide in West Covina on October 27, 1975
- Kidnapping, extortion, and rape in Buena Park on December 2, 1975
- Kidnapping, robbery, and sexual molestation in Whittier on December 7, 1975
- Kidnapping, robbery, and rape in Lakewood on December 9, 1975
- Kidnapping, robbery, and rape in Riverside on December 11, 1975
- Kidnapping, robbery, and assault with intent to commit rape in Lakewood on December 14, 1975

- Attempted kidnapping in Norwalk on December 19, 1975, followed by the last known case as of January 5, 1976
- Kidnapping and robbery in Downey. This one occurred just after the attempted kidnap in Norwalk on the same date

It was our custom during a major investigation for all the detectives to meet at least once a day, usually in the late afternoon. The purpose was to compare notes, talk about the progress of the investigation, and assign investigators leads to pursue or interviews to conduct. Often, new leads developed because of detectives talking to potential witnesses.

We met that same Monday afternoon at about three o'clock. We had two interviews set up that afternoon: one with Gina's stepfather and one with her husband. Captain Davis and I would do the interviews. Gina's autopsy would take place later that day and Detectives Schauperl and Storey would attend.[2]

On a hunch, Detective Chuck Collins contacted the Yellow Cab Company to see if they might have picked up a fare in the area where they found the Tisher car. This effort paid off, and a cab driver told Collins he had picked up a fare at approximately eight forty-five on Friday evening, January 2, 1976, at Chapman and State College, and he had dropped him off at Gilbert Street and Commonwealth in the City of Fullerton. He remembered he was a young white male in his twenties but could not describe him any further, and he was not sure he would be able to identify him. The location where he had dropped him off on that Friday evening would become very important later in the investigation.

In summarizing the investigation to this time, we knew we

---

2. It was a requirement of the Coroner's Office that police officers attend the autopsy for the purpose of observation and collection of evidence if needed. Both Detective Burks and Detective Storey were experienced in this detail.

were dealing with the same suspect and that he was responsible for several rapes and at least two murders we knew about at that point. The earliest crime we knew of, that he was probably responsible for, was in October of 1975. It was possible there were other incidents we were not aware of, either because they had not been connected by MO or they had not been reported by the victim. It was also possible some police agencies had not yet seen or responded to our teletypes requesting information on similar cases. There were several common elements of the MO that seemed to be present in most, if not all the cases:

- All the women we were aware of had been approached by the subject in public parking lots during the daylight or early evening hours.
- On some occasions, the perpetrator would tell them they had a flat tire to get them to get out of their vehicle.
- The suspect used a small handgun, probably a semi-automatic, to force his way into the women's cars and would then force them to move over to the passenger seat so he could drive.
- He would often randomly drive them around after kidnapping them.
- Most victims had been strangled, but not all were murdered. There was a distinct possibility the strangulation was for sexual gratification, not necessarily to kill them.
- All of them were young white females and very attractive. All except one were alone when approached. The exception was a young mother with two small children in car seats.
- Some, but not all the women, were robbed by the suspect during the encounter.
- If robbed, their purses were dumped out on the right front floor of their car, and any cash was taken.

- On more than one occasion, he had either attempted or had succeeded in extorting money from the families of the victims. These were small amounts of cash.
- Before abandoning the victim's car, he would wipe it down to destroy any fingerprints.
- Based on the testimony of the cab driver, there was a possibility the suspect lived around Gilbert and Commonwealth in the City of Fullerton.
- All except one of the incidents, the Riverside case, had originated in the southeast part of Los Angeles County or the north part of Orange County, indicating the suspect could very possibly work or live in that general vicinity.[3] A pin map was posted in the conference room of the detective bureau depicting the location of each of the events, and this clearly showed the events were "clustered" in the area indicated above.

At about four-fifty on that same afternoon of January 5, 1976, Captain C.D. Davis and I interviewed Donald Maloney, the step-father of Gina Tisher. Mr. Maloney had been informed of his stepdaughter's death previously. He had agreed to be inter-viewed and represent the family, as the other family members were too devastated to discuss the case with us at that time. Mr. Maloney told us that although he was the stepfather of Gina Tisher, their relationship was more like father and daughter. Visibly shaken by the death of his stepdaughter, Mr. Maloney struggled to recall the events of the past few days that might be important to the investigation.

He recalled that late on Friday evening he had received a telephone call from Gina's husband, Charles Tisher, who told him Gina had not arrived to pick him up from work and he was

---

3. It was later determined the Riverside case was not committed by the same suspect as in the rest of the cases cited.

concerned about her. Maloney said he believed Gina might be with her mother and he told Charles he would attempt to contact her to find out. When Mr. Maloney contacted his former wife, Betty Maloney, she told him Gina had been with her earlier in the afternoon and she had gone with Gina to pick up her check from Don Burns car dealership, then they went shopping at the Broadway in Anaheim and other shops in the immediate area. She said Gina had left Betty's apartment at approximately five o'clock and had told her mom she needed to go to the cleaners and the bank near her home in Whittier. Both were in the Whitwood Mall. According to Betty Maloney, Gina planned on taking surface streets because of the heavy rush hour traffic at that time of the evening. Mr. Maloney told Captain Davis and me that this should have taken her approximately one-half hour, which would have put her in the Whitwood Mall at five-thirty in the evening on the date in question.

After talking with his ex-wife, Mr. Maloney also became very concerned about his daughter's welfare as she was a very reliable and punctual person. He told us that at about eleven-thirty that night after she had not shown up, he became even more concerned and had driven to Whitwood Mall to see if he could spot Gina's car in the parking lot but was unable to locate it anywhere in the area. Mr. Maloney said that by that time of night there were very few cars at the mall. He also told us that after contacting all the family members and friends they could think of and having exhausted all their possibilities, Charles made a police report regarding his missing wife. Mr. Maloney confirmed no one in the immediate family had seen or heard from Gina since she left her mother's home in Anaheim on Friday at five o'clock in the evening. According to her mother, Gina was in a good mood when she left her apartment.

We asked Mr. Maloney if there were any possible associates of his daughter who might be able to offer some information concerning her disappearance, but the only one he could think of was a man his daughter had previously dated named David

Campbell who worked at McClure's Lincoln Mercury in Santa Ana, where Gina had also worked before her marriage to Charles Tisher. Maloney said he knew from conversations with Gina that Campbell had called her several times during the first part of December 1975 and had called again just before Christmas. He didn't know too much about Campbell but had heard he was a "gun nut" and that he too had gotten married. Mr. Maloney reported that Gina's mom said Campbell had attempted to contact Gina at Board Ford Friday morning, January 2, 1976, but had been unsuccessful in reaching her. Mr. Maloney also said his daughter was close to a girl named Bambi Carl, who lived in Claremont, California, and she might know something, but he did not have any other information about her.

It was later determined that David Campbell was actually the David Carpenter mentioned by Sergeant Saint of the Los Angeles Sheriff's Department, and Mr. Maloney had only remembered it as Campbell. At the time, Carpenter was our only viable "person of interest" in the case. Detectives also contacted Bambi Carl, but she had not heard from Gina for about a week.

Next, Captain Davis and I interviewed Gina's husband, Charles Tisher, who was very emotionally upset at the time of our interview. We asked him about any possible friends or associates of his wife who may have had some information about her whereabouts on January 2, 1976, after she had left her mother's house in Anaheim. Mr. Tisher told us he had thought of little else since his wife's disappearance, had been over and over the possibilities in his mind, and the only person who continued to surface was David Campbell (Carpenter), the same name obtained from Gina Tisher's stepfather. Charles Tisher said Campbell had dated Gina before their marriage, and he did not know much about him, other than the fact he had called Gina a few times after their marriage and had attempted to call her at Board Ford on Friday morning, January 2, 1976. He was told about that attempted contact by Gina after Campbell had also called and left a message on their home phone.

Charles Tisher also told us that last Friday he had worked until nine in the evening and Gina was supposed to pick him up at work, as she was driving his lease car. He said it was the same car in which they had found Gina in that morning, the Ford Granada. Tisher said he became worried when she did not pick him up as she was a very dependable person and would not typically be late. He tried to find her, first by calling her stepfather, Donald Maloney, but Maloney told him he had not seen Gina. The men had then checked with Gina's mother, but she had not seen Gina since about five o'clock that evening.

Tisher said, later that night, he and Mr. Maloney had attempted to make a missing report with the Whittier Police Department, but they had refused to take the report as she had not been missing long enough. Charles was not able to offer any further information about the activities of his wife since he reported her missing.

Late Monday afternoon, Detectives Schauperl and Storey interviewed David Carpenter at his home in Santa Ana. He told them he had known Gina since 1972 and they had dated for a while. He said he had worked with her at McClure Lincoln Mercury, until Gina left in 1975. Carpenter said he never saw her again after that but did talk to her on the telephone a couple times. He also admitted talking to Gina on Friday, January 2, 1976, in the early afternoon, again by telephone. (This differed from what Gina had told her husband about Carpenter having left a message.) Carpenter said he had called her at her home to talk about getting together for lunch sometime but did not have any physical contact with her on that day. Carpenter also said Gina told him she was happy to have moved out of the family home as her parents were going through a divorce, and there was a lot of tension in the family.

Carpenter had never used the name Campbell, and this error was probably the result of a faulty recollection from Charles Tisher and passed on to his father-in-law Donald Maloney. The detectives confirmed with Carpenter's employer he had worked on the day in question and had not left the business at any time. As a precaution, they asked him to strip down so they could see if he had any scratch marks or bruises on his body. Carpenter readily complied with the request of the detectives, and he did not have any visible scratches or bruises.

At five-forty that evening, Schauperl and Storey went to the Orange County Medical Center in Irvine to witness the autopsy of Gina Tisher. Also present at the procedure were James White and Mary Graves from the Orange County Sheriff's Crime Lab, who would continue their work in the handling of any evidence obtained in the investigation. In addition, Deputy R. C. Johnson from the Orange County Sheriff's Office was there to photograph any evidence found during the autopsy proceedings. Although it is necessary, detectives never look forward to observing an autopsy. It is, however, part of the job that is unavoidable. Like Detectives Storey and Schauperl, I have seen many autopsies, but have never really gotten used to it. Any time I could avoid witnessing one, I would. It was always a stark reminder of what had been done to the victim and, from that point of view, probably a good idea we attended them.

The autopsy was performed at about six-thirty that evening by Dr. Richards, a very experienced pathologist under contract with the county. He first examined Gina's backside and noted that there were ligature marks on the back of her neck. He continued to examine her from the top of her head to the bottom of her feet. Upon examining her anus, Dr. Richards showed Detective Schauperl what appeared to be tearing. This was an indication she was subjected to anal intercourse. Dr. Richards swabbed the area to check for sperm. It is important to remember this case preceded the discovery of DNA as a positive identifier by several years and, therefore, DNA was not a factor in this investigation.

Dr. Richards then viewed the front side of the body. He took swab samples from the victim's nose, mouth, and vaginal area. On the front of the victim's neck, there were ligature marks noted along with four marks that appeared to be scratches. On the right front side of the victim's neck, they located two more marks. Dr. Richards also located an apparent bite mark on the right breast of Mrs. Tisher, confirming earlier observations at the crime scene. Deputy Johnson photographed the suspected bite mark, and Criminalist White made a silicone cast of the bite.

Dr. Richards indicated in his report, "There is a ligature tied around the neck. The knot is in front, just to the side of the thyroid cartilage. It is sufficiently tied to produce a zone of blanching."[4]

After completion of the autopsy, Dr. Richards told the detectives he believed the cause of death was ligature strangulation, but before saying it was "the official" cause of death, he would await the results of the toxicological examination. This would take several days to obtain from the lab. Dr. Richards also said there was no other cause of death evident from the examination. As it turned out, he was correct, and strangulation with the use of a ligature was the official cause of death.

Tuesday, January 6, 1976

Detective Schauperl interviewed Gina Tisher's mother, Betty Maloney, in her Anaheim apartment the morning after the discovery of her daughter's body. Still in shock, and grieving over the violent loss of her daughter, Betty Maloney told Schauperl that Gina had come to her home on Friday, January 2, 1976, at about two in the afternoon. She and her daughter had gone to the Don Burns Volkswagen dealership to pick up Gina's check. From there they went to the Anaheim Shopping Center in the 500 block of North Euclid Avenue, where Gina had made a purchase from a store known as Country Kitchen. Next, they went to Robinson's department store where she bought a sweater as a gift for a friend. This information corresponded

---

4. A whitening effect on the surface of the skin.

with the receipts and the contents found in the Tisher car during the search the day before. According to Betty Maloney, they were both having a wonderful time spending the afternoon together. When they left Robinson's, Mrs. Maloney asked Gina if she would like to stop and get a Coke, but Gina said she didn't have enough money to stop for a Coke and she still needed to pick up some cleaning and go by her bank on the way home. Mrs. Maloney noted that when Gina dropped her off at her apartment that evening, the clock on the top of the California Federal Building near her home read five o'clock.

Detective Schauperl asked Mrs. Maloney to describe the clothing Gina was wearing when she was with her that Friday afternoon. She said Gina was wearing a scarf, a blue corduroy button-down-the-front dress, nylons, and shoes. She told the detectives that Gina was wearing a white gold wedding ring set with a diamond in the engagement ring surrounded by several rubies along with an older ring that was white gold with an emerald with had an onyx in the middle of the set. There was supposed to have been a diamond in the center of the onyx set, but it was missing, leaving an empty mounting in the center of the ring. She also indicated Gina was wearing a ruby ring of yellow gold and two necklaces, one set with stones.[5] Mrs. Maloney told Detective Schauperl that Gina had left her in a good mood. The last thing her daughter said to her was, "I love you, Mama." Mrs. Maloney never saw her daughter alive again.

The following is an example of the similarity of some of the other crimes to the Fullerton cases, taken from an article in the *Los Angeles Times* on November 13, 1975. The article describes a series of attacks on women in West Covina, all from the Fashion

---

5. Only the ruby ring was on Gina Tisher's finger when she was examined at the crime scene.

Plaza Mall, all occurring in October of 1975. It also demonstrates the fear that existed in the area because of these crimes. They were receiving a lot of attention by the news media and by residents of Southern California. Despite the obvious similarities, the West Covina Police had not yet been able to obtain a conviction in this matter.

> WEST COVINA--Reports of two attempted assaults and a murder have raised fears among some women about shopping at the new Fashion Plaza but Police Chief Allen W. Sill said the center is as safe as any in the valley. "We really haven't had that many problems there," Sill declared.
>
> However, six women picketed Fashion Plaza this week, carrying signs with such messages as: "Don't Park in Secluded Areas" and "Safety in Numbers." Sill said two women reported being accosted at the center last month by men who fled when the women resisted. The murder victim, Mrs. Sharon Aldridge, 23, of Monterey Park, was last seen alive shopping at Fashion Plaza Oct. 27. Her body was found near her car in the parking lot of a medical center a few blocks from Fashion Plaza.
>
> Sill said that Mrs. Aldridge made her final purchase at a Fashion Plaza store at seven-thirty in the evening. Her body was found at ten twenty-two, and the coroner's office placed her time of death at nine forty-five that same evening. She had been strangled.[6]

While the West Covina Police Department was unable to convict Ken Hulbert in their cases, the parents of Sharon Aldridge, a retired minister, and his wife, were convinced this was the same person who had killed their daughter. During the trial, they attended most of the hearings but never received the closure they had hoped and prayed for. At one point, Hulbert

---

6. Article by Times Staff Writer Mike Ward, in the *Los Angeles Times*, November 13, 1975.

asked his attorney to try to get them out of the courtroom because of the way they were looking at him. The judge denied his request. Sharon's parents never doubted that the person on trial, Hulbert, was responsible for the death of their daughter.

The following is a phone interview I conducted with Retired Pastor Max Siesser, father of victim Sharon Aldridge:

Early in September of 2018, many years after I had worked the case, I found out that my cousin, Winnie Long who owned a real estate office in the City of Downey, in Los Angeles County had been personal friends with the parents of Sharon Aldridge, the victim in the West Covina case in which Hulbert was not convicted. During the investigation, we became convinced that he was responsible for it, even though it couldn't be proven in court. Winnie provided me with a telephone number for the victim's father, Max Siesser, a retired pastor.

On September 24, 2018, I called Pastor Siesser and identified myself as the supervisor who had supervised the Hulbert investigation. He was willing to talk to me about his daughter's murder and the case itself.

Sharon's father told me that during this time, he had worked as a chaplain in the Los Angeles County Sheriff's Department and that he had an opportunity to talk to Kenneth [Hulbert] after he had been convicted of the Orange County cases while he was awaiting trial on the Los Angeles County cases. Pastor Siesser said that Hulbert did not confess to killing his daughter Sharon, but that Hulbert asked him, "What do you think of me now?" Pastor Siesser said that he took that as an admission by Hulbert that he was responsible for his daughter's death, even though Hulbert never directly said so.

Pastor Siesser said that he and his wife, Carolyn, who has since passed away, never missed a day of the trial in Santa Ana and that Hulbert definitely saw them in the courtroom. They also sat through the entire trial in Los Angeles County. On the first day of the trial, Hulbert saw them and recognized them from the Santa Ana trial. He asked the judge to have them removed from the courtroom. The judge had the bailiff ask them who they were, and they told him that they were the parents of Sharon Aldridge. The judge refused to ask them to leave and allowed them to remain in the courtroom throughout the trial.

Pastor Siesser did not know what had happened to Hulbert once he had been sentenced and entered the prison system. He said he often wondered how Hulbert was doing in prison and was not aware that Hulbert had committed suicide while there. I gave him that information during our conversation, but this news was not surprising to Pastor Siesser.

CHAPTER 3
LEFT FOR DEAD

Tuesday, January 6, 1976
Orange County, California

ON THE MORNING of January 6, 1976, Fullerton Detectives Storey and Collins had to take a break from the homicide investigation because the suspect in an armed robbery case they had worked required a court appearance in North Orange County Municipal Court in Fullerton. They were concerned the key witness in the case, the clerk from the Tic Toc , a small convenience store located at Placentia and Nutwood Avenue in east Fullerton, did not have a way to get to court. Of note, the Tic Toc was located less than half a block from where Gina Marie Tisher's car was found on Monday, January 5, 1976, just one day earlier.

They called the store and then transported him from his home at 517 Paula Street in southwest Fullerton to the courthouse in downtown Fullerton. Also of interest, his home was only a couple blocks from the intersection of Gilbert Street and Commonwealth Avenue where the taxi driver said he dropped off his male fare on the night of January 2, 1976, the night Gina Tisher was murdered. The detectives did not realize the clerk they were transporting to court was the killer of Gina Marie Tisher. They didn't make the connection until later when the killer was caught and confessed. That same day as his court appearance, he kidnapped a Fullerton College co-ed within a mile of the courthouse where the detectives had dropped him off. This was the second Fullerton case by this suspect.

Carmen Banderas circa 1975

From the transcribed confession of the killer:

I think the next one, that would be the next to the last one. I don't know her name, the girl at FJC (Fullerton Junior College). That was the same morning that I went to testify in court, I guess it was the sixth. I don't know what day it was, but you guys called me up and said I should identify that guy about the Tic Toc robbery, and I went over and did that, and you guys dropped me off, and I roamed around there for a while. I never had the job with the guy or any job interview or anything else I told you guys about. I was carrying a gun the day I went to court. At least I was carrying it for a while. Well, let's see, they let me off at Bob's Big Boy Restaurant right in front of the courthouse. I was carrying it, and I stashed it in the bathroom, in the trash can in the bathroom of the courthouse (they did not have metal detectors at the entrance back then). I went and got it after we were done. I went in the bathroom and picked it up, then went down and got in the car.

I told the detectives that I was meeting my boss at Bob's Big Boy. That I had to meet him for lunch, or I wouldn't have my job anymore. And the detectives dropped me off, and I roamed around that parking lot right below the courthouse thinking what am I going to do now, what am I going to do now? Then I saw some chick or something, and boom, it went off again. I followed her around for a while, and she went shopping or something, and I just walked away and walked around the parking lot looking for someone else. I don't know, I spent a half hour or forty-five minutes walking around that parking lot. Then I looked up and I saw the courthouse, and I thought, well, what am I doing here? I started heading home and started walking up Harbor, and I was going to hitchhike home. And I got to the corner, and I thought I'll go talk to a teacher over at FJC [Fullerton Junior College]. So, I started walking towards the FJC on, whatever that street is right there between Hillcrest and Fullerton Union High School. It was on Berkeley, and I was floating in and out of it again. I was getting paranoid, and I don't know, I was scared. I was sure everybody knew exactly what I was thinking, and I was going to turn around and go back to Bob's.

But I had to. I had to do it. I had to go over there and do it. All I knew was I had to go over there. So I went over to the JC, and I started walking through the parking lot of the JC, and I followed a couple of chicks around and started to move in on them, and then I didn't. I stopped and started to go see Roy, that teacher, and I thought, hopefully, that talking to him would bring me back down to earth or something. I got halfway over to where I thought he might be, and I see a chick again and turn around and start following her and went back and forth, back and forth for I don't know how long—fifteen, twenty, maybe thirty minutes. It was probably one-thirty or one o'clock by then. I remember seeing a clock, and it said five-to-one or some time in there. I don't know, but after going back and forth for a while, I was thinking I had to get the hell out of there. I couldn't handle it anymore, so I took off from the campus somewhere.

I went back up to Berkeley and started walking down Berkeley and around the campus and up across Chapman, over to Lawrence Street. I thought maybe some people I knew when I had lived there might still be there. I got over there, and they weren't there. I thought I'd turn around and started walking down to the school. I walked over to the parking lot by the tennis courts for a couple of minutes. I didn't see anything, and so I started walking back on campus. Then about halfway back on campus, over by the nursery, I saw a couple of girls, and then it was coming over me again. And so, I turned around and started following them, and I don't know if it was just paranoia, but they stopped and went into the Art building. And I knew that they were going in there to avoid me or something, so I just kept on walking, trying to be nonchalant. I was walking in front of the Art building, then across the tennis court parking lot, so I decided to keep walking. I didn't care where I went. I was just going to keep on walking.

I cut across the parking lot out to the sidewalk. I got to the driveway, and I was walking along the sidewalk, and I got to the driveway that ends into the tennis court parking lot, and this girl whips in front of me, pulled right into a driveway about thirty or forty feet from there. Something said, "That's her. Right now, go." So, I just started—I headed over there, and I walked up behind her car, and she was getting her books or something, so I walked on through it to the other side of the parking lot. And then I turned, and I just knew that it was the time to turn around and walk back.

So, I turned around, and I walked back, and just as I went back to the door, she had the door open to get out. I turned around, and I whipped my gun out and said, "Get back in the car right now." She said, "What are you talking about?" I said, "Get your fuckin' ass in the car." She said, "What the hell are you talking about?" I said, "It's a rip-off, I ain't going to tell you again, get your goddamn ass in the car, or I'll blow you away. Get over. Get over." She was fighting me, and I pushed her over. I get her over in the seat, and she said, "What the hell are you doing?" She kept hassling me, and I kept telling her to shut up! "Shut the fuck up, or I'm going to blow you away right here and now. Give me your goddamn keys! Put 'em in your ignition and shut up." She kept telling me she wasn't going to do it. I kept pushing the gun into her, and she kept saying that she wasn't going to do it. I kept pushing the gun into her, pushing it harder and harder, saying I was going to shoot her if she kept giving me shit. All I wanted to do was to rob her. She said, "Well, take my money now, and just get out of here and leave me alone." I said, "No, not here. I'm not getting out here where you can scream. I know better than that. Just shut up. Shut up and look at the dash or something." And, ah, then she handed me the keys, and I couldn't find the right key. I don't know.

Gun used in all of these crimes

Anyway, we ended up driving away. I was driving. That was about ten or fifteen minutes to get out of that parking lot—it's so wide. I don't remember what all happened. I just remember it was hectic in the parking lot. I turned left on Chapman, and I think I went up to Berkeley and turned right on that first street. I can't remember what it is. I turned left on it to Raymond and turned right up Raymond and went to the Riverside Freeway.

She was asking me, "Where are you taking me? What are you going to do?" And I was saying, "I'm going to drop you off out where there's some orange groves out in Placentia. I'm going to drop you off out there, and you'll be right by the police department. You'll have to walk a mile or so, and you can walk right to it." And she was saying she wasn't going to. I said I knew better, but that would give me time to get away. And so, I got on the Riverside Freeway. Got on the Riverside Freeway, and it's really a hassle because she is really giving me a hard time. I was going east on the Riverside Freeway and got off at a street called Lakeview, which is the first off-ramp after the Newport Freeway. I got off, turned right and was driving through some of those homes through the hills there.

Oh yeah, I remember now. I drove around in those hills; I

don't know for a half hour or so. Back and forth around the hills, while I was trying to get her to count up her money. I don't remember how much she had now, just a couple of bucks or ten bucks or, I don't know. Whatever it was, it wasn't enough. I wanted more. She kept telling me how she had a checking account that didn't have any money in it. She didn't know how much was in it, but she wrote bad checks, and her husband did the balance, and I kept calling her a liar, and she kept lying to me, and I kept calling her a liar. And we went back and forth and finally, we parked it up at the drive that overlooks the Riverside and Newport freeway junction somewhere. There was a little turnoff there, and we parked there, and she kept saying, "Don't give me this bullshit. Look, you got all my goddamn money, let me go."

She kept on hassling me, and I was getting pissed off, more and more pissed off. I think I slapped her up there somewhere. I think I slapped her and told her that that was just a sample and that if she didn't straighten up, I was going to slap her some more. If she looked at me again or lied to me again, I'd blow her away. And she better tell me exactly how much money was in her checking account because we were going to drive to a pay phone and call the bank, and she was going to tell them that she had lost her balance and wanted to know how much was in there. And if she didn't come within forty dollars of telling me how much money was in there accurately, I was going to blow her away. So, she said she thought she had a hundred and sixty or two hundred dollars, two hundred dollars roughly—I think. I drove around some more or something, and I kept saying, "You better be sure, you better be sure."

So, it floated between one hundred and fifty and two hundred and fifty, and finally, I said, "OK, we're going to go down the hill. I'm going to tell you exactly what to do, and you do exactly what I want." I told her some bullshit about I needed an "X" number of dollars for some reason. And so, I told her, "We're going to go down to the bank, and you're going to write out a check for cash." And I know I felt sorry for her. She was telling me about her car payments or something about they were going to take the car away or something, and so I told her, "Well, just write it for ninety dollars, and that will leave you enough to make a car payment."

Then we pulled inside the bank—so we pulled inside—no we stopped at a telephone booth and found out where there was a Barclays Bank. Her account was in Fullerton, I think. This was in Orange that we stopped, and we were on Tustin Avenue and drove into a parking lot, and I looked up the Barclays Bank, and there was one on—I can't remember if Tustin goes north and south or east and west. I know it was on Katella, and we went and turned-on Katella, then we pulled in the bank parking lot. I told her to write it out for cash and, ah, she better smile, and act normal like nothing's wrong. And if they hassled us about the check just to tell them to screw it, just give me the check back, and we'll go up to our own bank or something like oh God, I can't remember exactly.

No, we went to the bank. It was a drive-up on the wrong side. I really don't know. I think I was close to—I was impatient for some reason. I had to do it here and had to do it now. I thought about going to a different bank because the drive-up window was on the left side, and I wanted her to hand up the thing so that nobody would see me. For some reason, I had to do it right then, so I went ahead and pulled up and took the canister out and took her driver's license and the check and put them in the canister.

Anyway, that explains my thumbprint being on the check. Yeah, with all those things going on I don't exactly remember, but anyway, I put the check and the driver's license in the canister, and I said hello to the girl or something—nice day—I was carrying on some mechanical conversation. I turned around. I had my hand up trying to block my head or something, and I was turned around and was talking to her, saying, "Everything's OK. Keep up the act. Be sure to smile and everything." Then the girl said something about, "We'll have to call over to the other bank," or something, "to verify this, it would be easier if you came inside."

I told her earlier that if that happened, I would have to leave —that we would have to leave right then. And that if we took off and left her driver's license and the check at the bank, they'd know something was wrong, and they'd call the cops, and I'd have to kill her. So be sure and if anything like that happens, be sure and convince them to go ahead and cash it somehow. I don't remember how I told her, but I told her something like that. And so, she leaned over and said something or other to the teller, and the teller said something like, "Oh, yes, I understand that." Or something. But it would still be a lot easier if we'd just come inside. "Please come on inside." I said, "OK," and so we pulled out and whipped around to the front. She said, "Well, I'll just go in and get the money," and I said, "No way." And she said, "Well, you can come in with me then." I said, "No way, they've got cameras on both doors. I can't go in with you and you ain't going in without me. So, we're just going to have to split, and I'm going to have to kill you unless you think of some way to cash that check without going inside."

So, we sat there for a couple of minutes and talked—talked about different ways to get them to cash it or something. We ended up just driving back through the window again. I drove back, and we got in the longest line, and I figured well, they would have already verified it by now, and she's either been bullshitting me or else she's got the ninety bucks, and they'll go ahead and give it to us. So, I pulled into the line, and I pulled up to the window. She didn't recognize me at first and said, "Hi, may I help you?" Or something like that. "Yeah, did you get our check verified?" She said, "I asked you to come up to the window." I said, "What?" She said, "Well, we asked you to come inside." Then this other girl came up and she nodded yeah it was OK or something like that to the other girl. I said, "It's OK, right? There better be enough money in there to cover the check.

If not, somebody's in trouble." She said, "Well, could you just come inside then?" I said, "What's the problem?" And she said, "Nothing, just come on inside." I said, "OK, what the hell." I pulled around, and I told her, "That's it, we're splittin'." I was sure I was hot now, and I took off. Where the hell did we go?

We went back up Katella to—I think to the Newport Freeway —and got on the Newport Freeway, and we ended up by Irvine Park somehow. We drove up Katella to Irvine, and I don't remember where I was, but I was telling her I was really frustrated. We got to Irvine Park, and I went up Irvine Lake Road. I didn't know where I went; I just know I went a long way back into the hills. So, we were driving along, and she was hassling me and hassling me, "Where are we going? What are you doing?" I told her we were going to where my car was or something. Yeah, we were going to Riverside. That's where I left my car, and I rode the bus out to Orange County—rode the bus from Riverside to Orange County—and my car was out in Riverside, and that's where we were headed. Then I saw an OCTD sign along the way. Well, we're taking the same road back that I came in on, I don't know, I was really gone. I told her...... she had sunglasses that I kept telling her to take on and take off. I'm having trouble remembering everything. It is like watching a movie; it's hard to remember everything.

We were still driving out on Irvine Lake Road; it is a long road up and winds around. I've been out it a few times, but never past Irvine Lake, and I didn't know where the hell we were. We were past Irvine Lake though. I started telling her I was going to have to tie her up when we got out of there, so I had enough time to get to my car and get away. And I asked her what she had in the car I could tie her up with.

She went to the trunk, and she showed me different things. She said she had some battery cables or something, but I said that wouldn't do—did she have any old rags around I could tear up or something like that. And I was—I don't know—I was leading up to her clothes. And so, she got this old rag out and I said, "Well, that would be OK for—ah—for your hands but not for your feet. I need something long." And she didn't have anything. She had a blouse on that had a belt around it, a blouse or something. She had a cloth belt around it, and she took the belt off. I told her that would be OK for her feet, but I needed something to tie up her hands with. She said well, the only thing that she had was that belt unless there was something in this box or something... no, that wasn't right... the box came later....

I asked her if she wore a bra, and she said yes. I said, "I'm not getting fresh or anything, just turn your back to me so I can see whether it would be tough enough to... so she turned her back and lifted the back of her blouse up, and I looked at the bra and I said, "OK, that'll do OK, I'll probably use that" and to go ahead and take that off. She turned around and looked at me and I said, "You're going to have to take your blouse off to take the bra off so I can tie you up with it." She kept hassling me, asking why?" I kept saying, "So I can get away... so I can get away." So, she took her bra off and I told her to lay it down there with the belt in the... or something and to put her sunglasses back on and close her eyes and look out the window and don't look at me. And so, we drove around some more. I was looking at her blouse, and I could see her tits through her blouse. I undid my pants, pulled out my dick and started jacking off. All the time I was looking at her and thinking... all kinds of things... and that went on for a few minutes.

Then I asked her to get something out of the back seat, to turn around and keep her eyes closed and to get something out of the back seat, some scissors or something that I'd seen. I had her dump all her stuff out earlier from her purse, some art supplies and school supplies and everything. I saw a pair of scissors in there. Then I think I told her to get the scissors out of the back seat, and while she was doing that I was trying to look under her blouse. She turned back around and had her arms crossed. She couldn't find the scissors or something, so I said... I don't know... I said something or other... somehow, I ended up getting her to take one of her socks off so that I could jack-off and not get anything on me, and that was when I required her to see my dick.

She said, "What the hell are you doing? You said you weren't going to do anything." And I said I was pissed off and frustrated about the check and that that was how I got rid of my frustrations and it was not hurting her, and she doesn't have to watch if she doesn't want to. I kept watching her to see if she was watching, and she was watching me out of the corner of her glasses, getting more excited. She kept watching me, and I was telling her some story about my wife leaving me... two years ago... yeah, two years ago. She had taken the kids with her and how I'd never been able to have sex since then. I really loved her, and it really threw me for a loop when she split... and that this was the only way I could take care of my frustrations, and I couldn't find any sexual satisfaction with any girls, and no girls turned me on anymore... that she was the first one I saw that might.

As we came back out to the Riverside Freeway, I saw a sign that said Riverside Freeway three miles, and there were some houses, so I pulled up on a side road. I went back around up and down a couple of side roads looking for some place to park. They were all dead ends except this one that I had originally turned on. I started going down it about a mile or two. I got up on an off-ramp and pulled off the road. Then, somehow, I turned around and pulled over on the south side of the road. I pulled off and I headed back in the direction where we had come from.

I looked over at her, and she jerked away like she wasn't looking, and I looked back, and I looked out of the corner of my eye while she was watching out of the corner of her eye... and gave her some spiel about... I was still talking about... ah... now I remember... the story I'd been telling her was that I almost achieved orgasm with a girl for the first time in two years, just the other day. I told her it was with a cop's wife. Yeah, that was what it was, but, that he came home and that she put the make on me, but that he had come home and she had lied to me, because she told me that he was going to be gone for a couple of hours and he got home in forty-five minutes or something like that and that that was the reason I was on the run and had to get out of there, because he was going to kill me. And he would catch up with me because he was a cop and he had all kinds of resources available to find out where I was if I stayed in California, so I had to leave the state. And I told her I had to have money to leave the state, and that was the reason I had to have her write a check... that what she gave me wasn't enough to pay for gas to get out of the state. So, I was giving her this spiel... how I thought maybe she could help me... that I almost made it with this other girl. I wanted her to help me out.

She told me she had an ugly body and couldn't help me out, but from what I could see she had a nice body and she told me, "No I don't... I have stretch marks and ugly legs." I told her that she had nice looking legs. I told her I couldn't see 'em and to pull down her pants so I could see 'em, and she said no. I said "Look I can get off looking at your body and I can achieve something I haven't been able to do in years. I can get this over with and you can go home... and I can get out of here and I'll find somebody somewhere else."

So, she said OK and pulled down her pants, and I was building up pressure. I was still playing with myself all this time.... It must have been an hour or two by then. All I remember is I'd rubbed myself raw just about, so I asked her if she had any kind of baby lotion or cream or something to take the pain away and she looked around for a while and she came up with something... I don't know... all kinds of things... everything from lipstick to glue, I think.

So somehow, I talked her into putting it on for me and stroking it. She put whatever it was on and stroked me a few times and then pulled away and she said, "There, how's that?" and I was telling her how great it felt... so she pulled away and she said, "there, is that OK?" I said, "No, there's got to be something else"... so she tried something else and put it on and I don't remember, but I think she said how about some lipstick, and I kept saying, "try something else." She put something on and stroked me for a little while, and I'd say how good it felt, and she would pull away and I was telling her, "Don't stop." And she said, "That's what you wanted, and I got it on you." I'd say, "Well, then let's try something else." We went round and round, four or five different things… how about a lipstick, how about something or other.

So finally, I said, "Well, I think I can get off now if you let me see your belly or something." "No, I've got stretch marks." "I saw it before; you've got a nice belly." "No, I've got stretch marks." "No, you don't." "Pull it up, I'll show you the marks." She pulled it up, up to her tits… her blouse up to her tits… and I was all excited and I stroked and stroked and stroked and tried talking her into pulling her blouse all the way up, but she wouldn't do it and finally… I don't remember what I said…. Finally, I talked her into it. She said, "Just do it and get it over with, don't touch me." Then somehow, I talked her into letting me touch her anyway. Then I talked her into letting me suck on her tits and rub her legs, and I talked her into jacking me off while I was doing that. And then a Highway Patrol came driving by. I jumped back, and she jumped back and pulled her blouse down. I pulled up my pants and watched. He slowed down. I was watching him in the rear-view mirror. He was going five miles an hour or so, and he slowed down… anyway… he drove about a half mile or a mile or so… and he was watching us through his rear-view mirror.

So, I took my time and tried to be cool and casual. I got dressed and started the car up and just as he pulled up to the stop sign… he sat there just a second too long and I thought… I was debating whether to come back. I've got to make a move now or he's going to come back. I started pulling away, and so he turned off to the right and as soon as he did, I stepped on the gas and got up to the stop sign so I could see where he went and turned left… I went around in circles or something and then back at the same stop sign. I started driving around and she's saying, "Go home, I want to go home." I'm saying, "I'm not done, I'm not done."

I turned down some other road and ended up at the back side of the El Toro Marine Base or something. I didn't understand how that could be the El Toro Marine Base because I thought we were in Riverside. And, anyway, we turned around and went back. I turned up this road and it turned out to be an extension of the same road that we were on. It came off the road like that and went around. We came around and we were back where we were before. So, we parked again and started going through it again.

It seems like she jacked me off until I finally came, then, I think. I said "OK, now we can go find the car." I didn't know where the hell we were. I didn't want her to know that, so I told her I knew exactly where I was. I started driving around... around and around... going in circles about three times... trying to figure out where the hell we were. I was really getting pissed off because I couldn't figure out where we were, and I couldn't convince her that I knew where we were. We had gone around in circles, and she was starting to hassle me about going around in circles... a waste of time and her husband staying at home and "He's going to want to know where I am. I want to go home... you said I could go home." I kept saying, "Shut up, just shut up... I'll figure it out in a minute... I'm lost." So I went back down the road to the marine base, which was right there in front of me. I knew exactly where I was. I figured it out exactly where I was. I drove around the marine base on this back road going around the marine base and ended up around Redhill Avenue or something.

It was getting darker then, so I told her I'd just take her home and that we had to go back and get the check. The bank was open till five o'clock and it wasn't five o'clock yet so we'd go down the freeway and go back and get the check and her driver's license so that everything would be OK, and they wouldn't be chasing me, and I'd leave her in her car, and she could drop me off at the bus stop, and I'd just ride the bus back up to my car.

So, we got on the freeway, the Santa Ana, or maybe the San Diego… somewhere right there and we went the wrong way on the freeway. The signs were all messed up. I knew I was going south on the freeway instead of north. She thought we were going north, and she was telling me, "Everything's OK." And so somewhere in there I started goofing off again, and she was saying "This is too much" and I was saying, "That's why I'm doing it I guess, it's too much for me." She finally realized we were going the wrong way.

So I got off at the same road where we had been parked earlier. I started all over again. I was jacking off and telling her if she could just get me off, I'd make a deal with her, that she could drive, if she'd just jack me off one more time. She was saying "No"… and we were driving around in circles again. She said, "We are going to run out of gas." I said "No, we've got plenty of gas. All you gotta do is help me off one more time; it's been so many years. Help me one more time and I'll let you drive. There's the freeway right there. All you gotta do is get on the ramp going north."

She finally said, "OK." She said, "You'll let me drive, right?" I said, "Yes." So, I pulled over. She said, "Hurry up and get done so I can drive." I said, "No, you were going to do it for me." "No, I'm not going to do it anymore." "You're going to do it for me goddammit; you're going to do it." Then she said, "you told me you'd let me go, and you been telling me that you were going to let me go all this time, and you're not going to let me go. I don't believe you anymore." I told her, "I can't help myself, just one more time, just one more time… I can't help myself. Just jack me off then I can relax, and you can drive and drop me off at the bus stop." So, she said, "OK," or something… I don't remember exactly, but she ended up jacking me off.

And I was driving back, telling her we'd go right to the ramp while she was doing it. Well, we headed right for it, but about a mile from the ramp there were some orange groves and I said, "I'll just pull off this road here so nobody can see what's going on." I pulled over on this side road. I drove into a paved road that we pulled off on, and we went up just a block or two and there was a dirt road going off into an orange grove between some trees, and I pulled off there, and she said, "Promise you'll let me go after this." I said, "Yes, yes." And so, she started doing it... and I started touching her again and she told me not to and I said I had to, and I said, "Look, just lay in the back, just lay in the back, that's all." "No, I won't." Back and forth back and forth... she said something and finally she said, "OK. Lay the seat back here"... she thought she'd hurry up and get it over with. "No, I want you in the back." "I know what you're gonna do if you get me in the back... I know what you're gonna do." I said, "I can't help it... all those years, you're not gonna dump me now. You've got to help me. It means everything to me. Get up on the seat... get up there." "No, I can't." She said she can't.

I said, "Do it right now, get up there, get your ass up there." I stuck the gun in her neck or something and pulled my pants off, my shoes and my pants and my shorts and I think my shirt... climbed over on her. She was lying back on the seat. I climbed over on the seat in front of her. I told her to cock her legs. I started jacking her up... playing with her tits or something. I told her to sit on my dick. She wouldn't do it, and I told her to. She said, "You're not going to let me go, I know you're not going to let me go." She said, "I can't do it." I said, "Yes you can, get up" and I lifted her up on the seat so I could get underneath her. She said "OK, don't worry, I can do it." So, I sat her back down on me and it lasted a few seconds, and I came. I told her that what I had said was, that "she wanted to drive, not that she could."

"Now I know where my car is. I've been bullshitting you all along. You know that Ralph's Market we went by... yeah that's where it is... it's right over there. I've been bullshitting you all along. We'll go over to Ralph's. I'll still have to tie you up in the parking lot and jump in my car and split." She said, "I don't know my way home. I don't even know where I am." "I'll show you; I'll show you the way home. We'll drive and then we'll come back and get my car." "OK." And I showed her where the freeway was from Ralph's, and I said, "I can't tie you up right there in the parking lot, everybody can see us. Can't let anybody see me, because it would look awfully funny tying you up in the parking lot. I'll just go back out there a little way." "Well, I won't know where I am then." "Just watch."

We drove maybe a couple of miles to an orange grove. "We'll turn off and I'll tie you up and then we'll come back and go to Ralph's in the parking lot there. OK?" So, I drove back out there. I drove around... I couldn't find another orange grove like the one we were in before, so I tried finding the same one and I couldn't find it either. Then I remembered that I can't go there. I stepped out of the car and left my prints in the dirt. So, we drove around, and we drove around and there was something about a tourist attraction, I pulled up by it.

Anyway, we parked there. I got in the back. I told her to get in the back. I told her to get the belt and the bra. I got back there, and I was telling her something about I'd been doing this profes-sionally for years and that to tie a thirty-second knot or a thirty-minute knot. Well, she wanted to know how she could get undone. I said, "I can tie any knot that will take you from thirty seconds to get out to thirty minutes to get out, I'll show you." I tied a knot and I said, "you should be able to get out of that in ninety seconds." Right then somebody came driving out. I didn't know there was anyone around there. I jumped back in the front seat. She said, "Where are we going?" I said, "I'm not going to tie you up, yet I just want to show you that you can get out of my knot. Go ahead and get out of that one. Show you that I know what I'm doing."

I drove back towards the orange groves... back underneath the freeway and back up to the orange groves and down. She got out of it. I said, "See that was ninety-second knot... it took you eighty-five seconds to get out of the knot. I'm going to tie a twenty-minute knot on you when we get up here, and I'll give you plenty of time to get out of here." "You're sure, you're sure?" "Yeah, it will only be a twenty-minute knot." I kept telling her something about my disguises that I use ... that I had been using for all these years... that I made my living this way... that I had gotten a new fur coat I gave to my girlfriend last Christmas that way. And I found an orange grove... it looked concealed. I pulled off into it... I know this is where I did the number on her.

I had tied the knot around her neck before, that's when the guy came driving by. She couldn't pull too hard, or it would choke her probably. I think I started to put it around her neck then but that's when the guy came driving by. Then I found that place in the orange grove. It wasn't where I dumped her off either. It was a different one. I think it was the same place we parked in earlier. I got back there, and I know exactly what I did.

I got back there, and I tied her up somehow, and I told her that the belt I was putting around her neck was to make the knot last longer. I was pulling it tighter, tighter, tighter, tighter around her neck. "It's not too tight, is it?" Tighter... "it's not too tight, is it?" Tighter. "You're choking me. . . ." "It just feels tight... it's not tight." Then she started biting me. I pulled tighter and tighter. Somehow, she got rolled over or I rolled her over or something, and I had my hands around her throat. I was just squeezing harder and harder and harder. "Die bitch, die... die... you gotta die." She wouldn't die. I was crying... squeezing harder and harder. It seemed like I squeezed her for hours and hours. I was praying... don't let her die... die... don't let her die... die. She quit fighting.

I think I felt for her pulse or something. I felt a pulse. I thought I felt one... then I didn't. Then I couldn't find one. I thought, she's dead... I gotta get rid of her... gotta get out of here. I jumped back in the front seat and took off driving crazy… somewhere… just driving around, driving around, and driving around. I heard a noise in the back. I thought, God she's coming back to life. I gotta get away… gotta get rid of her.

I saw a road and it was out in the open. I thought, I can't go here, I gotta get rid of her, she's coming back to life. So, I looked up into this road and there was a ditch there… by an orange grove, but I think there was an open field there too, it was a dirt ditch. I pulled in next to it and a car went by, and as soon as it went by, I jumped out of the car and I grabbed her, and I yanked her out of there and pulled her down into the ditch. I threw her into the ditch. I picked her up and threw her into the ditch, and when I threw her in the ditch it was like the impact started her breathing again or something. She sucked in a big gasp of air… and I couldn't choke her anymore… I couldn't do it. I saw a rock there and I picked her up, and I slapped her head against the rock—the back of her head. She was still breathing. I reached down and I picked the rock up from underneath her and threw it in her face. I felt something all over my hands and it was all over the rock. I started running. I jumped into the car and then I remembered my footprints. I jumped back out of the car. I hung out of the car halfway or something and I used my hands to try to cover up my footprints.

I just wanted to get away, get a. I shook a bunch of dirt up real fast… got back in the car, and a car drove by, and I sat there and as soon as it was gone I started the car up… backed out of there and drove away I… I don't know where… I know I ended up at a gas station. I think it was in Tustin or somewhere… off the freeway. I had blood all over me. I had to get the blood off me. I thought, she had to be dead… she had to be dead. She couldn't come back to life. I don't remember when or how, but I just remember stuffing a bunch of dirt in her vagina. It probably was to cover up my semen, trying to cover it up… yeah.…

I pulled into this gas station, and I went into the bathroom and scrubbed and scrubbed and the fuckin' blood wouldn't come off me. I must have scrubbed for ten or fifteen minutes. I needed something else... I don't know what. I didn't wash the car; I still had her car.

I drove to the K-mart in Buena Park on Beach and... I think it's La Mirada Boulevard. I went to K-mart because I told Mollye that I would buy her an exerciser... an Exertrimer. That's the one you tie one of the ropes on the doorknob. I went and bought one. I bought an Exertrimer and I went over to the auto department and I bought a can of gas treatment or something.... Then I think I bought some darts for David. I bought them as a present because that's the only place that had darts for a long time.

Then I went to the parking lot at K-mart, and I took the gas treatment and dumped it on some kind a rag, and I started to do this at the K-mart. It was a piece of clothing or a rag or whatever it was... and probably... anyway it was a rag of some kind... and I started wiping the car down. I wiped the steering wheel down. I wiped the back seat, the back compartment down. I wiped the door down, both doors down, and then I wiped my fingerprints off it. I think I wiped everything down except for the seat that I was sitting in... and wiped the steering wheel because it had blood on it.

By then it was seven thirty or eight o'clock... I don't know what the hell time it was... I just knew I had to get home, my old lady would be worried and yell. So, I thought, well, where am I going to leave the car? I'm not going to leave it at the K-mart. I got back in it and I thought, well, I could take the car home. I need a car anyway. And so, I drove by the motel... what the hell are you doing, Ken... take this car.... How you going to explain having a car. I drove back to Beach Boulevard. I drove up and down Beach a couple of times... a couple more hours. I thought I'll go over to Winchell's and have a donut and cup of coffee and think about it... oh shit... I drove around and around and around in that damn car, and I finally ended up on Western coming up behind Albertsons Market.

I thought, I'll go into Albertsons. I'll get some more money in Albertsons. I didn't get any money. I only got five dollars. I've gotta have more money than that... cause I've gotta pay some bills, so I went around the parking lot at Albertsons and drove in and out a couple of times. And then I think... I don't know... I just gave up on it after a while. By then it was about eight o'clock... it was getting late, and I had to get home.

I drove around the back of Albertsons and pulled up by the box by some trash cans. I thought if anybody sees me back here, I'll get some boxes out of the trash cans. I got out and I started wiping the car down again. I got that gas treatment all over everything, spilling it and I thought man, that stuff is strong. So, I was wiping down the car again, and I was smoking a cigarette, and I was thinking this shit's flammable; I shouldn't be smoking a cigarette. I thought well, shit; I'll just burn the car up. I don't know why I didn't think of that before. So, I finished wiping everything down and then I found a couple of rags or something and set them on the seat and dumped a bunch of that shit all over the car and I thought, I wonder how flammable this stuff is?

So, I took a piece of one of the rags and I walked about twenty feet away from the car and stood there and lit up another cigarette and lit up my match on it and it didn't do nothing. I reached down and put my match on it and tried to light it on fire, and I lit the rag up and it started to burn pretty good. So, I threw that rag down into one of those driveways that go down to the dock... what was left of the burning rag... and I went back to the car and dumped some more of that stuff, and I think I took a rag and wiped the can off, and I laid the can down and I thought, well, there's still a half a can here.

I looked around and I didn't see anybody, so I took a match, and I lit it, and I tossed it on the seat, and it went out or something... I don't remember. I don't remember if I lit the whole book of matches or burned a couple of matches or what, but I got the rag started. I think I got one started on the floor, maybe even one started in the back, I'm not sure. I took off and started walking... towards Western. I know that one was burning on the seat and I think there was one burning on the floorboard and I dumped a bunch of the same stuff in the back on some rags or on the carpet or something, thinking that would catch fire eventually and give me enough time to get away that way....

I kept walking away thinking I'd forgotten something I'm not doing, something ain't right... what have I forgotten? I've got the Exertrimer... I've got the darts... I've got the keys... what the hell did I forget? I got to Western, and I walked around to the first street behind Albertsons and started walking a bit and I got about halfway up and... I'd forgot the gun... I forgot the goddamn gun in the car. I can't leave that there. The son of a bitch has gotta be in all the flames now. I gotta go back for that gun now.

So, I dropped my bag of stuff in the gutter, and I haul-ass back there and looked around the corner... I could just barely see a glimmer in the car, and I thought, man... that stuff is going to blow up in my face when I walk up to it. I know it. I've gotta do it. I walked up to it as fast as I could, and I looked and there was a smoldering rag on the... I think the one on the floor... had gone out and the one on the seat was just barely smoldering. It was all full of smoke though.

I opened it up and reached underneath the seat where I had stuck the gun... sometime ... I don't know when... sometime earlier... and I grabbed it and I threw it in my pocket, and I took some gas treatment out and I dumped it on the seat, and it lit up the rag... then I thought ... bus... bus... I had to hurry, or I was going to miss my bus. I knew there was a bus coming along... the buses ran every quarter hour or something like that... God, it must have been about eight o'clock... ought a be a bus coming at eight. Anyway, I knew I was going to miss my bus if I didn't hurry. So, I thought well, I gotta catch the bus, and I walked as fast as I could out of the parking lot around the corner.

As soon as I was around the corner, I looked back to make sure nobody saw me, and I ran.

While I was running, I peeled the keys off of the key ring one at a time and I wiped them off on my clothes. As I was running, I chucked them off in different bushes... along the street. I chucked most of them into... ah... there was a school there or something. I threw them into the playground into the bushes. Just as I almost got to the corner, my bus... my bus went by. I thought, piss on it I'll just go... then I thought, shit, I can't do that. I think the street on the north side of the street is Melrose... it's the first street.

I missed my bus, so I started to go to Winchell's, and I saw a taxicab over in the gas station, there's a self-service gas station there. And I ran over and asked, "Are you in service now?" And, he said... "ah...well, I"... he was a L.A. taxi or something. I never seen this taxi before. He was an English guy and he said, "How far you are going?" I said, "About a mile, a mile-and-a-half up the road, up Beach." He said, "Well, I gotta get back to the Santa Ana Freeway." He said, "I'm going right that way... jump in." I got him to give me a ride to Commonwealth and Stanton. I gave him a buck. I got out there and he went on up Stanton to the freeway, and I went home.

Another thing I remember when I first picked her up, I asked her if she had anything else of value. She said no. I said, "What about jewelry?" I don't know if she was wearing earrings or not. She had a watch. I know she had jewelry and I know I took it. She had a wedding set, and she said it was worth hardly anything. I told her I could get ten percent on whatever she had from a fence friend... two hundred bucks... would be twenty dollars in gas to get me out of the state. . . .

Banderas car after it was burned

CHAPTER 4
SHE'S ALIVE

CARMEN BANDERAS HAD lunch that day at her mother-in-law's home, not far from where she lived with her husband, Ronald, in Fullerton. She really enjoyed her mother-in-law's company and would have stayed longer, but she needed to leave to get to Fullerton College for a class that started at one-thirty that afternoon. Her family and getting a college education were what was important in her life. She left her mother-in-law's home with plenty of time to make the drive to the college, arriving at the parking lot that faces Chapman Avenue, where she normally parked, at approximately one o'clock. Usually, she would have to drive around the lot a few times, but today she was lucky. As she drove into the parking lot, she saw an empty space in the middle row near the center. As she parked, she saw a guy coming towards the general direction of her car. He was coming off the school campus and carrying a Pee-Chee[1] folder, like most other students did. She didn't think anything of it at the time.

---

1. A Pee-Chee folder is the brand name for a manila folder with artwork on the front that was commonly used by students, and still is, to organize and maintain notes from various classes.

Tuesday, January 6, 1976
Irvine California

A major development in the case occurred sooner than any of us would have expected, but, unfortunately, came as the result of another kidnapping and rape, with the victim left for dead in an orange grove in Irvine. We were notified of the incident by the Orange County Sheriff's Office shortly after they received the call at eight-fifty on the night of Tuesday, January 6, 1976, just one day after the discovery of the body of Gina Marie Tisher.

The Orange County Sheriff's Office had gotten a telephone call from a Mark Paulak, calling from a pay phone at Myford Road and Irvine Boulevard. Paulak had advised the Sheriff's Department dispatcher that he had picked up a young lady who was possibly the victim of a kidnapping and rape, and he had her at that location and she needed help.

Deputies Dunlap and Cook were dispatched to the area. Paulak told them that at approximately eight forty-five that evening, he and his wife were driving on Myford Road when they heard a young female screaming, "Help, someone is trying to kill me." The woman was hailing Paulak from the side of the road. Paulak stopped, put her in his car, and drove to a pay phone to notify the Orange County Sheriff's Department.

The two deputies then spoke with the victim, who was lying on the front seat of the Paulak car. They quickly identified her as Carmen Banderas, a white female, twenty-three years old, who lived in Fullerton and had been reported missing by her husband. Though seriously injured, she was able to tell the officers she had been at the Fullerton College parking lot, near the tennis court area, when a white male, approximately twenty years old, with light brown medium short hair approached her as she was getting out of her car. He pointed a small caliber handgun at her and told her to move from the driver's seat to the passenger seat then drove the car from the parking lot.

The deputies discontinued their conversation with Banderas

at that point because her forehead and face were severely lacerated, and her clothing and body were covered with blood. They contacted the dispatch center and requested an ambulance be sent to the scene. The two deputies then learned from Carmen that the suspect was very possibly still driving her car. They immediately contacted Orange County Communications Control One and requested a general broadcast for the suspect and the victim's car to all Orange County police agencies. Her car was a 1975 Datsun (now known as a Nissan) 210B, navy blue in color with a California license plate number 054KXV.

A few minutes later Doctor's Ambulance Service arrived and transported Carmen to Tustin Community Hospital, which was the closest trauma facility. When she arrived at the hospital, she was nude from the waist up, and Dr. Rettinger, the on-duty physician who examined her, would later testify in court that shortly after treating this young woman, he quit working in the emergency room due to the trauma of the terrible damage the suspect had done to her. Sharron Schauperl, the wife of Detective Leon Schauperl, was later a patient of Dr. Rettinger's in his private practice in Fullerton, and he would tell her the same thing. He also told Sharon that at the time of Carmen Banderas' admission to the hospital he did not expect her to live.

The two deputies remained at the hospital and between the doctor examinations and treatment they were able to continue to interview her. After her release from the hospital, she was also interviewed in detail by Detective Schauperl, at which time she completed a hand-written statement describing the entire ordeal.

During conversations with the doctors at the Tustin Community Hospital, the investigating officers learned that Carmen had debris, possibly rocks as well as dirt, packed into her vaginal canal. Doctors said they were not able to remove it at that time, apparently because they would need to administer an anesthetic and conduct an extended cleaning of the vagina. The deputies asked the attending physicians if they would notify the Sheriff's Office when they did the removal of the material so it could be saved for any evidential value.

The deputies made note of the fact that during the examination of Banderas at the hospital, they saw what looked like friction burns around her neck, which seemed to have been caused by a strip of unknown material. They believed that in addition to a severe beating, the suspect had strangled her to kill her.

At about eleven that night, the on-duty watch commander for the Orange County Sheriff's Office, Lieutenant Devereaux, decided, due to the seriousness of the case, to call Detectives Bruce MacAfee and Harry Kinder, and ask them to go to the hospital. When they arrived, they met Detective Schauperl, who had been called by the Fullerton Watch Commander after the initial broadcast by the sheriff's office. All of them immediately recognized that this incident closely paralleled the Tisher homicide investigation being conducted by the Fullerton Police Department. The Orange County Sheriff's Office investigators were advised that this new case had also originated in Fullerton. They continued to assist Fullerton in the investigation throughout the night and beyond.

By the time Detectives MacAfee, Kinder, and Schauperl arrived at the hospital, Carmen's husband, Ron Banderas, had also arrived from Fullerton. The detectives were able to interview him at that point. Mr. Banderas told the officers he was a schoolteacher at Saddleback High School, in Central Orange County, and he had left for work at approximately six forty-five that morning. He said he did not see his wife again until he arrived at Tustin Community Hospital that evening, but he had talked with her on the phone sometime during the morning hours. He told them he had been expecting her to get home at about three in the afternoon. He knew from his conversations with her and his mother that his wife had been at his mom's house in Fullerton for lunch, and she had left his mom's house at approximately one o'clock, headed for Fullerton College for a class. He told the officers that when his wife had not come home and he had not heard from her, he became worried about her, and began calling hospitals in the area in an attempt to locate her but was unsuccessful.

Banderas told the investigators that at approximately eight that night he had received a call from the Buena Park Police Department telling him his car had been found abandoned and completely burned, and his wife was not in it nor was she anywhere in the area. He was told by Buena Park Police to contact the Fullerton Police Department and make a missing person report on his wife. He did so and within minutes was advised by Fullerton officers his wife had been found and was at Tustin Community Hospital.

At this point, Detective MacAfee asked him to sign a release requested by the hospital allowing the Sheriff's Department to photograph his wife. He agreed to sign the release and stated he wanted to cooperate with the investigation in any way he could.

The detectives asked that all clothing be taken from the victim and collected as evidence. They also asked that fingernail scrapings and a rape kit be completed on her. In addition to this evidence, Crime Scene Investigator Sherlock had been able to locate an area he thought was near the initial crime scene and had collected a leaf with blood on it. He had also located a tennis shoe print in the same area, possibly belonging to the suspect.

Wednesday, January 7, 1976
Early morning hours
Irvine, California

At approximately one o'clock in the morning, the detectives were able to interview Dr. Rettinger about the medical condition of the victim. The doctor told them she had suffered severe trauma to her head and facial area and had a fracture around her left eye. There were several other injuries including lacerations both above and below the left eye. Ligature marks were evident on her neck. He also told them a preliminary examination of the pelvic area revealed a quantity of debris was present in the form of dirt. Until a more thorough examination was completed it was not possible to speculate on the amount of debris or the magnitude of any injury.

After talking to the doctor, it was determined that, given the extent of the injuries, it would not be possible to interview her at this time. For now, they would have to rely on the information obtained by the deputies while at the scene and in their interview following the victims' arrival at the hospital. The medical team was convinced that, if she lived, this beautiful young woman would probably carry these physical and emotional scars for the rest of her life. The detectives then made sure all the evidence was properly collected at the hospital before proceeding to the intersection of Myford and Irvine Roads to attempt to locate and further examine the scene.

They arrived while it was still dark. They were able to locate the crime scene area previously found by Sherlock, which was very close to where Mrs. Banderas had contacted Paulak and his wife. It was alongside the roadway in a drainage culvert near the intersection of Myford and Irvine Roads. Using only flashlights and the headlights of their cars, the detectives walked along the dirt road that ran parallel with the drainage ditch and saw what seemed to be recent tire marks of what would be a narrow wheelbase vehicle. They followed these tire prints for about fifty yards. The tracks appeared to stop at that point, and immediately south of the dirt road they found a large quantity of blood in the dirt, along with bloodstained leaves in the drainage ditch. They noticed a large rock in the same area that also appeared to have blood on it. The dirt area along the edge of the roadway at that location looked disturbed, indicating recent activity. This appeared to be the spot where Mrs. Banderas had been so brutally attacked and beaten.

Detective MacAfee then contacted the Sheriff's crime scene people to return to the scene for additional photographs and the collection of more evidence. Crime Scene Investigator Sherlock came to the area and completed the collection of the additional evidence at that time. They carefully expanded the search of this area and located a bloodstained blouse. It looked like the same material used to tie the victim's wrists and used to try to strangle her, as they were the same as the strips of cloth they had seen at the hospital. In addition, they found two pieces of a white sheet that had evidence of blood on them. All these items were collected by MacAfee and given to Crime Scene Investigator Sherlock for transportation to the Sheriff's Department Evidence Locker.

At about two o'clock that morning, Detectives MacAfee and Schauperl drove to Hunts Garage at 11th and Stanton Boulevard in Buena Park. The car belonging to Carmen Banderas had been towed there after being recovered by the Buena Park Police Department. The vehicle had extensive fire damage on the interior and a moderate amount of damage on the outside. It was extremely wet from the fire Department efforts to contain the flames. McAfee made arrangements to have the car taken from Hunts to the Orange County Sheriff's Office for further investigation. A tow truck came and took the burned-out car to the Orange County impound lot. Detective McAfee followed behind the towed vehicle to maintain the chain of evidence. When they got to the impound lot, McAfee tagged the vehicle for evidence and requested it be worked by the identification personnel, the crime lab, and the fire investigators for any remaining evidence.

At two-thirty in the early morning hours of January 7, 1976, a white male, generally matching the description given by our victim Banderas, was arrested by Buena Park Police Officers for a violation of section 148 of the California Penal Code, "Resisting an Officer." He had been drinking and was uncooperative and combative with the police officers who stopped him in the field. During the booking process, jail deputies observed blood on his undershorts and when questioned about it, he gave a vague answer. The arresting officers placed a hold on him for suspicion of violating section 217 (Kidnap) and 261.3 (Forcible Rape), and at eight o'clock that morning, Detective McAfee was notified of the arrest and the circumstances. He immediately contacted Schauperl and briefed him. Both detectives went to the Orange County Jail to interview the man. Due to the proximity of his arrest to the location where the Banderas vehicle was found and the blood on his person, the detectives were hopeful they had gotten a major breakthrough in the case.

Between ten and ten-thirty that morning they interviewed the arrestee in Interview Room #2 at the Orange County Jail. The interview was taped by McAfee. The subject was questioned about the blood on his shorts and attributed it to his being with his girlfriend during her menstrual cycle. Continued questioning revealed he was able to establish an alibi for all pertinent times relevant to the investigation. Detective Schauperl also questioned him about other dates and times involved in the Tisher homicide, but the subject also offered explanations for those dates. They also found out he was currently in the United States Army and was on leave from Fort Hood, Texas and would not have been in California when most of the incidents associated with the Tisher homicide, or the other known cases, had occurred. As a result of the interview, both detectives left the jail facility disappointed, convinced this person was not the man they were looking for.

After leaving the jail, they decided to go back to the hospital to see if they could get permission to interview Carmen Banderas in more detail. They also wanted to get an update on her condition. When they arrived, Dr. Shiffman, who was the doctor in charge, gave them permission to interview Banderas in the Intensive Care Unit. It was almost a quarter past two in the afternoon when they finally got in to see her.

She described the person who had attacked her as being between twenty-five and twenty-eight years old, 5'10" to 5'11", 170-175 pounds, with light brown medium length hair that she thought could be a military style cut. She said he had yellow teeth and on the back of his left hand was a tattoo that resembled a Nazi symbol. This tattoo would be important, later, in the identification of the actual suspect.

Some of the things she could recall were the suspect smoked Marlboro cigarettes and he smoked constantly throughout the ordeal. She said he told her at one point he was born in San Clemente and he was in the military service, possibly the Army, as he also spoke about events that occurred while he was in the service. She also recalled the incident where they went to Barclays Bank in Orange and attempted to cash one of her checks there.

Later that same day, Detective Storey went to the Barclays Bank on Katella Avenue in Orange to pick up the check and driver's license left by the suspect and belonging to Carmen

Banderas. Storey then took those items to the Orange County Sheriff's Evidence Locker and booked them in under the Sheriff's Office case number. Detective MacAfee notified Criminalist White and requested the check and driver's license be worked for fingerprints.

Monday, January 12, 1976
Fullerton, California

Some days later, after Carmen was released from the hospital, Detective Schauperl and Captain Davis drove her around, and she did a remarkable job of re-creating the route she and the suspect had taken on the afternoon of the sixth of January. Her account proved to be amazingly accurate when compared to what her assailant later confessed, as recorded in Chapter Three. At the direction of detectives, she also completed a detailed hand-written statement of her ordeal of January 6, 1976.

Carmen Banderas' Handwritten Statement
Monday, January 12, 1976
Fullerton, California

When I was parking, I noticed a guy coming in the general direction of my car, but he was carrying a Pee-Chee folder and appeared to be just another student. I turned off the ignition, reached over and picked up my purse off the passenger seat and was ready to take the keys from the ignition and get out of my car. I opened the door and put one foot on the ground when I felt a great force and I turned around to see this guy, the same one I had seen walking towards and past my car. He had a gun and told me, "Get in the car, move over and don't scream, because I'll blow your head off." He had the gun in my neck. I looked around to see if anyone was there and he says, "Don't scream, 'cause I'll kill you." At this point I thought it was a joke. The gun didn't look real, even though it felt cold against my neck. I said, "What is this? What the hell do you think you are doing? I don't think it is very funny." He said, "look, this is no joke, it's very real just like this gun is, and what it can do to you, so you better do like I say." And now I said, "What do you want?" He said, "Your money, but right now we've got to get out of here." I said, "But why? I can give you the money now." He was shaking and very nervous. Then he smiled and said, "well, I might need your car" All of this happened in the parking lot in about one minute."

Then he started the car and we drove off. I don't remember what streets we were on, but we ended up on the Riverside Freeway going towards Riverside. While driving in the lot, before we got out onto the street, he threw out his Pee-Chee folder. Now we're driving on the streets, before getting on the freeway. He had the gun in my ribs, and he had me looking down at the floor, so I would not look at him or seem suspicious to others, and we didn't talk. I started to say something, and he shut me up. We got on the freeway, and I asked, "where are we going?" He said, "Shut up and turn around, you ask too many questions." Then he asked me about my car, how much mileage it got, how far could he get with three quarters of a tank of gas. Then he said, "I'll have to put some license plates on this car, that's no problem." Then I said, "Well, you probably wouldn't get very far, you see something is wrong with my car. I took it into a garage to have someone look at it and they said there was a problem with it accelerating, and then slowing down." And, he said, "It needs a tune-up." I said, "that's all, for that they wanted eighty dollars?" At that time, we were still riding, going up a hill. Then I said, "Where are we going?" He said, "I have to tie you up and drive somewhere, because I am taking your car." I said, "Fine, take it, but just don't hurt me. You don't look like the type who would want to hurt anybody. I know you wouldn't hurt me because you are not, right?" And he said, "Just do what I tell you, don't go and do something stupid like the other girls. That's why I had to kill them, you see, they thought that they were smart because they've watched too much T.V." And, I asked, "Would you tell me what they did so I wouldn't do it?" He said, "Warning, screaming or jumping out of the car." I said, "Well, that really was dumb, don't worry I wouldn't do it. See, I have a little boy. He means the world to me." And, he didn't say anything. Instead, he told me to get a book, to open it and to start reading it. So, I did. We were still riding, this time down the hill, I'm not sure exactly where, and I asked, "Where are you taking me?" He told me, "To a place where there is no one around so I can leave before it gets any later." I asked him, "Why, are you in trouble?" He said, "Yes, I need some money so I can skip town. I am in big trouble; someone is out to get me" Then he slapped me and said, "You bitch, you talk too much", and he hit me again. Then he told me, "OK, give me the money" and then he made me empty my purse and wallet on the floor-board. He then asked me what I had in the car. He made me open the glove compartment and asked again, "What else do you have? What's in the back?" I answered, "Just school supplies, papers and books."

He then asked me, "Do you have a spare and a jack?" I said, "Yes." He then asked me, "Do you have any jumper cables?" I told him that I didn't know. Every time he would ask me about something my heart would jump because I was afraid he wouldn't like the answer and would hit me again. He said, "I hope you do, and I hope the wire is nice and sturdy, or is it the cheap kind?" I told him, "I don't know," and he hit me again and said, "You don't seem to realize how serious this is, do you? You talk too much, and you don't seem to be afraid. What's wrong with you? Are you made of steel? You're supposed to be scared." Then I got mad and said, "Of course I am scared. What do you want me to do, cry?" He smiled and said, "I don't care what you do if it makes you feel any better. He left me alone for a few minutes, but then he asked me how much money my husband and I had in the checking account. I told him I really didn't know. He got mad again and was threatening to kill me right there. He said, "you have to know, don't lie to me." Then he asked me, "Do you think you might have two-hundred dollars?" "Maybe," I answered. He told me, "You just better pray to your God that you might have at least two-hundred dollars, because as you can see, twelve dollars wouldn't take me very far." I told him, "Look, you've got everything I have, my money and my car, please let me go."

He ignored me and said, "Take off your rings and the watch too." I told him how much my wedding rings meant to me. He just said, "Would you rather die?" So, I gave him my jewelry, a set of wedding rings, one turquoise, white gold ring and my watch. He put them in his pants pocket and continued to drive."

He asked me if I lived in a house or an apartment and if there was any money in my home. I told him that there was no money at our home and that my in-laws were at our house. They weren't, but I didn't want him going to our home. I was afraid for my husband and my son, and I didn't want him to know where I lived. He came back to the issue of the check and asked me where our bank was and if we usually walked in or used the drive-through. I told him that it was in Fullerton, and that we did both. He then told me, "We'll go somewhere else." He asked if I knew where there was another Barclay's Bank near the area, and I said I didn't. He thought a minute and then said, "Well, I do. There's one on Katella and we're going there." He drove around and then he pulled in where there was a phone booth and he looked up the address for the bank. He told me to wear my sunglasses and to cover my eyes. The next thing I knew, we were at the bank, and he told me to write a check for ninety-dollars and ten cents, so I did, and he put it in the canister at the drive-through window. He told me to smile and be nice to the teller or else he would shoot me. The teller looked at the check and then she told us to park the car and come into the bank, because they had to call our bank to verify the check, so, he calmly said, "All right, and thank you."

We pulled away and parked in front of the bank and he

began threatening me again, saying, "You've got to have enough money in the bank. There's no way we can get inside the bank." I said, "Why not?" He furiously said, "Don't you know they have cameras and guards in there. Who the hell do think I am? I know better than that!" So, I suggested that I would go in and he would be behind me with his back to the camera, and he said, "Don't be stupid. That wouldn't work. I don't trust you." I told him, "You have got to trust me, and don't you see I want to go home. I want to do the right thing. Please let me go." I had hoped to get him into the bank where I might have been able to get help, but he ignored my pleas and said, "We're trying once more and if it doesn't work outside, I am killing you right here." I said to him, "Look, if you shoot people will hear you." He told me, "Well, all I have to say is that it better work this time." So, he pulled around the bank one more time and got into the same row with the same tellers as the first time and she said, "Oh, you have to come in." So, he said, "Oh, I'm sorry, I thought you said to come back. Well, thank you and have a nice day." At that we left the bank and turned left onto Katella. He followed that road again towards Irvine and I asked him again, "Where are you taking me?" He answered, "To a place where there's nobody around, out there in the middle of nowhere. You see, I'm taking your car, so you would have to walk about ten miles if you can walk that is, before you get to a police station and cry for help" Then he added, "Have you ever been to Placentia? Oh well, it doesn't make any difference anyway, there's nothing but orange groves and farming area where I am taking you, so now you know." He was driving further into the country, nothing but trees, roads, hills, and mountains. It was about three-thirty or four because he told me that by this time my family would be wondering about me, school was out, and I wouldn't be home. He started to masturbate himself. He told me, "Too bad if this bothers you, I have to do it every time I get upset or nervous" I said, "I don't care, just let me go, please" He laughed again and said, "No, not yet no way." Then he took this different road and told me that if I masturbated him he would let me go. I refused and told him, "No way. I love my husband very much, and I also love Jesus Christ and I wouldn't do anything to hurt either of them." So, he told me, "I guess you'll never get home to your husband and your son." So, I had to do it. Then we left the area, and he supposedly was taking me to the parking lot where his car was, somewhere in Placentia and I noticed that we were going around in circles. I saw the same street sign about five times and the same places. I saw a sign that said, "Cemetery', another that indicated, "Lake Forest', the marine base and finally a sign saying "freeway', so he said, "We're lost."

We were going to take the freeway to L.A. so we could get on the Riverside Freeway to Placentia, but he didn't do it. He took the freeway going south, the opposite direction. I told him that and he got off the freeway. By this time, it was getting dark, about five or five-thirty in the evening. As we were driving, he saw a police car, and we pulled into this shopping center. He parked in front of a 31 Flavor ice cream place, and I asked, "Now, why are you parking here?" He yelled, "Look bitch, shut up! I know what I'm doing. Don't you see the pig? What if the bank called because of the check? They know the car. They probably got the license number too. I'm not taking any chances; just in case he stops we better have our story together. You're going to say you didn't feel good, so you left the bank without picking up your driver's license. Or, you can say that you passed out in the car, and I am driving you home. No, he would not fall for this one." Then he said, "Of course you can say that you are pregnant and had a miscarriage, so you better remember, or else you know what will happen." I still wasn't sure what story he was going to go with if we got stopped. I wouldn't have known what he wanted me to say."

We waited there for about five minutes until the police car was out of sight. From here I don't remember what route he took, but we ended up in a shopping center in Tustin, I believe it was. I believe that it was at First and Newport in Tustin. It was here that he said he was going to tie me up and leave me there. He told me to get in the back seat of my car and to take my shoes off and my knee socks because he needed something to tie me with. He suggested that I take off my bra, so I gave it to him, and he was stretching it or testing it for strength. He said that it wouldn't do the trick, so he had me look for something else in the car. He told me, "Take off that sash from your blouse." I took it off and gave it to him. He tied my feet with the knee-high socks and my hands with the sash. He told me that it was a "24 minute" knot and he wanted to see how long it would take me to untie myself. He just watched and about one minute later, I untied myself. He was furious at me again and he drove off with me still in the back. I noticed that we were heading toward Tustin once more. We saw orange groves and avocados also. He was looking for the right spot.

We ended up somewhere in Irvine, a farming area. He was driving around not knowing where he wanted to go. We came around the same farm about three times. Finally, he pulled over on the side of the road. He started to masturbate again, and he asked me for cream. Then he started the engine and said, "Shit, there's a pig. We've got to get out of here," and I turned around and saw a vehicle from the Orange County Sheriff's Department, and he yelled at me and said, "Turn around and look the other way" (the opposite of him). He was upset, even shaking. I told him not to worry; everything was going to be fine. He told me, "If he stops, I've had it. This is kidnapping, you know, and it's a federal offense. You have any idea how many years they'll give me for this?" I told him, "Look, if he does stop, I'll tell him I am here because I want to be, calm down." I thought he was going to kill me right there. The sheriff's car just passed us and went on. He started masturbating again and told me to take my blouse off. I said, "No way. You'll have to kill me first. I'll yell my head off. I know where you're heading to, but no way. I'd rather be dead." He drove away, very mad, accelerating to about 70 miles per hour and calling me names as he drove. From there, we just drove around aimlessly. He wanted me to believe we were lost but I know we were not. He knew exactly where we were. About half an hour after we had been riding around in Irvine, or El Toro, I began to pray. He was making fun of me because I was praying out loud. He laughingly told me, "We'll see if your God gets you out of this one." I got mad then and told him, "You're liable to go wrong someday. You'll make a mistake. They'll catch you and lock you behind bars forever. What about the fingerprints you'll leave behind?" He answered, "Don't worry; I know what I am doing. I know my procedure." We were driving again, and we passed a dirt road, then came back to it, but saw that it led to a house. He drove out again and passed another. Again, he came back, and he drove in, and told me, "O.K. baby, take your clothes off." I refused and he poked my stomach with the gun and told me, "Unless you want this. Here you can scream all you want; nobody will hear you." He raped me there. After this he drove back to another shopping center. There was a Ralph's grocery store and a bank, but he drove right out, and he went back to the same dirt road where he had raped me and stopped. He said, "Thank you for being so nice, and for helping me." I said, "Help?" He said, "yes, because since my wife left me, I wasn't able to have normal sexual intercourse and you've helped me that way." I said, "You're sick." He answered, "Maybe I want to be sick." Then he added, "Well, this is it. I guess it wouldn't make a difference if I tell you that everything, I said to you was a lie. Get in back face down." At first, I thought he was going to just tie me up and let me go, but now I knew he was planning to kill me. My heart was pounding. While I was in this position, he had both of his knees on my lower back. He was doing something. I couldn't see but I heard. He was clipping or cutting something. I saw he put down a pair of scissors I had with all my school supplies. He tied me up and I felt a string around my neck. He started to strangle me. I was fighting him off me. I remember I was running out of air. I don't know if I scratched his face, but I was thinking about doing it, but I don't know if I did. He pulled the string until I blacked out. I don't know how long I was gone, but when I came to, I was in the back seat of my car. My hands were still tied up. I could see trees along the road. I knew we were driving on a dirt road because of the way the car was moving and jumping. That's all I remember because I went unconscious again. I don't know if he hit me while I was still in the car. When I gained consciousness again, I was in a deep ditch. My vision was poor. I was trembling and freezing cold. I couldn't feel my body. I couldn't get up or sit up. There was a road nearby because I could see the headlights of vehicles. I laid there like a vegetable for God knows how long. There I was looking straight up into the sky. I was praying because I felt I was going to die. I thought of my son, and my husband and I told the Lord I couldn't die. So, God told me to try to get out. My blouse was next to me. I thought of flagging it and maybe someone would see. I saw a total of three cars go by and the third one stopped. Before I knew it, I was in this car. Two people were in the car, a man and a woman and they got help for me.

How she could remember so much detail after the terrifying events she had suffered through was a mystery to me at the time —and still is.

CHAPTER 5
WORKING THE CASE

ALL THE DETECTIVES assigned to the case continued to interview possible witnesses in the area where both Gina Tisher was found and the site where our second victim, Carmen Banderas, was abducted. We were desperately seeking anything that could help us identify the suspect who had murdered Gina Tisher and kidnapped, strangled, and beaten Carmen Banderas before abandoning her for dead in the Irvine orange grove. We continued to pursue promising leads that ultimately went nowhere. The murder book got bigger, but we were no closer to finding the person responsible.

Wednesday, January 7, 1976
Fullerton, California

At the end of the day, Wednesday, January 7, 1976, we again met to summarize what we knew about the case up to that point. Clearly, the fact Mrs. Banderas had survived was not only remarkable, but a major break in the case, for as it turned out later, all her information was extremely accurate and was critical to making the case against the suspect when he was finally located and identified. Our body of knowledge about the suspect was growing slowly, but we knew each of the following facts would get us closer to an arrest. Here is what we knew to that point:

- We were dealing with a serial rapist and murderer. Based on what we had at that time, it appeared the series of crimes had begun in October of 1975.
- All the victims we were aware of had been approached while in public parking lots during the daylight or early evening hours.
- On some occasions, the suspect would tell the victim she had a flat tire, to get her out of her car.
- The suspect used a small handgun, probably a semi-automatic, to force his way into the victim's vehicle and would then force her to move over to the passenger seat so he could drive.
- The victims would often be driven around randomly during the time following the kidnapping.
- Most had been strangled, but not all killed. There was a distinct possibility the strangulation was to produce a sexual gratification for the suspect, and not necessarily for the specific purpose of killing them, although what happened to Carmen Banderas would not support that conclusion.
- All the victims were very attractive young, white females. All were alone when approached, except for one who had small children in the car with her. The victim in this case, however, had thwarted the suspect in his attempt to kidnap her and her children, and there were no other cases where small children were involved that we knew of.
- Some, but not all, of the victims had been robbed by the suspect during the incident.
- The victims' purses were dumped out on the right

front floor of the vehicle and any cash was taken by the suspect.

- On more than one occasion the suspect had attempted or had succeeded in extorting money from the families of the victims. These were small amounts of cash.
- Based on the testimony of the Yellow Cab driver, there was a good chance the suspect lived around Gilbert and Commonwealth in the City of Fullerton.
- Before abandoning the victim's car, the suspect would wipe it down to destroy any physical evidence.
- All except one of the incidents, the Riverside case, had originated in the southeast part of Los Angeles County or the north part of Orange County, indicating the suspect could very possibly work or live in that general vicinity.[1]
- The suspect was a white male in his 20s and was probably between 5'10" and 5'11", weighed 170 to 175 pounds, and had light brown medium-length hair.
- The suspect had a tattoo of a swastika on the back of his left wrist.
- The suspect had yellowing teeth.
- The suspect smoked Marlboro cigarettes.
- The suspect may have been in the military.
- There was a possibility of identifying a suspect through the bite pattern found on the breast of Gina Tisher. This was, however, a new process and still being refined. While we considered the possibility, we did not know how successful this would be.
- The suspect had handled the driver's license and check from our second victim, and there was a chance of fingerprints that could identify him. We would

---

1. It was later determined that the Riverside case did not involve the same suspect as the other cases.

follow up with the Orange County Crime Lab on this in a few days.[2]

- A good deal of personal information was given to Banderas by her abductor; however, there was no way to determine if any of it was true, at least at this stage of the investigation.

- The last crime we knew about probably involving this same individual, prior to the two cases we were working at that time, was on December 19, 1975, in Downey, California in southern Los Angeles County.[3] The two cases we had, one a homicide and the other an attempted homicide, had occurred only four days apart. Tisher, in all probability was killed on January 2, 1976, and Carmen Banderas was kidnapped on January 6, 1976. It looked like the incidents were occurring with more frequency, adding to the urgency of finding this suspect.

- In the previous ten cases, only one victim had been murdered, and that case occurred in West Covina, back on October 27, 1975. Since then, there had been seven incidents where the victims were not killed. That string of survivors ended with the death of Gina Tisher on January 2, 1976.

Because of the cases in Los Angeles County, Sheriff Peter Pitchess of the Los Angeles County Sheriff's Office had called the Fullerton Chief of Police, Wayne Bornhoft, to offer any assistance he could in working this high-profile case. Detective

---

2. While having a fingerprint was a very positive development in a case, this was before the days of the computerized/automated fingerprint systems that could take a single print and match it to an individual if the person's prints were already on file. So, while having a fingerprint was valuable, it could only be matched when the police had developed information on a particular individual where his or her fingerprints could be obtained and then matched with the latent print.

3. This case was documented by the Downey Police Department.

Schauperl happened to mention to the chief he needed a good artist, and Chief Bornhoft was able to arrange for a police artist from the Los Angeles County Sheriff's Office to help us.

On January 8, 1976, Detective Schauperl transported the police artist to Tustin Community Hospital, where Carmen Banderas was still recovering. With her help, a sketch of the suspect was completed at that time. It was distributed to over three hundred law enforcement agencies the following day plus given to the newspapers and television stations in Orange, Los Angeles, Riverside, and San Bernardino Counties. It was then picked up by the wire services in many other parts of the country. The distribution of this drawing resulted in over two hundred leads, all of which had to be pursued and eliminated, but this drawing would ultimately lead to the actual killer.

We were contacted early that same afternoon by Detective MacAfee who said Identification Technician Hayes had found numerous prints on the check booked into evidence by Detective Storey. MacAfee had requested Hayes go to the Barclays Bank in Orange and get elimination prints from all persons who may have handled the check while it was at the bank. He also requested elimination prints from Mrs. Banderas at the hospital. Hayes completed both tasks that afternoon.

At nine-thirty that night, Detectives McDermott and Sharp from Los Angeles County's Norwalk Station, came to the Fullerton Police Department and told the on-duty desk officer, Ron Rowell, they had information that might be of assistance in investigating the recent attempted murder, kidnapping, and rape case that had occurred on January 6, in the city of Fullerton.

According to the detectives, their agency had experienced two incidents, the first, an attempted kidnapping occurring on December 19, 1975 at the La Mirada Shopping Center, and the second, a kidnap and attempted rape, occurring at about six-thirty in the evening on the same date, in the area of Lanning and Mills Street in La Mirada. They told Rowell they had a composite drawing of the suspect done by the daughter of the victim in their first case, and it matched the description given of the suspect in their second case. They said there was a possible suspect vehicle described in the second case as a light blue older model Chevrolet along with a vehicle seen in the first case, described as a red Toyota pickup truck with a white camper shell partial California plate 155. The detectives also said their office was currently forming a task force in reference to the above-noted cases through their station, which could result in further information which might be of assistance to us in the local investigation.

Later that evening we received copies of the reports from the Los Angeles Sheriff's Office of the first case that had occurred in the Norwalk area on December 19, 1975, and probably involved our suspect. This one had occurred in the La Mirada Shopping Center at Imperial Highway and Norwalk Boulevard. The twenty-two-year-old victim, Donna Margaros, described the suspect as a white male, twenty-five to thirty years old, approximately six feet tall, weighing about one hundred sixty pounds, and wearing a blue denim jacket and blue faded jeans.

She told the responding officers she had been shopping at Montgomery Ward with her two small children, ages one and four, and had just returned to her car at around noon. Margaros placed the children in car seats in the front passenger side of the car, then entered her car on the driver's side. As she got into her car, she observed a white male standing at the rear of a red Toyota pickup truck with a white camper shell parked next to her car. He had several packages in his arms and looked as if he was trying to open the camper shell to place them inside. After she was seated in her car, he told her that her back tire was flat. When she opened the door of her car to look, the suspect then attempted to enter her car, pushing her on the left shoulder and ordering her to slide over in the seat. She was prevented from moving over by one of the car seats attached to the middle of the front seat. She began honking the horn to get the attention of someone in the area. He then pointed a gun at her, which she described as being a small automatic pistol, chrome and black, and told her, "If you want to see Christmas, you better tell the little boy to get in the back seat, move the baby's chair and slide over. He repeatedly stated, "You want to see Christmas, don't you?"

Margaros told him she couldn't move over because of the car seat and she felt like she was going to faint, and if he would just leave, she wouldn't tell anyone. He then threatened her, telling her she'd better not tell anyone what had happened then walked into Montgomery Ward and stood just inside the doorway until she drove away.

According to the reporting officer, Margaros didn't know the location of the closest sheriff's office, which would have been the Norwalk office, so she drove directly to the Pico Rivera Substation and made the report there.

From the description of this incident and of the male perpetrator given by the victim, there seemed, at the time, little doubt this was the same person who had murdered Gina Tisher and left Carmen Banderas for dead. The fact he attempted to kidnap this particular woman, with two small children in the car, again added to the urgency we felt in catching this guy as soon as possible.

Unfortunately, the next real break in the case did not occur for almost three weeks. In the meantime, teams of detectives followed up on the almost two hundred leads provided by the public from posting the composite drawing done with the help of Carmen Banderas. There was extensive coverage of these crimes and, due to that, leads were coming in from as far away as Texas and Illinois. There were over three hundred pages of police reports generated because of information coming in from the public alone. Other law enforcement agencies were also investigating leads in their cases, trying to identify the suspect before he kidnapped another woman.

When a lead provided sufficient information, detectives would attempt to identify the possible suspect by name, obtain a picture and fingerprints and submit them so that person could either be identified or eliminated. Many of the leads named specific individuals and even provided addresses, making the job a little easier. Some of the photographs were from drivers' licenses obtained from the Department of Motor Vehicles, while others were Polaroids, taken by the detectives. Any that were even close to the physical description we had were shown to Carmen Banderas. She had no difficulty eliminating them immediately. We were very fortunate she was such an intelligent and stable person and that she was willing to help us in the case. As indicated earlier, the artist drawing she helped to develop turned out to be an extremely close likeness to that of the actual suspect.

The media is often criticized for their repeated coverage of events, especially in today's world of continuous 24-hour cable news channels and talk radio stations. But the coverage on this case, while not nearly as constant as in today's news cycles, was very intense for that time, and resulted in a high level of awareness on the part of the public. This proved to be very helpful in generating continued interest and many leads. People also began to pay more attention to their surroundings and report suspicious behavior they probably would not have reported otherwise. The constant and repetitive running on television of the artist drawing kept tensions high in the Los Angeles and Orange County areas, but also resulted in a more alert public, willing to help.

One reporter in particular, Sylvia Palmer of the now defunct Fullerton News Tribune, was especially helpful in keeping the public informed, and her efforts did not go unrewarded. The tip we received on January 30, that ultimately led to the arrest of the responsible person, came as a direct result of the local newspaper coverage. Sylvia was the police reporter for the newspaper for many years, and after the newspaper closed its doors, she went to work for the City of Fullerton. She served as the City of

Fullerton public information officer until her recent retirement. She was a favorite with us "cops" and had earned our respect because she kept confidences and always treated us fairly.

After the conclusion of this investigation, Captain Davis would tell the local newspapers, and later the Orange County Probation Department, this case had stirred more citizen concern and panic than any other case in his twenty-four-year career with the Fullerton Police Department.

At the end of each day, we would meet to discuss our progress, or lack thereof. At these daily meetings, which were sometimes informal, we would brainstorm ideas and talk about anything we might be missing. Ideas generated were to be followed up on in the days ahead.

For example, during one of these meetings, we discussed the Carmen Banderas case and what had transpired during the initial contact between Banderas and the suspect in the Fullerton College parking lot. She recalled he was carrying a notebook, like what a student might carry, and that he had left it in the parking lot. We had searched the parking lot for the notebook but had not pursued the issue further. After it was brought up in one of our meetings, we sent Detective Chuck Collins back to the college to see if someone had turned it in. They had not. It was this kind of routine follow-up and detail that consumed many hours during the early days of the investigation. There were detectives working seven days a week, trying to ensure that information didn't elude us during this critical time. Detective Leon Schauperl worked continually on this case for over a month without any days off. He was determined not to miss anything, and to get the person responsible for these vicious crimes.

Despite all the leads being checked out, we were making very little progress. Adding to our frustration was the realization our suspect would most likely commit another crime, if he had not done so already. Each day we failed to find him meant we were closer to finding another victim. But we knew that if information was coming in, we were closing the gap. We were confident we would find him, hopefully before another young woman was kidnapped, raped, or murdered. The urgency to catch this guy was increasing daily. Unfortunately, we were one day too late to prevent another woman from becoming his victim.

CHAPTER 6
THE LAST VICTIM

Thursday, January 29, 1976
Norwalk, California

JOYCE ROGUS HAD no reason to fear anything on that warm afternoon in late January as she chatted with a friend outside the Kinney's Shoe Store in the Paddison Square Shopping Center in Norwalk. It was her twenty-first birthday, and she had just bought a pair of shoes with money she had gotten from her family. She had no way to know her life was about to change forever.

There would be one more victim in this series of crimes committed by what the media had named the "Fullerton Parking Lot Rapist." Less than twenty-four hours later we would have our suspect identified and in custody, but not in time to prevent one more young woman from being subjected to the terror of being kidnapped and raped, not knowing if she would live or die. This time it occurred in her own home.

From the transcribed confession of the suspect:

OK, the most recent thing was Thursday. Last Thursday. I was supposed to go to work at the Chevron. It was on Thursday, January 29. I took my boy to school, and I went to… instead of going to work after that I went to…. It's really fighting me now man. Ah! I went to a shopping center where I drove around for a couple of hours. I drove around Orange County for a couple of hours… around Buena Park and La Palma, and a couple of hours later I ended up in Norwalk."

"I had been trying to get it to cut loose. OK. Ah. I pulled in there with the intention of committing a robbery and rape. I spent an hour or two roaming around in the parking lot. I think I parked and walked around, in and out of the stores, and around the parking lot for about an hour or so, and I don't know. I was trying to decide to do it, not to do it, whether to go to work, whether to do it. Fighting myself. Finally, I gave up, and I went and got back in the car, and I drove for a while around in Norwalk and Downey. I just drove for an hour, another hour or so. I went to a park. I don't know the name of it or anything. I went… I'm not sure, but the girl can probably tell where it was.

Anyway, I went to this parking lot I think it's on the edge of Norwalk, on the west… southwest corner of Norwalk some-where. If I had a map, I could pick it out but… anyway, I went in there. I don't know how much time I spent… doing the same thing, roaming around, and I saw this girl talking to this guy in front of a Kinney shoe store. And so I went, and I parked behind the building and sat and watched and waited for about fifteen minutes, and the guy finally went back inside the store. Maybe he was a shoe salesman or something. Anyway, she drove away, she pulled out… she took off out the parking lot and I followed her. I think it was off Pioneer Boulevard.

She pulled out of the parking lot onto a street and just went a hundred yards or so and made a left onto Pioneer Boulevard and then I followed her for ten or fifteen minutes up Pioneer Boule-vard. And she turned off on some side street, and I turned around on the side street, and she pulled in some apartments, and I pulled up. I pulled the car up in front of the apartments and jumped out and ran around the alleyway that she pulled into, looking for her car, with the idea that I would catch her in her car in the carport where I'd be safe from view, and she would be isolated. But she was way down the alleyway, and I ran down there and found her car, and she wasn't in her car. And so, I started to turn around to leave but there was a doorway out of the carport, and I thought that the doorway went through the apartments or something, so I started to walk through it and opened it up, and it was opened onto a patio, to the patio of her apartment.

And, she was standing there, and I said, "Uh, excuse me." I was trying to get through the apartments through to the center or something, and she said, "Well, you can cut through my apartment, that's OK." And so, I walked into her apartment and started cutting through it and went to the front door. And I saw there was no one there but her, and so I turned around, and I asked her if I could use her telephone. She walked back into the kitchen where the telephone was and said, "Here it is right here."

I walked back up to her and pulled out my gun and grabbed her shoulder, or something, and put the gun to her head and told her this was a rip-off. "I don't want to use your phone. Get in the bedroom." She asked me something. Like she asked me what I wanted, and I told her to shut up and get into the bedroom and directed her into the bedroom and told her to lay down on the—. No, first I asked her how much money she had. She told me about ten dollars, and I told her to get it all out. I spent a couple of minutes asking her if she had any money hidden anywhere that she wasn't getting. And she said no. So, I told her to lay down on the bed and put her face in the pillow and not to look up or not to look at me. If she looked at me, she could identify me, and I would have to kill her. And so, she did. She laid down with her face in the pillow, and then I took a piece of clothing or something that was lying on the floor, and I started going through her drawer with it looking for some money or something hidden. I pulled the drawer out that had underwear in it, and so I started sorting through her underwear, and I pulled out a slip which, I don't know, appealed to me or something, and I told her to take off her pants and put the slip on.

I made her take off her clothes and put the slip on. And I was asking her about money. How much money did her family have to pay to get her back alive? And she told me that that they were broke and didn't have anything. And I told her I didn't believe her and was pushing the gun in her face and telling her I was going to kill her, and she ought to be worth something to her family. And she said they might have a hundred, or two hundred dollars at the most, that was all they had. So, I told her that we were going to get it, but first, she was going to fuck me and fuck me like she never fucked anybody else before, and she was doing it for her life. She said "OK."

In the meantime, I had taken off some of my, all my clothes except my underwear, and so I told her to roll over on her back, and to stick my cock in her, and to pull down her pants. And she did it, and I kissed her a couple of times on the neck—ear lobes or something—and spent a couple of minutes in agonizing her and telling her that she wasn't doing a good enough job and that she better work harder until she got into it a little more. She got into it a little more, and it was—I was thinking a bunch of things at the time—I don't know. I got off and said, "It wasn't so bad, was it?" She said, "No." I said, "OK, get up, and go into the bathroom."

I followed her into the bathroom and told her to get in the shower. She tried to shut the door, and I said, "No, leave the door open, and stay in the shower." And when she went to get in the shower, I turned around, and I walked away, and I walked back into the bedroom. I was doing something in the bedroom. I don't know what I was doing. I think I was getting dressed, and then all of a sudden, I had my... I got my pants on, and she went running out the door of the bathroom. And I ran and chased her, and she ran across the living room, and I ran into the door to the hall, to the entry running into the living room, and I yelled, "I'll shoot! I'll shoot!" She just kept running, and she grabbed the door and ran out the door screaming.

I turned around and ran back into the bedroom and grabbed up my clothes. And I ran out the back door, and I ran over to the corner of the carport and started to jump over onto a roof behind the carport, and I realized that I had left my shirt in the apartment—my Chevron shirt—so, I ran back inside for it. I ran in there. I ran up and locked the front door and ran back inside. It was a real mess in the bedroom. I was tearing things apart looking for my shirt. I finally found my shirt, grabbed it, and ran to the carport, put on my shoes and started running up the alleyway back to the car. I could hear her screaming all the way back to the car. I got my shirt on and I ran out and I jumped in the car and she was still screaming. I don't know where she was, she was somewhere in the apartment complex or something.

I jumped in the car, and I started it up and I took off. I went down the side street and ended up next to the 605 Freeway. I got on the 605 Freeway going north, and I got off at Whittier Boulevard. I went on up Whittier Boulevard a way and I saw a Chevron Station, and I pulled into it and put some oil and a couple dollars' worth of gas in the car. Then I went over to the telephone and called Mollye to tell her I was going on my lunch break or something and was everything OK. I got back in the car and drove on up Whittier Boulevard until I got to Beach. I turned down Beach to... to my job... it was about one-thirty then. I was just going to go ahead and go to work.

I called... I remember now... I had called into work that morning from... ah... I called in twice, the first time I don't remember where. I called in from somewhere and told them that Ruby had had a stroke, a light stroke, and that I had to take her to the hospital, and I'd be a couple of hours late. And then, about eleven o'clock when I was in the Paddison Shopping

Center parking lot that I saw the girl at, I called into work again and told them that the doc said that Ruby had brain damage and probably wasn't going to make it, and I was going to spend the day with her, and I would be in tomorrow, Friday the first... yeah, Friday.[1]

---

1. His landlord, Ruby Patterson had actually suffered a stroke; however, it had occurred on January 28, 1976, one day earlier than what had told his employer.

CHAPTER 7
IN CUSTODY!

The Special Bulletin Sent to News Media and Law
Enforcement

IT WAS ON A FRIDAY, January 30, 1976, when a much-needed break in the case came, and the pieces of the puzzle began to fall into place. As is often the situation, this break-through came from a completely unknown and unexpected source. Involving the media as a "partner" in an investigation was something we frequently did, and sometimes it paid off. This was one of those times. The publicity the case created throughout the Orange County and Los Angeles area resulted in a citizen who thought he knew who we were looking for.

Friday, January 30, 1976
Placentia, California

8: 20 a.m. Detective Schauperl received a telephone call from a man identifying himself as Ronald Rockenbach. He told Schauperl he was a volunteer counselor for the Alpha Center, a non-profit counseling center, located at 106 Chapman Avenue, Placentia, the city just east of Fullerton, and he had information on the person he believed might be the "Fullerton rapist," also known as the "parking lot" rapist in the press.

Rockenbach told Detective Schauperl he had been counseling a couple named Mollye and Ken Hulbert for a marital problem, and had been for several months, off and on. He said that yesterday, the twenty-ninth, he had been contacted by Mollye Hulbert, who had come to his home to see him. She told him she suspected her husband, Ken Hulbert, was responsible for the rapes and murders appearing in the newspapers.[1] At five-thirty that same afternoon Mollye gave Ronald's wife, Linda Rockenbach, an envelope containing women's jewelry. This occurred when Linda had gone by the Hulbert residence on south Paula Avenue, in Fullerton. Mollye Hulbert revealed to Linda that her

---

1. At this time, Mollye Katherine Selfies was not and had not been married to Kenneth Hulbert, although they lived as husband and wife.

husband, Ken Hulbert, had told her he had raped and kidnapped two girls.

When she returned home, Linda shared this information and the envelope with her husband. Mr. Rockenbach told Schauperl he had looked into the envelope and saw it contained a wedding set, an emerald and onyx ring, a watch with the engraving of the name "Teri Muzic," and one pair of onyx earrings. Mr. Rockenbach was familiar with the case from the accounts in the newspapers, and knew that, according to newspaper reports, the suspect in the rapes and murder cases had a swastika on the back of his left wrist. After looking at the jewelry, Rockenbach called the Hulbert residence and talked to one of the children, David. He wanted to confirm that his father had a tattoo on the back of his left wrist. The child told him, yes, his dad did have a tattoo on the back of his left wrist, and it was a "Nazi tattoo."[2]

Detective Schauperl asked Mr. Rockenbach if he could bring the envelope and the contents he had described to the Fullerton Police Department. Schauperl immediately recognized description of the watch with the engraving "Teri Muzic," as that was the name of a victim in a case that had occurred in Los Angeles County in December of 1975.

Schauperl then notified Captain Davis and me of the conversation and that Rockenbach was on his way to the station. This news soon spread quickly around the detective bureau, and there was an air of excitement and anticipation among all the detectives. Every one of the detectives involved in the case had been present in the "bullpen" area of the detective bureau, where each had a desk, when the news came in. It seemed we had gotten a lucky break in the case far sooner than we had anticipated.

9: 00 a.m. Ronald Rockenbach arrived at the detective bureau

---

2. This was a "stepson" of Ken Hulbert's who lived with his mother, Mollye Selfies, at the time of the murders. His biological father resided in Lafayette, Mississippi. The tattoo had been described by Carmen Banderas back on January 7th, 1976.

and met Detective Schauperl who took custody of the envelope he had in his possession. Schauperl examined the jewelry and immediately realized the wedding set and emerald ring appeared to match the description of the missing jewelry of the murder victim, Gina Tisher. On closer examination he saw there was a stone missing in the emerald ring, just as described by Tisher's mother, Mrs. Maloney.

The envelope contained the following items of jewelry:

One ring with emerald and onyx set (with a set missing from the center)

A wedding ring set (consisting of two gold rings)

A pair of earrings containing what appeared to be onyx stones

A Timex brand watch with the name Teri Muzic engraved on the back

All the jewelry was subsequently matched with several of the victims in both Los Angeles and Orange Counties. The property was photographed then booked into evidence by Schauperl.

Mr. Rockenbach confirmed again his wife, Linda Rockenbach, had received this envelope and jewelry from Mollye Hulbert at the Hulbert residence on January 29, 1976, at five thirty in the evening.

After receiving this information from Rockenbach, Schauperl ran a record check on Kenneth (Ken) Richard Hulbert through the Department Records Bureau. Our local records did not reveal any criminal record that would lead a person to believe Hulbert could have been a violent killer. The check revealed he had been arrested two and a half years earlier for possession of marijuana in the City of Fullerton. We also learned, based on information given by other police officers, that Hulbert was the son of a Fullerton Fire Captain. Schauperl then requested fingerprints and a "mug shot" (booking photo) on Hulbert.

9: 20 a.m. The fingerprint card was taken down to the Fullerton ID Technician Jim Babcock to compare with the fingerprints that had been obtained from the check we had picked up from Barkley Bank in the Banderas case. Detective Schauperl then put together a photo lineup of six pictures, one of which was the booking photo of Hulbert taken over two and a half years earlier on May 14, 1973. In this particular photo Hulbert had shoulder length hair and a moustache.

Ken Hulbert Fullerton arrest photo 1973

9: 30 a.m. Carmen Banderas was called by Detective Schauperl, and she came in immediately to view the photo lineup, which included the picture of Ken Hulbert. Schauperl showed the photo lineup to Banderas. I noticed that, when she came in, the scars were still very clear on her face, but she was calm, determined, and ready to view the photo lineup. During the course of this investigation, Banderas had already been shown over forty different photographs and had eliminated them all.

Before viewing the six pictures, Banderas was admonished that the responsible person may or may not be in the group of photos. She was also told it was her duty to eliminate the innocent as well as to identify the guilty person, and if she was able to identify someone, she should be absolutely certain. Detective Schauperl then handed the photo lineup to her, and she began looking through the pictures. Upon coming to the picture of Hulbert, she immediately said, "That's him." Schauperl then asked her to what degree of certainty she was identifying him with, and she replied, "I am absolutely positive." She told Schauperl, "The only difference is that in this photo he has long hair and a moustache, but I am certain that's him." This remarkable woman had come through again. Despite the tension and the terror she had been subjected to on that day in January, she had been able to retain almost a perfect recall of the facts and identify her assailant from a photograph taken two and a half years previously, and where the suspects appearance was very different than when she encountered him.

9: 37 a.m. Detective Schauperl received a telephone call from Ronald Rockenbach who expressed concern Hulbert was probably aware Mollye Hulbert had contacted him regarding her suspicions. Rockenbach had no real evidence Hulbert was aware of this but was fearful that the lives of Mollye and their children might be in danger. He told us that if Hulbert did know, he would, in his opinion, probably either attempt to flee or to harm Mollye or the children.

After the photo identification by Banderas, everyone was anxious to find Hulbert, but Detective Schauperl, as was typical of him, slowed the process down, and continued to methodically put together all the information and evidence so probable cause for the arrest would be solid and hold up in a court of law. He was waiting for the identification technician, James Babcock, to come back up with the print taken from Carmen Banderas' check and confirm a positive identification of Ken Hulbert. Until he had that final piece of evidence, he would not move forward. Chief Wayne Bornhoft and Captain C.D. Davis were watching this process, and I overheard Davis comment, "You can't rush Leon." It was exactly this characteristic that made him such an effective homicide investigator.

9: 40 a.m. ID Tech Babcock informed detectives there were twenty-six points of identification in the latent print found on the check positively identifying Hulbert as having handled the check that was subsequently recovered from the Barclays Bank in Orange. This amounted to an absolute positive identification. We now knew for sure we had our suspect and that he was identified beyond a reasonable doubt.

After receiving this information, Leon met with Captain Davis, the other available investigators, and me to plan our approach to the Hulbert residence.[3] It was decided we would divide into several teams and set up a surveillance perimeter to prevent Hulbert from escaping from the area. Schauperl, accompanied by Captain Davis, would go to the closest location to the suspect's home in preparation for an emergency entrance if necessary. This decision was based in part on the telephone call received from Rockenbach and his concern for the safety of Mollye and the children. After all units were in place, Rockenbach was instructed to place a call to the Hulbert residence to determine if Hulbert was in the house, or if Mollye was there alone with the children. If he was able to make contact and Hulbert was there, he would attempt to get Mollye to take the children and leave.

9: 50 a.m. All officers were in place and the Hulbert home

---

3. This address was only a few blocks from the intersection of Gilbert Avenue and Commonwealth Avenue, where the cab driver had let his fare out on the night of January 2, 1976. The cab driver was never able to positively identify Hulbert, but Hulbert himself admitted to taking the cab in later interviews.

was basically surrounded by teams of police officers. Rockenbach placed the call from the Fullerton Police Department;
however, no one answered the phone. We were concerned
Hulbert was, in fact there, but not answering the telephone.
There was also the very real possibility he had injured or killed
Mollye and/or the children. These possibilities were discussed
by Detective Schauperl and Captain Davis, and Davis made the
decision to enter the residence to attempt to locate Hulbert and
to make certain no harm had come to any family member.

10: 00 a.m. Schauperl and Davis approached the home, and
when they tried the front door, they found it was unlocked. They
entered the home and made a visual check of the interior to see if
anyone was there or not. No one was found inside the house,
and the two of them left and resumed the surveillance of the
home from the street.

10: 32 a.m. While this was going on, Detective Jerry Storey
and I were staked out in a position on West Avenue, about one-
half block west of Gilbert Avenue and a couple blocks north of
the suspect's residence on Paula. This was just one block south of
the location where the cab driver had dropped off our suspect on
Friday evening, January 2, 1976.

Jerry was driving and I was in the front passenger seat,
armed with a shotgun loaded with double ought buckshot. We
were parked at the north curb facing west. In the rear seat was
Wayne H. Bornhoft, the legendary Fullerton Chief of Police, who
rarely came into the field to participate in an investigation or
arrest. His presence that day was an indicator of how high a
profile case this had become, not only in the community, but in
the State of California and beyond.

As we waited at our location, we saw a car coming toward us
from the west but did not recognize it as Hulbert's until it was
almost on top of us. We glanced at the driver and realized immediately it was him. There was a female passenger with him in the

front seat. It was also clear from the startled look on his face, that he had recognized us as police officers. He immediately accelerated and continued eastbound on West Avenue and then southbound on Gilbert at a high rate of speed.

Chief Wayne H. Bornhoft circa 1970s

Storey made an instant U-turn in pursuit of the Hulbert car. I called in the information on the police radio and other officers began to converge on our location. This was the first and last time I was involved in a pursuit with the Chief of Police in the car with me. Our detective units were, for the most part, old and not always very fast.

I remember one exchange that occurred during the pursuit, between the chief and Detective Storey, that still causes me to laugh when I think about it. When we first made the U-turn and started the pursuit, I had a fleeting thought about how the chief was going to react, given the discipline he had handed out for officers involved in pursuits in the past. But I need not have worried. Going south on Gilbert we were having difficulty catching up to Hulbert's car, and Chief Bornhoft began pounding on the rear driver's seat and yelling for Storey to go faster. Storey angrily yelled back he was going as fast as this "piece of crap will go," referring to our second-hand Dodge. After that it was no longer the chief in the back, but just three police officers in pursuit of a murder suspect.

10: 35 a.m. Fortunately for us, Hulbert made a series of turns back into the residential area to the west. He ended up in a cul-de-sac and stopped in a driveway at the south end of the street, where we were able to catch up with him. I jumped out of the passenger side, racked a shell into the Remington 12-gauge shotgun I was carrying, and ordered Hulbert out of the vehicle and onto the ground. He did not respond right away, so the order was repeated by me then by Jerry Storey. Jerry had also gotten out and was standing behind the police vehicle's open front door pointing his weapon at Hulbert. Chief Bornhoft was outside the right rear door, just behind me, watching the whole thing take place.

There were a few tense moments when it looked like he was not going to comply with our instructions. Finally, however, he opened the driver's door, got out of the car and, following our directions, walked a few steps away then lay face down in the driveway. Jerry conducted a cursory search for the weapon we knew he owned then handcuffed him. The weapon was not found.

As it turned out it was good Hulbert had followed our directions and exited the car, because when we walked up to the driver's door, we realized there was a baby in a car seat in the middle of the front seat next to Mollye, and she and the baby had remained in the car as ordered.

Margaret Place where the pursuit ended on January 30, 1976

Area Map of 600 Paula Drive, Fullerton

No one was injured during the pursuit or the arrest.

Detective Storey got on the radio and notified the dispatcher Ken Hulbert was in custody. A uniformed officer, Mike Maynard, came to the scene, transported the suspect to the Fullerton Police Department, and accompanied him into an interview room and stayed with Hulbert. Maynard would remain with him until Schauperl and I arrived, as we would conduct the first of what turned out to be three interviews with our suspect, Ken Hulbert, later that morning.

10: 37 a.m. Detective Schauperl and Captain Davis came to the scene of the arrest and interviewed Mollye Hulbert. She was asked if she would come to the department for further questioning. She told Schauperl she would go with them, but first needed to go back to her residence and get diapers and milk for her baby. We agreed to this and escorted her back to the house where she obtained the items she needed. She was then taken by Schauperl to the department for interviewing. While on the way, Leon asked Mollye if, in fact, Hulbert had told her about kidnapping and raping girls. Mollye told him he had told her he had kidnapped and raped two girls, but he had also told her he was just fantasizing.

10: 45 a.m. They got back to the station and Schauperl continued the interview with Mollye. She told him she was not legally married to Ken Hulbert, but they had been living together for the past two years, and she had been using the name of Mollye Hulbert. She stated she had met him here in California, but they had moved to Mississippi for a short time in 1974 to visit with her parents. She said they moved to Nebraska in July of 1974 and lived there until July of 1975. Mollye said she and Hulbert got along very well at first, but while living in Nebraska they began to have money problems and the relationship began deteriorating after that.

Detective Schauperl again asked her about the statement made by Hulbert when he told her about kidnapping and raping two girls and about where she had found the jewelry she had given to Linda Rockenbach. She told Schauperl she didn't want to hurt Ken and became reluctant to answer any further questions. After several attempts to get her to reveal more of what she knew, the interview was terminated. Mollye asked if she could stay at the department until she knew what was happening with Ken, and she was allowed to do so.

Right after the arrest of Ken Hulbert, Patrol Officer Ben Hamner was posted at the Hulbert home on Paula Street, until a search warrant could be obtained. This was to ensure the integrity of the scene and the admissibility of any evidence recovered.

10: 50 a.m. After discussions with Schauperl, I requested Detectives Deveney and Collins obtain search warrants for both the residence on Paula Avenue and the person of Ken Hulbert, as soon as possible. I also asked Deveney to serve the search warrants and assist in the search of the residence. I told him the house was secured and a police officer would remain there until the search warrants could be obtained and the property could be searched. Deveney and Collins, not having been personally involved in all facets of the case, were having some difficulty with the affidavits in terms of establishing the probable cause for the arrest, so Detective Schauperl had to leave one of the interviews and assist in this process. During his absence, Detective Rex Stricklin stayed with Hulbert. A detailed analysis of the evidence collected is described in Chapter Eight.

12: 40 p.m. Detective Schauperl and I began the first of three interviews with Ken Hulbert. Some of the details of the transcriptions from these interviews are also detailed in Chapter Eight.

The home on Paula Avenue where Hulbert lived in at the time of his arrest

The .25 auto Found in Search of Paula home

1: 00 p.m. Detectives Deveney and Collins planned to meet with two of the Orange County District Attorney's Homicide Division attorneys, Frank Briseno and Oretta Sears. Both Briseno and Sears were very experienced with homicide cases and prepared to assist us in the search warrant process. With their assistance the detectives compiled an eight-page affidavit outlining the particulars of a single rape, assault, and kidnap homicide investigation being conducted by our department. We could always add more charges later. The affidavit requested that the detectives be allowed to conduct a search of the premises where Hulbert was residing on south Paula Avenue in Fullerton as soon as possible. Specifically named in the affidavit were items in the envelope as well as items turned over to the counselor:

One wedding ring set, white gold color, no stone in the wedding band, small diamond in the engagement ring

One ladies' Timex watch, silver metal, oval-shaped, light blue face with Roman numerals at the 3, 6, 9, and 12 positions on the dial

One lady's white gold ring with a blue stone

One .22 to .32 caliber handgun, semi-automatic, blue steel

They also completed an affidavit to obtain a search warrant for the person of Ken Richard Hulbert to include samples of head hair, pubic hair, saliva, dental impressions, full dental casts, wax bite impressions, and photographs of each of these, all to be taken in a medically approved manner.

3: 30 p.m. Schauperl and I took a break from the interview with Hulbert to allow him to use the bathroom and get something to drink.

3: 39 p.m. Ken Hulbert was taken to the main area of the jail and booked on the current charges. He was fingerprinted and photographed at that time. Detective Schauperl asked him if he wanted to make a telephone call, and he said he wanted to call Ruby Patterson but did not want to make the call at that time.

4: 50 p.m. Hulbert was returned to the Investigation Division interview room and the questioning continued. This second interview was also tape recorded and videotaped. The interview was concluded at approximately five forty-five p.m. Nothing of value was obtained and Hulbert was very nervous and uncooperative, which led us to discontinue the interview at that time.

5: 50 p.m. Detective Schauperl requested a specialist from the Orange County Sheriff's Office obtain physical evidence from Hulbert. Criminalists Mary Graves and Jim White were contacted and asked to come to the Fullerton Police Department. A request was also made for Dr. Vale, a forensic dentist and consultant to the Los Angeles County Coroner's Office, to come to our station. Detective Schauperl had become aware of Dr. Vales' work while attending one of the Los Angeles/Orange County Homicide Investigators' monthly meetings where the subject was discussed. Dr. Vale agreed to assist us and came to the station.

6: 00 p.m. Schauperl interviewed Mollye again. Even though she was becoming increasingly uncooperative, this time she told him she had found the jewelry she gave to Linda Rockenbach in a small cardboard box located in a dresser drawer in their bedroom. She said she had found it approximately one week prior to giving it to Linda Rockenbach. She was shown the jewelry in question and identified it as the same jewelry she had found in the cardboard box. She told the detective that when she first found it, she thought Ken was seeing another woman. Mollye also said that, in the past week, a neighbor had contacted her with a newspaper containing the composite drawing of the person responsible for the Fullerton kidnapping and rapes and had commented about the closeness of the drawing to Ken Hulbert. She said that because of these comments by the neighbor, she confronted Ken with her suspicions, but he had assured her he was not responsible for these crimes. Throughout both interviews she was reluctant to reveal the full information regarding her conversation with Ken or her discussions with Linda and Ronald Rockenbach. She did, however, admit to giving the jewelry to Linda Rockenbach on January 29, 1976.

6: 37 p.m. Meanwhile, Deputy D.A. Briseno had arranged with Superior Court Judge William L. Murray to review the affidavits in anticipation of obtaining the warrants. Detectives Collins and Deveney went with Briseno to the judge's home in Santa Ana. After reviewing the affidavits, Judge Murray issued the search warrants as requested. He also issued an order that the suspect be held without bail in the case.

7: 00 p.m. Detectives Deveney and Collins returned to the department with the search warrants. A team of detectives and patrol officers was selected to do the search of the Hulbert home, while Detective Glenn Deveney would serve the search warrant on Hulbert himself.

7: 37 p.m. Deveney served the search warrant on Hulbert for the collection of any suspected physical evidence from his person. Present at this search were Captain Davis, Detective Schauperl, Orange County Criminalists James White and Mary Graves, Dr. J. Vale, and Dr. Burg, who was a doctor at the UCLA Medical Center and who had come with Dr. Vale to assist us in the case.

The criminalists obtained a pubic hair sample and a saliva specimen and transported the samples to the Orange County Crime Lab for further evaluation.

7: 40 p.m. While the warrant was being served on Hulbert for the collection of any physical evidence from his person, I accompanied Detectives Collins, Storey, and Goulet, and Officer Ben Hamner to the Paula Avenue residence to serve the search warrant. It was served on Howard Patterson, the twenty-eight-year-old son of the owner, Ruby Patterson, as she had suffered a stroke and was still hospitalized. We spoke with Mrs. Patterson on the phone and confirmed her son was acting as an agent for his mother. We also told Mrs. Patterson we would be conducting a search of her property on South Paula, in accordance with a search warrant we had obtained.

8: 00 p.m. Ken Hulbert was transported to the office of a local dentist by Detectives Schauperl and Deveney and Captain Davis. Dr. Donald Tormey had made his dental facilities available to us so Dr. Vale and Dr. Burg could obtain a dental impression from Hulbert, also in compliance with the search warrant. At about eight-ten that evening, they began the process of obtaining the impression. It was kept by Dr. Vale for further evaluation and comparison later.

This was a relatively new technique at the time, and one that was not practiced by very many forensic dentists. After completing his examination, Dr. Vale was not able to positively confirm the bite mark was a match to Hulbert. There were many indications it was, but it could not be conclusively established. His report read, "Evidence of consistency between Mr. Hulbert's teeth and the tooth marks on the decedent's breast can't eliminate Mr. Hulbert. He could have inflicted the marks on the decedent's breast. I can't make a definite conclusion in this matter."

10: 30 p.m. Detective Schauperl allowed a visit between Mollye Selfies and Ken Hulbert in the Fullerton jail. This conversation was recorded, but it was inaudible due to interference in the jail and because both Mollye and Hulbert were whispering.

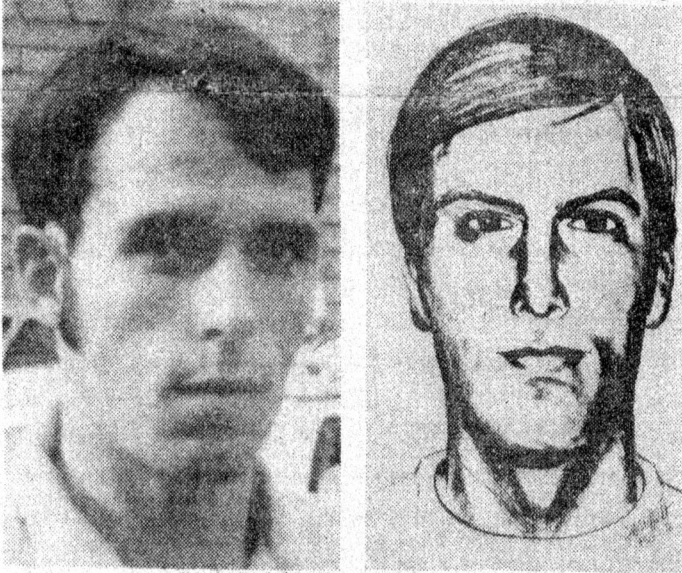

Photo, Sketch Compared

Photo by Jess Andresen Jr.

At left is a photograph of Kenneth R. Hulbert, arrested yesterday as a suspect in a slaying and series of assaults on women during the last three months, and at right is a composite sketch of the suspect made from witnesses' descriptions by a police artist earlier this month.

Newspaper copy of photo of Hulbert compared to the Drawing

10: 40 p.m. During a review of the case, we realized we had failed to include a blood sample in the original search warrant for Hulbert, so Detective Deveney again contacted District Attorney Briseno, who told him to get another warrant for this. Deveney and Collins prepared the additional affidavit and took it to the home of Judge Murray for his signature.

Saturday, January 31, 1976
Fullerton, California

11: 10 a.m. At the request of Detective Schauperl, Dr. John

Hunter, a neuropsychiatrist, came to the department to interview and examine Ken Hulbert. The interview was tape recorded, subsequently transcribed, and lasted until 1: 40 p.m.

In his written report, dated February 3, 1976, Dr. Hunter related the following:

"In the course of this protracted psychiatric examination, I found nothing which would suggest that this defendant is either psychotic or insane in either the medical or legal senses. However, his entire past personal background would indicate that he shows all the cardinal attributes of the sociopathic personality disorder. Evidence of this lies in his prior known police and antisocial record which consists of indiscriminate and extensive use of illegal drugs, inability to conform even in jail—where he continued to use contraband materials—convictions for grand theft auto, burglary, and armed robbery, "hustling" as a male prostitute, living many years on "hand outs and what he could steal', writing bad checks, and sexually deviated activities which I suspect were admitted to me only in part.

"He shows pathological confidence in his belief that he can completely explain away all involvement in the offenses with which he is now charged, despite the overwhelming evidence against him. He shows absolutely no overt fear or guilt responses.

"It would be most unusual, if not impossible, for a defendant, even if innocent, to show this type of smug confidence and total lack of fear and/or concern. All the above would identify an individual who does not put the proper values on anything. He shows poor judgment in everything he does, he does not profit by past experiences, and he does not have a conscience which causes him to have guilt feelings about any of his anti-social behavior. These are the attributes of the sociopathic personality."

12: 49 p.m. Judge Murray approved the search warrant allowing for the drawing of blood from Hulbert.

2: 02 p.m. Orange County Criminalist DeGowin took the

blood sample from Hulbert at the Fullerton jail facility and transported it to the Orange County Crime Lab for evaluation.

4: 10 p.m. Carmen Banderas came to the department at the request of Detective Schauperl to view the jewelry that had been recovered and see if any of it belonged to her. Mrs. Banderas immediately identified a Timex watch, one ring, and one engagement ring as being hers. These three items also corresponded to three stolen items she had described to officers in the initial police reports. We couldn't help but continue to be impressed with her as we had been from the first days of the investigation. It was remarkable she was able to remember almost every detail of her ordeal, despite the circumstances and the fact she was near death when found that night. Even with the scars that gave evidence of the beating she had undergone, she was still a very beautiful young woman and an articulate, accurate, and competent witness.

4: 15 p.m. Charles Tisher, Gina's husband, came to the department at the request of Detective Schauperl for the purpose of viewing the jewelry brought in by Ronald Rockenbach the previous morning. He immediately identified a wedding ring set, an emerald and onyx ring, and a pair of stud earrings as belonging to his wife. He confirmed she had been wearing these items on that Friday, January 2, 1976.

4: 50 p.m. Detective Schauperl called Mollye and asked her to come to the police department. Mollye Selfies had already moved out of the Paula Avenue house and was living in an apartment in Anaheim. Selfies came to the station but told Schauperl she did not wish to make any further statements. After their conversation, Schauperl again allowed her to visit with Hulbert in the jail facility.

CHAPTER 8
GOING FOR THE COPOUT

Friday, January 30, 1976
Fullerton, California
The First Interview

AS INDICATED EARLIER, the first interview with Hulbert, took place at twelve-forty p.m. on the same day as his arrest. He was interviewed in one of the two small interview rooms in the Detective Bureau, located on the main level of the annex building, completed in the early 1970s. The room was small and contained a table pushed against the center of one wall and three metal chairs. There was a two-way mirror on the wall opposite the table, which allowed detectives to observe someone placed in the room or to monitor the actual interview. The interview was recorded with video equipment, and an audio recording was made with a small diskette style tape recorder. Interviews are always a tense time in an investigation, and this was no exception.

When Hulbert was brought into the interview room, he appeared a little apprehensive about his situation but still displayed an air of confidence that this would all be over soon. He was advised of his constitutional rights, and he told us he understood his rights and agreed to talk about the case. This entire interview was videotaped and recorded. He listened closely to what we said to him and responded to every question.

As the interview progressed, he seemed to get more and more nervous and smoked heavily throughout the time we were there. Although Hulbert did not admit to any crimes, there was a lot of valuable information obtained, mostly as the result of some very skilled interviewing by Leon Schauperl. Some of the things we learned included the following:

- About a year before, he and Mollye had lived in Nebraska. This became relevant later as there was a similar incident that occurred in Red Cloud, Nebraska, where they had been living. Nebraska authorities looked at him closely as possibly having committed this crime but were never able to put their case together. The murder remains unsolved.
- Hulbert had been employed at the Tic Toc minimarket on Placentia Avenue in Fullerton during December 1975. This was relevant as it was less than one-half block away from where the body of Gina Marie Tisher and her vehicle were abandoned.
- Hulbert had testified in court on January 6, 1976, having been transported there by Detectives Storey and Collins. This put him near the Fullerton Junior College on the date and approximate time Banderas was kidnapped.

Through the interview techniques used by Detective Schauperl, Hulbert was moved closer to admitting to the crimes he was arrested for. One of these techniques was to reveal small amounts of the evidence we had that connected him to the crimes, letting him know this was not a "fishing trip" but was based on solid information that would hold up in court. This began to dissolve his cocky attitude and assurance he could "beat the charges." Hulbert was slowly but inevitably maneuvered into a corner of facts and seeming coincidences he could not escape from. The information given to him were the kinds of evidential material we could safely reveal without jeopardizing the case or a subsequent confession by Hulbert.

Two of the most critical were that we had positive identification from a witness, and that his right thumb print had been found on a check left at Barclays Bank and belonging to Carmen Banderas.

Here is a part of the transcript from the interview where the issue of the fingerprint was discussed. Hulbert is shown a copy of the check with his fingerprint on it:

Schauperl: "It's true; I haven't shown you all the evidence in the case. I haven't really gone into that much detail about a lot of things, but I am saying that in my mind I know you did these things."

Hulbert: "Putting myself in your place, in my mind, with what I've said, well, I don't know where the hell I was from December the first to today except for a few days here and there. And if that's my defense and my wife's saying yes, he was here and ah... unless I can come up with specifics or something like that as opposed to this check that is somehow connected and whatever, you know, all the of the things that have been mentioned, well, then I can see how you're sure in your mind. I can see how that would work."

DeVore: "But, what about this Ken?" (I am holding up the copy of the Banderas check with Hulbert's thumbprint on it).

Hulbert: "I can't say nothing. What, what the hell can I say? I don't even know how the hell it's connected; I don't know how it could 'a got there, I don't know..."

Schauperl: "I'll tell you how it's connected..."

Hulbert: "OK."

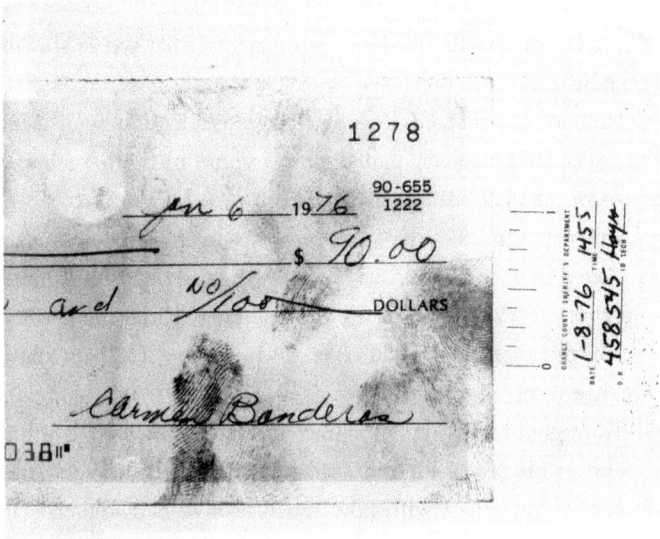

1278

90-655
1222

$ 90.00

NO/100   DOLLARS

Carmen Banderas

038

Banderas Check with Hulbert Fingerprints

Schauperl: "Ken, you put that check just like that, with your right thumb… along with a driver's license into a canister and sent it into a bank with this young lady that said that you talked about avocado pizza, you talked about liking the country, and that same young lady you took her check that you asked her to write, and you stuck it in a canister, and you sent that check into the bank."

DeVore: "It was left there, and we picked it up."

Schauperl: "And it was left there until we picked it up. And that check was processed and there's the print on that check. That's just a photograph of it but we have the check. That is how that print got on that check. And the young lady described all those circumstances. Not only did the young lady describe the circumstances, but the people at the bank also. And, that is your right thumb, I mean that's conclusive. That is your right thumb."

Hulbert: "If the experts say that's my right thumb, then that's my right thumb and there ain't nothin' I can say about that except, I don't know a goddamn thing about it."

Schauperl: "Well, OK, Ken, you analyze what we've shown you here so far, and that's just a portion of it, OK?"

Hulbert: "Like I said, looking at it from a legitimate or legal hangover, or whatever, that's, even I come up with probable cause for me to be sitting where I'm sitting right now."

Hulbert admitted that the previous evening Mollye had suspected he was responsible for the crimes and had confronted him about it. He also acknowledged he knew about the jewelry and the fact that Mollye had given it to someone. He even knew who had received it from Mollye.

Throughout this part of the interview, Hulbert shifted around in his seat a lot and appeared to be very nervous and obviously concerned with how much Mollye had told us. He was unable to establish an alibi for himself for the days and times these crimes took place and had no witness to any of his activities. Again, here is part of that conversation taken from the transcript:

Schauperl: "Let's go on further... to the point where you are in your... ah... home atmosphere. Say Mollye realizes that you might be the one responsible for these things. Something happened that..."

Hulbert: "Yes she did."

Schauperl: "OK. And talked of how you..."

Hulbert: "Talked about how I was... schizophrenic."

Schauperl: "Wouldn't that upset you?"

Hulbert: "It upset the hell out of me. It still is upsetting the hell out of me."

Schauperl: "Then did you have any discussion with her about that?"

Hulbert: "Sure we did."

Schauperl: "And what was that discussion about?"

Hulbert: "How whether or not I'm the guy... or..."

Schauperl: "Did she believe that you were?"

Hulbert: "She questioned it… ah… I thought it was a joke at first."

Schauperl: "Then when she had the jewelry… it wasn't a joke was it? Could you explain that jewelry to her?"

Hulbert: "I'm saying that's not my jewelry. Are you telling me that Mollye gave you that jewelry?"

Schauperl: "Not directly, no."

Hulbert: "She gave it to somebody who gave it to you?"

Schauperl: "Then you know about the jewelry. Then you talked about that, and you talked about kidnapping and rape… to…"

Hulbert: "To Mollye?"

Schauperl: "Mollye."

Hulbert: "She asked me about it and I…"

Schauperl: "And you told her that you thought you had."

Hulbert: "No, did she tell you that?"

Schauperl: "At one point in time…"

Hulbert: "You gotta be speculating…"

Schauperl: "No, no I'm not speculating, I'm not speculating, I'm saying at one point in time didn't you yourself tell her that you had kidnapped… ah… some gals… ah… coming from you to her without you questioning her?"

Hulbert: "I didn't kidnap any gals, and so I wouldn't have told her that. She questioned me about it when that photo… ah… it was a Sunday, I think.

… or Saturday or a Sunday and one of the neighbors brought it over. We were talking about it or heard about it or something. That was when I saw that newspaper thing the neighbor brought it over and gave it to her or gave it to me and I gave it to her, and she went outside, and she came back. That's when I thought it was a big joke but she… it turned out she was half-assed serious. So, I thought I had convinced her that… that she was just … imagining it."

Schauperl: "But, she wasn't, was she because she had jewelry that she had found. She was serious and she had something substantial that she was trying to find out. And you talked to her about it."

Hulbert: "I don't remember talking about it. I remember telling her I didn't do it and no mention of jewelry or anything else except that from the fact that I fit... you know... fit the description generally and the picture looked something like me and... the fact that I'd been out sometimes and hadn't told her where I was... I'd been out late or..."

Schauperl: "Now, do you think this is all imagination? These things have been happening."

Hulbert: "I'm sure..."

Schauperl: "Mollye believed that things that she found... jewelry..."

Hulbert: "Well, I don't like to throw names around. I don't think Mollye found

That..."

Schauperl: "Am I now telling you how we came by it?"

Hulbert: "Why... that's why I'm saying I don't like to throw names around but I'm telling you that..."

Schauperl: "In connection with..."

Hulbert: "I don't know, you say that Mollye had that jewelry or gave it to somebody that gave it to somebody that gave it to you or..."

Schauperl: "All of this is in connection with Mollye's concern and her conversation with you about this. The fact that it came to us by some means, the fact that we have a fingerprint on a check which there's no... no question is yours. Mollye, its true is unaware of your fingerprint. She's unaware of your identification... and in her mind she was still convinced, wasn't she?"

Hulbert: "She questioned it."

Schauperl: "No, she was convinced."

Hulbert: "This won't last..."

Schauperl: "She must have been serious... she must have been..."

Hulbert: "OK, she was seriously questioning, or halfway

convinced last night, I guess, but the deal with Ron, she sure wouldn't have gone through all that through what we did last night."

Schauperl: "What did you have to go through last night?"

Hulbert: "What went on with her… well, I'm sure you know what happened… 'cause I'm sure Ron must have got in touch with you."

Schauperl: "I'm trying to say to you that Mollye, I believe, was convinced or she wouldn't have done the things that she did do."

Hulbert: "From your conversation with her do you believe she's convinced that I did it?"

Schauperl: "Oh no, not just that, but the fact that we got this jewelry in our possession at this time."

Hulbert: "That you say that you got from her directly or however… and what did she say about that?"

Schauperl: "What did she say about it? What did she say to you about it?"

Hulbert: "She didn't say nothing to me about it."

DeVore: "What happened last night, tell us about that?"

Hulbert: "Well, I'm sure she must have told you about it."

DeVore: "Why don't you tell us what happened last night?"

Hulbert: "Well, she questioned me again last night cause I… ah… missed work and she took the kids over somewhere… to ah… to Ron's place and apparently, she… obviously she told him ah… her suspicions which I imagine is the reason I'm here. I don't know why he waited until this morning…"

Schauperl: "She told you that?"

Hulbert: "What?"

Schauperl: "That she went to somebody's house?"

Hulbert: "Well, I went over there and picked my kids up, yeah."

Schauperl: "OK, did your discussion take place after you picked your kids up? Your discussion with her… did it take place after you picked the kids up? Did you know she was over at somebody's house? Did you have any more discussion with her?"

Hulbert: "In relation to this?"

Schauperl: "Yeah."

Hulbert: "We talked before we picked the kids up. That was the idea of taking the kids over there, so that we could talk..."

Schauperl: "Well, what was her purpose in going to Ron's house?"

Hulbert: "Ron was a therapist... is or was or... psychologist or therapist or something that we went to see for a while. Apparently, she just continued to see him. She kept in contact, I haven't, last night was the first time I've seen him in a long time."

Schauperl: "Well, what I'm saying though..."

Hulbert: "Since we first..."

Schauperl: "Did she tell you that she had told this Ron her suspicions?"

Hulbert: "Yeah."

Schauperl: "Don't you have anything to say about that?"

Hulbert: "She went to see Ron because she thought her mental state was bad. I guess it was."

Schauperl: "Why, she didn't want to believe it herself?"

Hulbert: "Well, I sure wouldn't. She was just freaking out, so she called him up. I don't know, I don't really know what she did. All I remember is she told me that she called him up and told him that she... well, she talked to him and asked him to keep the kids for a while so that when I got home, we could talk in private about it."

Schauperl: "Well, what did she say?"

Hulbert: "She wanted to know where the hell I was."

Schauperl: "When?"

Hulbert: "Yesterday."

Schauperl: "Oh, yesterday. Where were you yesterday?"

Hulbert: "I wasn't where I was supposed to be... I wasn't at work... so."

Schauperl: "Well, do you remember where you were at yesterday?"

Hulbert: "Yeah, I was… most… I told her where I was anyway. That's… that's when we went and got the kids and then it was after that she told Ron. I don't know if it was before or after, but anyway…"

Hulbert: "… jewelry or gave that jewelry to you directly or indirectly."

Schauperl: "Well, how do you think we got it?"

Hulbert: "I don't know where the hell it came from. I only know that you're telling me that it was my jewelry and that…"

Schauperl: "Not your jewelry."

Hulbert: "OK, well, that it was… that I was in possession of it. Now you're telling me…"

Schauperl: "How do you think we came by it?"

Hulbert: "That Mollye found, I don't know how you came by it. I don't know how you came by this either."

At that point, to continually keep Hulbert off-guard, Schauperl changed directions and began asking him about any guns he might own. He admitted to having owned a small .25 caliber semi-automatic pistol but claimed to have sold it. It was recovered later that same day during the service of a search warrant on his home on Paula Avenue. It was also determined he had purchased the gun from a gun store during the time he had lived with Mollye in Nebraska. Here is what he told us in the interview:

Schauperl: "Do you own a gun now?"

Hulbert: "Do I own one?"

Schauperl: "Yeah."

Hulbert: "I used to own one… a couple of 'em but I sold 'em."

Schauperl: "What kind of guns did you have?"

Hulbert: "A twenty-five pistol and a twenty-two rifle."

Schauperl: "What was the pistol like? What kind of a pistol was it?"

Hulbert: "A twenty-five automatic."

Schauperl: "Automatic?"

Hulbert: "... twenty-five. That was a little cheapie automatic."

Schauperl: "Do you still have that? Was it a small one?"

Hulbert: "I also know that it was... a small automatic pistol or something like that was used. They put that into the newspaper article. I also assume that's what you were looking for when you searched today, for any kind of a weapon."

Schauperl: "Do you have it there in the house?"

Hulbert: "No."

Schauperl: "When did you sell the twenty-five automatic pistol?"

Hulbert: "After we came out here."

Schauperl: "Who did you sell it to? You said when you came out here back last year?"

Hulbert: "Yeah that was a condition of my probation, that I get rid of it."

Schauperl: "How did you go about selling it?"

Hulbert: "I sold it to a guy under the table."

Schauperl: "Do you know who he is?"

Hulbert: "No, I just ... I had to get rid of it... I needed the bread."

Schauperl: "Do you remember what you sold it for?"

DeVore: "Was it to somebody you work with?

Schauperl: "How did you meet him? How did you know he wanted to buy a gun?"

Hulbert: "Just talking. I know I sold the rifle. I don't know who I sold that to either."

[I hadn't picked up on this sentence when he said it during the interview, but later when we were reviewing the transcript it stood out as it seemed like a slip up on his part. He indicated he knew he had sold the rifle, and by inference, didn't know if he had sold the pistol. We typically would have re-interviewed him on this issue later but didn't have the transcripts completed at the time of the second interview, and the third interview was initiated by Hulbert and took a completely different direction.]

Schauperl: "Do you remember where it was at that you were talking to him?"

Hulbert: "Yeah it was in a bar."

Schauperl: "Do you remember which bar?"

Hulbert: "No. That's a violation of probation right there." (Hulbert was on probation for writing bad checks while he and Mollye were living in Nebraska.)

Schauperl: "What's that?"

Hulbert: "Being in a bar."

Schauperl: "There's no way you can remember who you sold the gun to?"

Hulbert: "No. I think I still have a box of shells."

Schauperl: "Where are they at?"

Hulbert: "I think they are in the car. Half a box, it's a half a box. I was trying to make a full box. I found a bunch of cartridges the other day, and I was going to try and get em reloaded and make a full box and sell 'em. I know other people that might buy 'em."

Schauperl: "Well, I'll tell you right now. We're obtaining a search warrant, and probably have it by now and they're over searching the house... and the other place that you used to live in over in Buena Park."

Hulbert: "OK."

Schauperl: "Are they are going to find something there? Are they are going to find the shells, Ken? They weren't in the car, were they?"

Hulbert: "I don't know where they are then. I know I've got 'em around somewhere 'cause there was a seven dollar box of shells that I thought I lost six months ago, and I just found 'em recently.... There's about twenty or twenty-five. There's about half a box, anyway... I had a bunch... I was up at a dump and found a bunch of shells that somebody had been shooting or something, and I found a bunch of twenty-five cartridges. I mean there was about twenty of 'em. I have a friend that reloads, and I figured I'd get him to reload 'em and put 'em back in the box and re-sell the box for seven dollars."

Schauperl: "But there's no way that you could find out and know who you sold that gun to?"

Hulbert: "I don't know where that gun is. I don't have the slightest idea. I thought I knew where the shells were. I'm sure I put 'em somewhere so I wouldn't lose 'em. And... unless somebody copped 'em, I'm sure they were in the car."

Again, Schauperl changed directions in the questioning to another subject. He continued to do this at various points in the interview when he thought he had all he was going to get at that time on a particular subject under questioning. He began to question Hulbert about his continual burping, which had become quite noticeable during the interview and was one of the characteristics of the suspect as related by victim Carmen Banderas. From the transcript:

Schauperl: "Do you have a stomach problem?"

Hulbert: "Why, is it growling or something?"

Schauperl: "No, I was just ... you were burping."

Hulbert: "Do I, am I burping?"

Schauperl: "Yeah."

Hulbert: "I thought that was you knocking on the bottom of the table."

Schauperl: "No, it was you burping."

Hulbert: "Oh, well, bad nerves, I guess. Hungry too, I ended up with a half a donut today."

Schauperl: "Does that happen when you get nervous?"

Hulbert: "What, burp?"

Schauperl: "Some people do."

Hulbert: "I don't know. I didn't notice it with me. Could be. I burp, I have a lot of gas all the time and I burp a lot and I fart a lot."

Schauperl then switched again and started questioning Hulbert about the Terri Muzic case. As previously discussed, one of the items of jewelry found in the bag given to us by Mollye was a Timex watch with her name engraved on the back. This watch had been described in detail by Muzic in the police report documenting he assault, rape, and robbery.

Schauperl: "Do you ever get around over in Lakewood?"

Hulbert: "Is that supposed to be my handwriting or something?"

Schauperl: "No... no."

Hulbert: "Do I ever what?"

Schauperl: "Do you ever get over around Lakewood?"

Hulbert: "I've been through Lakewood once or twice since we've been out here. Lakewood and Bellflower, I think. I haven't done any jobs out there, and I haven't raped or robbed or killed anyone or . . ."

Schauperl: "Well, what about that incident out at the . . ."

Hulbert: "If it's a police incident it's not me."

Schauperl: "Is that right? Did you see that watch there that we have?" (Detective Schauperl pointed directly at the watch so that Hulbert could see it. All the jewelry items were in the interview room as a reminder to Hulbert that we knew he was the responsible party in these cases.)

Hulbert: "The one that's tagged?"

Schauperl: "Yeah. The one with the Roman numerals on it?"

Hulbert: "The what?"

Schauperl: "With the Roman numerals on it. This watch."

Hulbert: "It was taken off a body or something?"

Schauperl: "Not a body, a person."

Hulbert: "No, I didn't take it. Has the watch got my thumb print on it too?"

Schauperl: "No, but it has the name of the victim that it was taken from engraved on the back... Terri Muzic.... It was described in detail in this report."

Hulbert: "That watch like the rings was in my possession at one time and was... that's another article that Mollye was supposed to have passed to you, right?"

Schauperl: "There's no question about that. There's no question about that—that's a fact."

Hulbert: "OK."

Schauperl: "OK?"

Hulbert: "You said that."

Schauperl: "Well, believe me, it is."

Hulbert: "Well, I believe you believe it. I believe you expect me to believe it."

Schauperl: "Well, I think you believe it."

Hulbert: "I believe you expect me to believe it."

Schauperl: "No, I think you do believe it, otherwise you... ah... you know. First of all, that you wouldn't be here today, and Mollye wouldn't be here, and we wouldn't have that property here in our possession here today. And that's why you believe it, that's why you know it for a fact."

Hulbert: "I didn't say so."

Schauperl: "No..."

Schauperl then made another change of course to a discussion of avocado pizza from the recollections of victim Carmen Banderas from her time driving around Orange County with her kidnapper, prior to being raped, beaten, and left for dead:

Schauperl: "Have you ever eaten any avocado pizza?"

Hulbert: "Yeah."

Schauperl: "Do you like avocado pizzas?"

Hulbert: "Yeah. I like avocados a lot."

Schauperl: "Where do you get avocado pizzas?"

Hulbert: "My wife makes 'em."

Schauperl: "Does she?"

Hulbert: "Why, did she say something about 'em to you?"

Schauperl: "Do you know of anyplace else in town where you can get an avocado pizza?"

Hulbert: "No, especially not now"

DeVore: "No place locally around?"

Hulbert: "Uh-uh. Why?"

Schauperl: "Perry's? Does Perry's Pizza have avocado?"

Hulbert: "Is that the one that used to be Binky's... Blinkey's?"

Schauperl: "Uh-huh... yeah."

Hulbert: "Right. They had 'em."

Schauperl: "They have?"

Hulbert: "We've got avocado pizza there before. It was avocado and shrimp and cashews."

DeVore: "They have the whole variety there."

Hulbert: "Yeah, they have everything there. They used to."

Schauperl: "Didn't you tell that to the young lady in the car out towards El Toro?"

Hulbert: "No. I wondered what the hell you were fishing for, no."

Schauperl: "Yeah."

Hulbert: "Uh-uh. They don't have 'em there anymore anyway. Did I tell her that too? I did? Bullshit."

Schauperl: "You think that's something I just dreamed out of my head?"

Hulbert: "I don't know what the hell you're talking about."

Schauperl: "Huh?"

Hulbert: 'I ain't been in no goddamn car in El Toro, I'm tellin' ya!"

Schauperl: "But, do you think that's something I'm just , ya know, dreaming up?"

Hulbert: "I don't know, I thought maybe Mollye said something about that."

Schauperl: "Why in hell would I think of avocado pizzas?"

Hulbert: "I don't know, I thought maybe Mollye might have told you something about her avocado pizzas."

Schauperl: "The young lady in the car said you told her about that."

Hulbert: "Avocado pizza?"

Schauperl: "Pizza at Perry's Pizza House on Orangethorpe... and..."

Hulbert: "While I was raping and..."

Schauperl: "No... that's..."

Hulbert: "... and killing her...?"

Schauperl: "No, not while you were doing that. It was when you were driving."

Hulbert: "Well, I've had avocado pizza at Perry's before, we all have. It's a family occasion and my wife makes 'em now when we can get avocados."

As Schauperl continued to back him into a corner, Hulbert was chain smoking Marlboro cigarettes and appeared to be getting increasingly anxious as the questioning continued. He kept looking around the small room, was burping pretty much continuously, and was becoming more hostile toward us. Leon then brought out several more "coincidences" for Hulbert to think about as he moved toward the conclusion of this first interview.

Schauperl: "You just took out a pack of Marlboros. The person responsible for these things smokes Marlboros. The person responsible smokes Marlboros."

Hulbert: "I can get you on that one."

Schauperl: "Can you, how can you get me on that?"

Hulbert: "... 'cause I just changed back to Marlboros about... ah... six weeks ago."

Schauperl: "That'd be about right. Turn your hand over, let me show you something else. Turn it all the way over. See that swastika? That's another thing. Oh… you don't believe? Do you believe that I'm putting you on Ken?"

Hulbert: "I believe I'm really getting set up or you're putting me on, whatever."

Schauperl: "Oh, hey listen, before I even knew your name Ken, some of these things came to light before I ever knew your name. In fact, all these things came to light. You see that bulletin there that we have? You see the description on that? What is that?

Hulbert: "I see it's a swastika… now I see it."

Schauperl: "OK, that's the description of the person responsible… with a swastika."

Hulbert: "Is it a left hand?"

Schauperl: "It's on a wrist."

Hulbert: "Well, you know how many swastikas there are…"

Schauperl: "Oh, I have no doubt, I won't argue with that point."

Hulbert: "I can damn sure tell a left hand from a right hand, and I'll tell you…"

Schauperl: "It's not just one isolated piece of evidence, or one isolated incident. We're not relying on, say, one piece of evidence, like a tattoo."

Hulbert: "Yeah… like a tattoo, or rings… or pizza…"

Schauperl: "Or a tattoo or Marlboro or the fact you burp or the fact that you like avocado pizza."

Hulbert: "Or …"

Schauperl: "But you start putting those things all together and all of a sudden, boom, you got a picture, right?"

Hulbert: "Right."

Schauperl: "A complete picture. You know we're belaboring the point in a sense because there is just so much there. It's those kinds of things that are just there in this case. Do you believe that you did it, Ken?"

Hulbert: "I know I didn't."

Schauperl: "I'm trying to understand what, you know, would cause it... realizing that I'm convinced, and I feel right here and now that you're convinced, too, even though you haven't said it... and I've... talked to enough people to know what I'm talking about."

Hulbert: "Hell, if I was in your position, I can see why you can't hardly figure out anything other than what you're saying."

Schauperl: "Well, now I can't sit here and put my finger on all the facts, but that is why I know, and also that I've talked to enough people to know what happened."

Hulbert: "Yeah, well, I mean you can't sit here and say well, I'm kind of wishy washy I don't know whether you should be here or not, whether you should be in custody or not."

Schauperl: "Oh me? Oh no, there's no question in my mind."

Hulbert: Well, I know, I'm talking about your position, you can't. You have to believe it, or you don't have any business doing it."

Schauperl: "Well, I've seen enough evidence over the years. I've been in the business for sixteen years. You know what evidence is and what kind of evidence it takes to make a case in court and things like that. I've been honest with you. I've laid it on the table... part of it... the evidence on the table and this evidence... can and will be hooked up."

Hulbert: "... eyewitnesses and fingerprints..."

Schauperl: "All the other information. The purpose in our being here is not necessarily to explain this evidence to you, as much as to listen to you and try to understand... you know... why these things happened and how they happened. That's the purpose..."

Hulbert: "I'm not a killer. I'm not a killer."

Schauperl: "In saying that Ken, you notice how you are feeling right now. I notice that your eyes... are tearing."

Hulbert: "Does that mean... does that mean I'm telling a lie or something?"

Schauperl: "it tells me that... I believe that you're giving some of those symptoms... that you're realizing that I know what I'm talking about. And, in a sense I think you want to just bleat it out... you know... but you... there's things holding you back. And I don't think it's necessarily clear what's going to happen in court... more what people are going to think of you, what Mollye's going to think of you..."

Hulbert: "I know what... I know what Mollye thinks of me, and I'm not concerned with what a whole lot of other people think of me. I'm only concerned with being with my family and..."

Schauperl: "Well, I'm just saying some reasons why a person might not want to say to the world 'I did it,' you know?"

Hulbert: "If I did it, I should remember it. I'd have that much more reason than anyone else does."

Schauperl: "I think you remember it. I think you remember the incident. I'm more convinced that you... you want to tell us about it, but you can't find a way to do it."

Hulbert: "[Inaudible.]"

Schauperl: "Well, not only that... not only that but listening to what you have to say as to why these things happened. Maybe you can shed some light on... on the degree of these things."

Hulbert: "Well, I'm saying there's a hundred thousand reasons why those things could happen to anyone, or why anyone could do those things, but..."

Schauperl: "That's right."

Hulbert: "Hmmmmmmm?"

Hulbert: "Like I said, looking at it from a legitimate or legal angle, or whatever, that's, even I come up with probable cause for me to be sitting where I'm sitting right now."

With plenty for Hulbert to think about, the interview was concluded at that time, and he was taken back to his cell.

At approximately four-fifty in the afternoon of January 30,

1976, we again interviewed Ken Hulbert. This interview was more of a continuation of the earlier session than a separate, new interview. This second interview only lasted about an hour, and we gained very little ground with Hulbert before deciding to quit for the time being. As pointed out in Chapter Seven, Hulbert had become increasingly restless, argumentative, and uncooperative since our first interview. This second interview didn't result in anything helpful to the advancement of the case. I think the more time he had to think about the facts, the more he realized there was no way out for him.

CHAPTER 9
PUTTING THE CASE TOGETHER

AN OLD DETECTIVE told me years ago that the key to being a good investigator was 5% inspiration and 95% perspiration. Over the years I worked as a detective and supervised detectives this would prove true over and over. It was certainly true with this case. Even after identifying Hulbert as the suspect in these crimes, there were still weeks of work by all the detectives assigned to the case to get it ready for presentation in court. There were over four hundred pages of police reports generated in this matter. Most of them were just following up on information that never materialized as far as being useful to the case but were necessary to investigate to put together a complete, professional investigation that would stand up to the scrutiny of a judge and jury.

As a result of the search warrant served on the Hulbert residence on Paula Avenue, Detective Collins was able to obtain several items of possible evidence from the home, the most important of which was a Titan .25 caliber pistol. Other items taken included the following:

1. One yellow gold necklace with an oval religious

medallion encased in plastic in the center, located on top of the T.V. set in the living room.

2. Recovered from a white & red ceramic basket located on top of the TV set in the living room were a ladies' Benrus wristwatch with a white metal band, a gold bracelet with simulated pearls, a strand of simulated pearls with what appeared to be 4 diamond chips on the clasp, and a key chain containing two keys and a folding manicure knife.

3. One pair of men's Puma black and white tennis shoes. These were found on the floor in the middle of the living room.

4. One yellow gold multi-stone bracelet. This was in the coin pocket of a brown wallet in a purse on the sofa in the living room.

5. One General Motors key located on top of the TV set in the living room.

6. One dark brown wig in an afro style, located on top of the dresser in the master bedroom.

7. One Kodak Instamatic camera and a brown plastic carrying case, "Smile Saver" model. The camera was on frame #17 and was located on top of the dresser in the master bedroom.

8. Twenty expended .25 caliber rounds of ammunition on the dresser in the master bedroom.

9. One silver ladies' Timex watch, 17 jewels, located in a clear plastic bag on the floor in the master bedroom.

10. One pink rag with an unknown substance on it, located on the floor in the master bedroom.

11. One white gold ladies' ring with a blue stone, on the headboard in the master bedroom.

12. One white gold ladies' ring with three possible diamonds, located on the headboard in the master bedroom.

13. One white gold ladies' ring with white, blue, yellow, green, and red tulip type flowers with the inscription "Thailand Sterling", located on the headboard in the master bedroom.

14. One child's nightgown with blue elephant pattern, feet tied in a knot, possibly with bloodstains, located in the master bedroom.

15. One yellow-gold mood stone ring with adjust able band, located on the floor under the bed in the master bedroom.

16. One box of .32 caliber ammunition containing six live rounds, located in the nightstand in the second bedroom.

17. One Titan .25 caliber blue steel automatic with white metal trigger, hammer and clip release, Serial No. 298809, and one empty clip for the weapon. They were in the living room beneath the sofa.

All the above items were brought to the Fullerton Police Department and booked into property evidence. Not all of it would prove relevant to the crimes under investigation, but we did not know it at the time and took items we thought could be of evidential value.

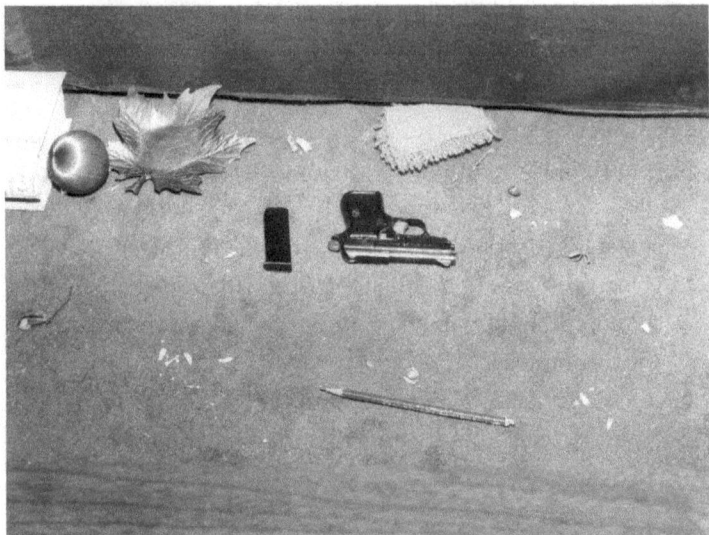

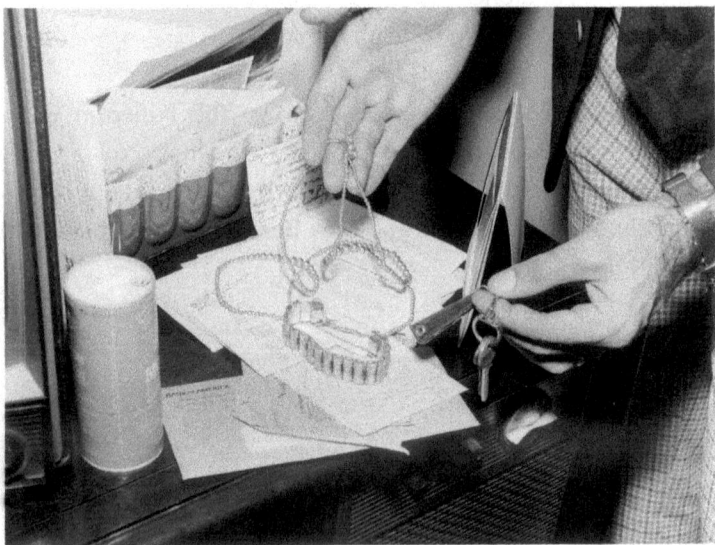

gun, jewelry, Banderas watch

Sunday, February 1, 1976
Fullerton, California

8: 00 a.m. Detective Schauperl again interviewed the witness Ronald Rockenbach regarding his relationship with Ken Hulbert and Mollye Selfies. This time the interview was considerably more in-depth. Rockenbach reiterated he was a volunteer counselor for the Alpha Center, in Placentia, located in a church just east of Fullerton. He explained he was currently completing a thesis for his master's degree and did counseling part time. He told us that on August 1, 1975, the Hulbert family was referred to him for counseling regarding marital problems. He said he met with Mollye on that date, but Ken Hulbert did not come. Mollye seemed disturbed and explained that her "husband" was out looking for a job and he had been having trouble finding work. She told him they had just returned to California from Nebraska, where they had been living. According to what he was told, they were then living on Commonwealth Avenue in the City of Buena Park. He said that from what he could learn from Mollye, their problems seemed to stem from the fact that Ken was unemployed, and they had no money.

He said he spoke with Ken on August 4, 1975, and they just discussed general problems and didn't get into anything specific.

Rockenbach went on to say that on the thirteenth of August 1975, he had returned a call from Mollye Hulbert, and she told him about a conversation she'd had with Ken. She said Ken had told her that a girl picked him up while he was hitchhiking, and he had made her take her clothes off and then had taken the girl's jewelry.

Rockenbach confirmed the conversation his wife had with Mollye about her concerns that Hulbert was the parking lot rapist. He also confirmed Mollye had given his wife the jewelry we had taken as evidence in the case.

Rockenbach said he also met with Ken Hulbert on that same day, August 13, 1975. During the conversation, Hulbert told Rockenbach he could not discuss some of the things that had happened to him when he was in New York. Hulbert told Rockenbach he had gone to New York on his way to Canada, and from there he had planned to travel the world; however, he never did so.

Mr. Rockenbach said his next appointment for Mollye and Ken was to be on August 31, 1975, but he was contacted by Mollye who told him Ken Hulbert was in jail on check charges. Mollye said Hulbert had written "insufficient funds" checks in the state of Nebraska for four-hundred sixty dollars. She had called to cancel the appointment.

Rockenbach told Detective Schauperl that Mollye Hulbert had called several times after that asking for help with food. He said he helped her to obtain welfare and food stamps. He said he and his wife also held a garage sale to try to raise bail money to get Ken out of jail after he had been sent back to Nebraska on the bad check charge. Rockenbach told Schauperl he had lost contact with the Hulbert family in early September of 1975 and he was next contacted by Mollye Hulbert on January 29, 1976, which was the incident that led to Hulbert's arrest.

Linda Rockenbach told Detective Schauperl that on January 29, 1976, at about five-twenty in the evening, Mollye Hulbert had contacted her by telephone and had wanted to talk to her husband Ron. Linda told her Ron was not home, and Mollye began talking to her. She told Linda she was calling because Ken might be involved in something. She told Linda Ken did not want her talking with Ron. She went on to tell Linda she thought she was crazy or that Ken was lying to her. Linda asked Mollye why she felt that way, and Mollye told her Ken would go away from home and then come back, with no explanation as to where he had been or what he had been doing.

Linda said Mollye also told her Ken had gotten a job a week before at a Standard gas station on the corner of Harbor and La Habra Boulevard in the City of La Habra. She said that earlier in the day, Thursday, January 29, 1976, she had called the station while Hulbert was supposed to have been working and was informed by whoever answered the phone that Ken had not been to work. She also said that, the night before, she and Ken had been up most of the night talking about his strange behavior. Mollye explained to Linda she thought Ken was "going out on her." After she discovered Ken had not gone to work on the 29th, she decided to make an appointment with Ron Rockenbach. Linda invited her to come over, but Mollye said she did not have a car.

Mollye told Linda she wanted to stay home and talk to Ken when he returned but was concerned about her children's safety. She asked Linda to come and pick them up and told her to hurry as she wanted them to be gone when Ken got there. She claimed Ken had beaten her up twice in January and Ken had a gun in the house. Mrs. Rockenbach agreed to come get the kids and take care of them. She arrived at the Hulbert home at about seven-thirty that evening. As she entered the house, she observed Mollye put something into a manila envelope. She said that as the objects were dropped into the envelope they jingled. Mollye placed the envelope on the coffee table in the living room. They then sat down and talked. Linda asked Mollye if she would like to have a third person there when she talked with Ken. Mollye sent her young son out of the room and said, "I know it would be smart to have another person present, but Ken confessed to me something he had done and if I were to bring this out, the other person might feel it their duty to look into it." Linda said she then told Mollye, "Don't you think the other person might think it confidential?" Mollye responded by saying "No." She added that Ken was on probation, and she did not want to take any chances of getting him in trouble if he was still doing "these things."

About that time, they heard a car approaching the home, and Mollye jumped up to see if it was Ken. It was not. She returned to the coffee table and handed the envelope to Linda Rockenbach and told her, "If I don't get in touch with you before tomorrow, take this to the police. I know it sounds corny, but it is the only thing I can think of to do." Mollye then told Linda to take off her wedding ring so Hulbert would not know she was Ronald Rock-enbach's wife and she should pretend to be the "babysitter." Mollye then changed her mind and told Rockenbach, "Maybe it would be better if you left now." She then got Mollye's children ready to leave, and after giving Mollye directions to her home, left with the couple's children.

Linda told Detective Schauperl that when she arrived, her husband was home. She left the envelope in her purse and placed the purse on the kitchen counter. Ron asked her why the Hulbert children were at their home and Linda explained about the telephone call from Mollye and her conversation with Mollye at the Hulbert home.

Ronald Rockenbach said he then called Mollye and asked her what was happening. He said he told Mollye, "I want you to tell me exactly what is happening." Rockenbach said that after some hesitation, Mollye confided in him that she believed Ken was involved in kidnapping women. He then told her, "OK, give me the specifics." Mollye said she had confronted Ken when he came home about her suspicions. She told Rockenbach she had asked him, "Did you read in the paper about the girl who was left for dead?" Mollye said Ken confided in her and told her he had kidnapped a woman that day. She then asked him, "Did you beat her or rape her?" He replied, "No."

Mollye told Rockenbach that on one occasion recently, Ken had come home, walked into the house, and then would not let her touch him or his clothes, and would not talk to her for about two hours. She said he looked "all messed up." He later told her four guys had beaten him up.

Ron asked Mollye to give him more of the specifics, and she told him Ken had been bringing home purses; that she had found two purses and some jewelry in their home. Mollye then told him to look into the envelope she had given to his wife. Rockenbach told Schauperl he did not know about the envelope as he and Linda had not discussed it, but his wife then told him about the manila envelope in her purse. He opened the purse and took out the envelope, opened it, and found a slip of blue paper and the jewelry. Mollye told him to look at the blue slip of paper, which he did. She said she had found those names on identification in the purses she had found. She told Rockenbach, "Ron, I think he's been involved in these rapes. I've been calling newspapers, trying to find the names of the victims. Is there any way to find out the names of the victims without telling Ken's name?"

Ron told Mollye to leave the house, go to a restaurant, and call him in half an hour. He then called the La Habra Police Department and talked to the on-duty watch commander. The watch commander told Ron that the rapes had occurred in Whittier and in Fullerton so he should call them. The watch commander did run the two names Ron had gotten from Mollye on the blue slip of paper, but he was unable to find out any information about them. The La Habra watch commander did tell Rockenbach that the suspect in the case had a swastika tattooed on his hand. Rockenbach called the Hulbert home and asked David if his father had any tattoos and David confirmed that his dad did have a tattoo of a swastika on his left wrist.

After learning this, Rockenbach called the Fullerton Police Department watch commander and asked if a check could be run on the two names he had. He was told he should contact Detective Schauperl in the morning to obtain that information. This could have been a critical error on the part of whoever took this call, as they apparently did not obtain the name and telephone number of the caller. Fortunately, Rockenbach followed through and called Detective Schauperl the following morning.

At about nine-ten that evening Rockenbach again called the Hulbert residence and spoke with Mollye. She had not gone to a restaurant as he had previously suggested. He asked Mollye not to tell Ken who she was talking to but to get out of the house and come to his home. He then waited until almost nine forty-five p.m. when Mollye had not shown up at his home, so he called the Hulbert residence again. Mollye again answered the phone, and he again asked her to get out of the house and come to his home.

Rockenbach said he waited until ten-twenty p.m. when both Ken and Mollye showed up at his home to pick up their children.

Rockenbach told Detective Schauperl he had received another telephone call from Mollye Hulbert at seven-forty that morning, January 30, 1976. He told Schauperl that Mollye told him, "I think I was just imagining this," and she cancelled their appointment. She seemed nervous and acted like she wanted to get off the phone as quickly as possible.

By this time, Rockenbach was convinced Ken Hulbert was involved in these crimes, so he called Detective Schauperl that morning as suggested by the officer he had talked to the previous evening. His diligence in this situation helped lead to the case being solved.

It was also clear from this interview that Mollye knew what Hulbert was involved in and had chosen to not report it to the police.

11: 00 a.m. Hulbert was taken from his cell into the interview room of the jail facility. Jim Babcock, the ID technician took several photographs of him at the request of Detective Schauperl. He photographed his face, his face with his left wrist showing the swastika, and his private parts.

12: 35 p.m. Detective Schauperl and I again interviewed Ken Hulbert. This interview was also recorded and videotaped. Prior to any questioning, Hulbert was again advised of his rights and acknowledged he understood them and would talk to us about the case. This interview was much more an "in your face" approach designed to shame Hulbert into admitting his involvement, while continuing to prove to him we had the evidence to convict him even if he did not.

When he came into the room, Hulbert did not have the "air of confidence" we had seen the first time around. He was very restless and had difficulty concentrating at first. His attitude seemed more defensive, and the frequency of his belching had increased considerably. He frequently glanced around the room, nervously. He chain smoked Marlboro cigarettes throughout the interview.

Schauperl began by telling him about the investigators who would be coming from other jurisdictions to interview him later that day on their outstanding cases. Hulbert was also told that the Fullerton case would go to the district attorney the next day, Monday, February 2, 1976. I could see he was visibly shaken by those facts and probably realized he was close to the end of his game. As this interview progressed, he became surlier and more defensive in his answers. The following excerpts from transcripts of the interview gives an idea of the techniques Schauperl used and Hulbert's responses. Schauperl had decided to hit him hard and see if Hulbert would finally admit his guilt. Although he didn't admit to the crimes during this interview, I believe this interview led Hulbert to call out to the jailer at 9: 00 that Sunday evening and tell him he wanted to talk to Leon Schauperl and he would make it worth his time.

Schauperl: "OK, we'll be discussing the case with the district attorney tomorrow, and at this point, it is your opportunity, prior to our doing that, to listen to anything you want him to understand, or anything you want him to know. This is your opportunity to do so."

Hulbert: "I'm going to tell you I am "not guilty" still."

Schauperl: "Well, I kind of figured that you'd do that. As you realize, a lot has happened since Friday night. You've experienced a lot of search warrants and, as you probably realize by now, your whole body is some type of evidence, right?"

Hulbert: "Ummmmmm."

Schauperl: "Like I said before, Ken, all this evidence is continuing to build up and continuing to identify you as the person responsible."

Hulbert: "I said I'm not guilty."

Schauperl: "Do you remember the things we discussed on Friday? Are some of these things still puzzling you as to why they're so accurate in relation to these crimes, why some of the things we've discussed are so accurate? And yet you say you're not responsible for them?"

Hulbert: "I don't have any explanation for it."

Schauperl: "No explanation? Do you feel like you have a conscience?"

Hulbert: "You mean feeling guilty whenever I do something wrong?"

Schauperl: "Yeah"

Hulbert: "Yeah, I feel guilty when I do something wrong."

Schauperl: "Do you have any feeling or remorse for it?"

Hulbert: "Of course. If I didn't, I'd continue doing it."

Schauperl: "Well, then, can you give me one good example of when you felt that way?"

Hulbert: "I can think of a hundred thousand things."

Schauperl: Well, I'm just asking you to pick out one and…"

Hulbert: "Why?"

Schauperl: "I'm just trying to determine something in my own mind."

Hulbert: "Like whether or not I know what a conscience is?"

Schauperl: "Well, maybe, but I think you know that. I'm trying to find an incident where you can show me that you have a conscience. In that way, maybe I would know too. There must be some instance?"

Hulbert: "Everyday living. You run into it always, in everything you do."

Schauperl: "OK, I'll pick one for you. Remember the circumstances of that armed robbery you were involved in?"

Hulbert: "I remember feeling guilty, and I remember feeling remorse."

Schauperl: "And, how old were you then?"

Hulbert: "Sixteen."

Schauperl: "Did you admit it to the policeman?"

Hulbert: "Well, I don't remember the policeman I talked to, but I know I admitted doing it because I did it."

Schauperl: "OK."

Hulbert: "I remember that I admitted it in court."

Schauperl: "Then you must have a conscience then."

Hulbert: "Well, if that means that I have a conscience, yeah, I know I have one."

Schauperl: "Now, sixteen and an armed robbery, it isn't near as serious as what you are facing now. You're facing a murder charge, right? And I can understand that if I had murdered someone, I wouldn't be able to live with myself."

Hulbert: "If I murdered someone, I wouldn't be able to live

with myself. I wouldn't be concerned with what I'm facing, like now."

Schauperl: "And what if that evidence showed that you did murder somebody?"

Hulbert: "Why I'd say the evidence was wrong."

Schauperl: "OK. Ken, do you remember your mother very well?"

Hulbert: "Yeah"

Schauperl: "OK, did she have any daughters?"

Hulbert: "Did she have any daughters? Yeah, I have a sister."

Schauperl: "How old is she?"

Hulbert: "About two years younger than me, two-and-a-half years."

Schauperl: "That would make her…"

Hulbert: "Twenty-one, no, she is twenty-two now."

Schauperl: "Like I said, I'm not the judge or jury on this, and I'm not going to find you guilty, but I've seen the evidence and I know in my mind, OK? And I believe you killed Gina Tisher, and I believe you beat the hell out of the other gal. And I'm saying what if it had been Mollye, or if it had been your sister and I'm trying to rouse some conscience in you. Only about three weeks ago, sitting in that chair where you're sitting now, we had the mother of Gina Marie Tisher, and she couldn't understand why her daughter's dead, but she's dead. I believe that you, Ken, can explain to me why she's dead. I believe that. And like I said before, the only way your side of the story is going to come out in this is if it comes from you. All this evidence we've been talking about, building up, it's identifying you as the person doing these things but it's not saying why you're doing it. I personally would like to know why so I might be able to explain to somebody. I might be able to explain to somebody, maybe a mother, or a husband, why their daughter or wife is dead."

Hulbert: "Are you still looking for an explanation?"

Schauperl: "Uh-huh."

Hulbert: "It's the same explanation that I've given you twice and on two different dates."

Schauperl: "But you and I both know that that's not the explanation."

Hulbert: "No, you believe it."

Schauperl: "You do too, you do too Ken."

Hulbert: [Inaudible.]

Schauperl: "See, there's a difference in a crime. Some are looked upon as being a lot more serious, and that makes a difference on whether a person will face up to it and admit to the world that he did it, you know. I understand why you're not doing it… being man enough to look at Mollye and say, 'Mollye, I killed her… I raped her and I killed her.' You aren't man enough to go up to that court and admit to the world that 'I killed that Tisher girl.' Because you and I both know you did it, don't we? And you know I know. No question about it, you know that I know, and you aren't man enough to do it. It takes some conscience, some feelings…"

Hulbert: "I got all kinds of conscience and feelings."

Schauperl: "You do?"

Hulbert: "Yeah, I do."

Schauperl: "But, no guts. Your thinking of one thing and that's saving your own hide so you might get back out there and get involved in it again. Instead of feeling that…"

Hulbert: "I just want to get back with my family, to get involved with living where I belong…"

Schauperl: "Oh bullshit! You and I both know that's bullshit!"

Hulbert: "Well, you know that's your prerogative."

Schauperl: "You had a family over there, and you were out prowling around in the afternoon and evening hours. You dumped one body in Fullerton, and you dumped another one out in Orange County, believing she was dead. Is that what you mean by wanting to be home with your family?"

Hulbert: "That's your prerogative to think that."

Schauperl: "No, I know that. Ken, you know exactly what you did. You know exactly what you did to those girls."

Hulbert: [Inaudible.]

Schauperl: "Right. You know exactly where you stand."

Hulbert: "I sure do."

Schauperl: "You sure do. All these items of evidence are just coincidental, aren't they? They are just some physical coincidences, right?"

Hulbert: "I guess there is no explanation."

Schauperl: "Right, no explanation. No explanation."

Hulbert: "I don't have to explain shit to you…"

Schauperl: "You're right. Not for me, but on your own behalf… someday…"

Hulbert: "I know what the hell I've done, and I know where the hell I've been, and I don't have to explain a goddamn thing to you. And I know where you stand, and I know what you're saying, so it would be futile."

Schauperl: "Is that right?" That isn't it, that doesn't take any guts to say you're not guilty for something that you are." That's just the opposite."

Hulbert: "You got guts enough to stand up and say you're right, you son of a bitch. I've got my head set and that's the way it is. And there ain't nothing you can say that changes it."

Schauperl: "Is that right?"

Hulbert: "Yeah."

Schauperl: "You know why?"

Hulbert: "Sure I know why."

Schauperl: "You have no shame, no conscience, and no compassion for other people's lives. No remorse. Life is cheap to you; it has no meaning. But it had a hell of a lot of meaning to a father, a hell of a lot of meaning, Ken. But no meaning to you. You carried those rings off that dead girl's hand to your house. You took them from one house and moved them to another house. What kind of remorse, what kind of conscience is that? Was that a trophy, Ken?"

Hulbert: [Inaudible.]

Schauperl: "What kind of a human being would attack a dead girl, rip her rings off her fingers, carry them home with him and stash them away as a trophy? What kind of a human being is that, Ken? What kind of rights does this dead girl have? What kind of rights do the parents of that dead girl have? Her husband? You tell me. She's the one that is six feet under... you're not."

Hulbert: "No, but you sure would like to put me there, wouldn't you?"

Schauperl: "What I want doesn't enter into this."

Hulbert: "No?"

Schauperl: "Where do you think you are here Ken, where do you think you stand?"

Schauperl: "I'm seeing what the evidence is, Ken. We're seeing black and white. It's as simple as two and two...and black and white, you know. Are those rings my imagination? Is that gun my imagination? Is that swastika my imagination? That face of yours, is that my imagination? That dead body out there, is that my imagination? Talking to that mother over there about three weeks ago, is that my imagination?"

Hulbert: "I never said..."

Schauperl: "That's reality, Ken... that's reality. Those are the plain simple facts.

Hulbert: "I don't know what you do with the facts."

Schauperl: "Nothing. I don't do anything; just present them to the court. They do something with the facts."

Hulbert: "You've got an obligation to everyone. You've got an obligation to keep an open mind."

Schauperl: "I've been sitting here Ken for...let's see...from Friday, and all the other evidence we've been obtaining. I am sitting here today, waiting, and listening for something I can believe and understand. Is that not an open mind?" You've been here with me. Have I not been sitting here listening and waiting to hear something, an explanation for those rings, an explanation for the gun, an explanation for all these other things, the fingerprints? I'm waiting, you know. I'm listening. You tell me what the explanations are, and I'll listen. I'll have an open mind. I had an open mind when I looked at the evidence. Now here I am listening for your side of the story and…waiting for it."

Hulbert: "I didn't do it."

Schauperl: "I have done this for sixteen years, Ken, and I've listened with an open mind to people with problems. I had compassion for their problems. That is people who are willing to face up to what they have done."

Hulbert: "Well, I haven't done anything. You just keep belaboring it, by going over it again and again and again. Because I'm telling you I didn't do it, and you're telling me I did do it and so there you are! I keep saying, 'I didn't do it.' You keep saying, 'Yes you did, you're a lying son of a bitch.'"

Schauperl: "You could put it aside and come back to this thing and talk about it as a human being, man to man, but you aren't doing that."

Hulbert: "That's because I ain't a man, and I ain't got no nuts, I ain't got no conscience, I'm just an animal."

Schauperl: "You said it."

Hulbert: "I'm just quoting you."

Schauperl: "I didn't say that."

Hulbert: "Bullshit, you sat right here and said it."

Schauperl: "I called the person who killed Gina Marie Tisher an animal."

Hulbert: "OK, then you were talking about me, 'indirectly' calling me an animal."

Schauperl: "Ken, you are going to live with this the rest of your life."

Hulbert: "Yeah, we'll both live with each other for the rest of our lives."

Schauperl: "But, I'll be in an entirely different state of mind, won't I? Because I know I didn't kill Gina Marie Tisher."

Hulbert: "And, I know I didn't."

Schauperl: "You can say the words, but up here you know the truth.

The interview was concluded at 1: 35 p.m., and throughout this discussion I closely watched Hulbert. It was clear the evidence Schauperl was presenting to him was getting to him. He had become increasingly agitated as the interview progressed; he had difficulty maintaining eye contact with Leon and seemed to be more and more frustrated by the evidence stacking up against him. While he maintained his innocence, his denials were less convincing and indicated a lot less confidence than he had shown before.

1: 35 p.m. Two homicide investigators from the Los Angeles County Sheriff's Office, Detectives Adams, and Gainer, came to the jail to interview Hulbert. He was brought back to the interview room and the investigators talked to him for about an hour. Hulbert had denied being involved in their cases and was sullen and uncooperative throughout the interviews. They learned little to help their investigations.

5: 30 p.m. Leon called Mollye Selfies and asked her to come to the department to give a handwriting exemplar. When she got there, she refused to make any further statements or to give a handwriting sample. We again let her visit with Hulbert for about an hour, and we recorded it. They again whispered to each other, and we were unable to pick up the conversation. After this visit, I released everyone who was still at the station working the case so they could go home and spend a little time with their families and try to get some rest. It had been pretty much nonstop for all of us from Friday morning through the weekend.

9: 00 p.m. We believed we had a solid case against Hulbert, even without his admitting to the crimes, but it was about to get even better. At 9 o'clock that Sunday evening, Captain Davis, who was at home, received a call from the on-duty watch commander, telling him Hulbert had informed the jailer he wanted to talk with Detective Schauperl. He told the jailer, "It will be worth his while to come back." Captain Davis called Schauperl at home and requested he come to the station.

He arrived ten minutes later. Hulbert was taken from his cell by Captain Davis and Detective Schauperl and walked to the Investigation Division for an interview. When they sat down, Hulbert told them, "I have been thinking about this, and I have decided I want to confess to the charges."

Schauperl then asked him, "Is this decision to confess to the crime yours or is there any other influence upon your decision?"

Hulbert responded by saying it was his decision to confess. He advised, however, that prior to making a statement, he wished to discuss his decision with Mollye Selfies and with his brother, Dan Hulbert. He was then allowed to call both Mollye and his brother, both of whom came to the department to visit with him.

10: 00 p.m. Mollye and Dan arrived and visited with Ken Hulbert for approximately forty-five minutes. This conversation was recorded, but as with the others, we were unable to understand much of what was being said. They were all talking barely above a whisper, and the quality of the recording equipment we had, even though very good for that time, didn't give us an audible recording of the conversation.

10: 50 p.m. After Hulbert had visited with Mollye and his brother Dan and had discussed his decision to confess to the crimes, he was taken back to the interview room by Schauperl and Davis. Before any questioning, he was again advised of his constitutional rights. He said he understood these rights and wished to discuss the charges against him. Hulbert then, very freely and without any hesitation, admitted to the following crimes:

- Kidnapping, robbery, rape, and murder of Gina Marie Tisher on January 2, 1976.

- Kidnapping, robbery, rape and attempted murder of Carmen Banderas, the Fullerton College coed, on January 6, 1976.
- Robbery and rape of a victim in a residence in the Norwalk area, occurring on January 29, 1976, only one day before we arrested him in Fullerton.

The above three cases were each described in a very chilling and detailed confession by Hulbert. He discussed the crimes as if he was seeing them reenacted in his mind, switching between what he had said and what the victims had said. His ability to remember details was astonishing.

By the time he finished it was one thirty-five on Monday morning. Because of the detailed accounts of the crimes he was giving, it would have taken the remainder of the night to finish the interviews, so Schauperl asked him to identify all other crimes in which he had been involved and said they could discuss these crimes in more detail later.

Hulbert related the following additional crimes:

- Kidnapping and indecent exposure occurring in July of 1975, at Raymond and Commonwealth in Fullerton, where he had taken the female victim to an apartment area close to Knott's Berry Farm in Buena Park. This crime apparently went unreported as we were never able to locate a police report on the incident.
- Kidnapping of a female victim from the Buena Park Shopping Center.
- Kidnapping and robbery of Teri Muzic, which occurred in the Lakewood area in Los Angeles County.
- A kidnapping in the Bellflower area.
- Kidnapping and extortion, which he believed to have occurred after the Bellflower incident, which occurred in the Whitwood Mall (the same place where he

kidnapped Gina Marie Tisher on January 2, 1976). In this case he extorted $160.00 from the father of the victim.

- Kidnapping of a seventeen-year-old female in the City of Downey. Hulbert told detectives the girl jumped out of the car. He stated he had taken her purse home and had given it to Mollye. He described the purse as orange-brown in color, and had the identification of the victim in it. He said that after the victim jumped out of her car, at the Orange Mall in the City of Orange, he left the car and took the bus back to Fullerton.

As with the others, the entire interview was recorded, video-taped, and later transcribed in its entirety. It was from this transcription that the detailed statements by Hulbert about the Tisher and the Banderas cases were taken in Chapters Two and Three of this book. As is evident from these two cases, Hulbert's recalling of the incidents was extremely thorough. It was almost as if he were reliving the crimes or watching them on a movie in his head. In all my years in law enforcement I have never seen a more detailed or vivid account of such vicious crimes as we witnessed with Hulbert. When I listened to the tape recordings and watched the videos later the next day, I could not believe the detail and the minute-by-minute, blow-by-blow description of the crimes, even to the words he had said and what his victims had said to him.

In the early morning hours, Captain Davis decided to discontinue the interview and take it up again in the morning when both Hulbert and the officers were fresh. As it turned out, this was probably not a good call, because early the next morning, a public defender showed up at the jail. He demanded to see Ken Hulbert, claiming to represent him. He had a court order, signed by Judge James Cook, appointing the Public Defender's Office to represent Hulbert. This kind of "end run" on police investigations was happening more and more in these high-profile cases, even though the defendants were never interviewed to establish whether they even met the criteria to be eligible for a public defender or not.

After that visit, Hulbert would no longer talk with the police. Fortunately for us and for the families of the victims, we had the blow-by-blow confessions to the Tisher homicide and the Banderas abduction and rape, so little more was needed. We also had Carmen Banderas who had been left for dead and could identify Hulbert and give detailed information on the crimes committed against her.

Leon's decision to have Hulbert list out the other crimes he had been responsible for turned out to be a very important decision in the prosecution of cases belonging to the other police agencies. That information was used in the Los Angeles County trial charging Hulbert with the crimes that occurred in that county.

Monday, February 2, 1976
Orange County, California

10: 00 a.m. Early the following day, Monday, February 2, 1976, Detective Schauperl called Deputy D.A. Frank Briseno and made an appointment to meet with him at ten o'clock. He and Captain C.D. Davis told the deputy D.A. what had transpired with the interview the night before and laid out all the other evidence then available. Based on this evidence, Briseno issued a ten-count felony complaint charging Ken Richard Hulbert with the following crimes:

Count 1: Murder, with a special allegation of murder during robbery, murder during kidnapping, and murder during rape

Count 2: Kidnapping
Count 3: Robbery
Count 4: Attempted murder
Count 5: Rape
Count 6: Kidnapping
Count 7: Kidnapping
Count 8: Robbery
Count 9: Rape
Count 10: Sodomy

That same day, Detective Schauperl drove to the North Orange County Municipal Court in Fullerton and filed the complaint with the District Attorney.

Later that day, Hulbert was interviewed by the following investigators from their respective police agencies:

Los Angeles Sheriff's Department Investigators Adams and Gainer
Whittier Police Department Lieutenant Shelter and Detective Lee
West Covina Police Department Detective Dan Leonard
Alhambra Police Department Detective Bennet
Riverside Police Department Detective Osborne

Because he had "lawyered up," and would not converse openly with the investigators, they were not able to obtain a lot of information that was helpful to their cases. As indicated previously, it was later determined the Riverside case did not involve Hulbert and did not really fit the pattern of the others.

Tuesday, February 3, 1976
Fullerton, California

8: 10 a.m. On Tuesday morning, Leon and I transported

Hulbert to the North Orange County Municipal Court building in Fullerton for the first of many hearings. He was arraigned on the ten count complaint, and the "no bail" order from Judge Murray remained in effect. He was remanded to the custody of the Orange County Sheriff's Office then taken to the Orange County main jail in Santa Ana.

8: 15 a.m. Early Tuesday morning, the officer assigned to the front desk received a telephone call from Gary Kelley, the owner of a Chevron Service Station in Whittier, California, telling him he had information that might be pertinent to the investigation. He came into the Fullerton Police Department to be interviewed by Detective Glenn Deveney about the information he had on Ken Hulbert.

Mr. Kelley told Deveney that Hulbert had applied for employment through the Work Incentive Program sponsored by the State of California Department of Employment. According to Kelley, Hulbert had applied to participate in the program on January 2, 1976, and had been sent to Mr. Kelley for consideration of employment (which was the same day he kidnapped and killed Gina Marie Tisher).

Kelley ended up hiring Hulbert to begin employment on January 23, 1976, to work the hours of 10: 00 a.m. to 7: 00 p.m. Kelley produced records showing Hulbert had worked on January 23, 24, 25, and 26. Hulbert, according to Kelley, was off on January 27, 1976, and returned to work on January 28, as scheduled, and worked the entire day.

Kelley told Deveney that, on January 29, he received a telephone call from Hulbert at about 9: 30 in the morning saying he would like to be excused from work for at least part of the day because the owner of the home he rented had suffered a stroke, and he was going to have to transport her to the hospital. Kelley told Hulbert he could be excused from work for the day, given the nature of the emergency.

Kelley said he then received another call from Hulbert at

about two in the afternoon on that same date, and at that time Hulbert told him it looked like the woman might die and he would like to take the rest of the day off.

Later the same day, at approximately 4: 00 p.m., Kelley got a telephone call from a female subject, who he believed to be the wife of Ken Hulbert. She asked him, "Could you tell me what Ken wanted?" She then went on to tell Kelley that Hulbert had called the house, but she had been sleeping, and the children who answered the telephone were not able to relay the message. Kelley told her Hulbert was not at work and related the information given to him earlier by Hulbert. According to Kelley, the female then told him, "Oh, that's right, maybe he's at the hospital. I'll check there. Our landlord did have an attack."

The following day, Kelley learned from news reports that Hulbert had been arrested by the Fullerton Police Department for a series of rapes and homicides.

Thursday, February 5, 1976
Fullerton, California

After filing a request with the federal government, we received a copy of a Federal Alcohol, Tobacco and Firearms purchase form, showing that the .25 caliber Titan pistol found in the Hulbert residence on the day of his arrest had been purchased by Hulbert on July 18 1975, in the State of Nebraska. We knew then that the gun we found was his and he had lied about selling it.

FPD CAS # 76-226

DEPARTMENT OF THE TREASURY BUREAU OF ALCOHOL, TOBACCO AND FIREARMS	TRANSFEROR'S TRANSACTION NO.
FIREARMS TRANSACTION RECORD PART I – INTRA-STATE OVER-THE-COUNTER	1569

NOTE: Please read and carefully follow instructions on reverse. Prepare an original only.

SECTION A – TO BE COMPLETED BY TRANSFEREE OR BUYER

1. TRANSFEREE'S (Buyer's) NAME (Last, First, Middle) (Mr., Mrs., Miss.)	2. HEIGHT	3. WEIGHT	4. RACE
Ken R. Hulbert	6	175	W.

5. RESIDENCE ADDRESS (No., Street, City/State, Zip Code)	6. DATE OF BIRTH	7. PLACE OF BIRTH
R.R. 2. Red Cloud Neb	9-16-51	

8. CERTIFICATION OF TRANSFEREE (Buyer) – An untruthful answer may subject you to criminal prosecution. Each question must be answered with a "yes" or a "no" inserted in the box at the right of the question:

a. Are you under indictment or information in any court for a crime punishable by imprisonment for a term exceeding one year?	No	d. Are you an unlawful user of, or addicted to, marihuana, or a depressant, stimulant, or narcotic drug?	No
b. Have you been convicted in any court of a crime punishable by imprisonment for a term exceeding one year? (Note: The actual sentence given by the judge does not matter – a yes answer is necessary if the judge could have given a sentence of more than one year.)	No	e. Have you ever been adjudicated mentally defective or have you ever been committed to a mental institution?	No
		f. Have you been discharged from the Armed Forces under dishonorable conditions?	No
		g. Are you an alien illegally in the United States?	No
Are you a fugitive from justice?	No	h. Are you a person who, having been a citizen of the United States, has renounced his citizenship?	No

I hereby certify that the answers to the above are true and correct. I understand that a person who answers any of the above questions in the affirmative is prohibited by Federal law from purchasing and/or possessing a firearm. I also understand that the making of any false oral or written statement or the exhibiting of any false or misrepresented identification with respect to this transaction is a crime punishable as a felony.

TRANSFEREE'S (Buyer's) SIGNATURE	DATE
Ken R. Hulbert	7-18-75

SECTION B – TO BE COMPLETED BY TRANSFEROR OR SELLER

THE PERSON DESCRIBED IN SECTION A: ☐ IS KNOWN TO ME ☒ HAS IDENTIFIED HIMSELF TO ME IN THE FOLLOWING MANNER

9. TYPE OF IDENTIFICATION (Driver's License, etc.)	10. NUMBER ON IDENTIFICATION
	A45-7141

On the basis of: (1) the statements in Section A; (2) the verification of identity noted in Section B; and (3) the information in the current list of Published Ordinances, it is my belief that it is not unlawful for me to sell, deliver or otherwise dispose of the firearm described below to the person identified in Section A.

11. TYPE (Pistol, rifle, etc.)	12. MODEL	13. CALIBER OR GAUGE	14. SERIAL NO.
		25	298809

15. MANUFACTURER (and importer, if any)
TITAN.

16. TRADE/CORPORATE NAME AND ADDRESS OF TRANSFEROR (Seller) (Hand stamp may be used)	17. FEDERAL FIREARMS LICENSE NO.

18. TRANSFEROR'S (Seller's) SIGNATURE	19. TRANSFEROR'S TITLE	20. TRANSACTION DATE

ATF FORM 4473 - PT I (6-74)   EDITION OF 9/73 WILL BE USED

Documentation on Purchase of the gun

10: 15 a.m. Detective Schauperl, along with detectives Chuck Collins and Glenn Deveney, checked the pistol out of evidence and test fired it on the indoor Fullerton police range. Schauperl shot seven rounds with the gun to determine if it was operable. All rounds fired and all hit the target. This was witnessed by both Collins and Deveney.

Detective Schauperl and the other investigators continued to follow up various "loose ends" that needed to be addressed before we went to trial.

Tuesday, January 17, 1976
Orange County California

9: 00 a.m. Schauperl contacted Helen Covington, who had been the teller working the drive-up window at Barclays Bank in Orange on January 6, 1976, when Hulbert attempted to cash Carmen Banderas' check. Schauperl showed her a Polaroid photo lineup that included the photograph of the suspect Hulbert. Covington was not able to identify him from the lineup as the one who had attempted to cash the check. She told Schauperl she had not observed the individual closely enough to ever make an identification of him.

4: 00 p.m. Later the same day, Leon interviewed Ruby Patterson, who had recovered, for the most part, from the stroke she had suffered and had moved back into the home at 517 S. Paula Avenue in Fullerton, after it was vacated by Mollye and her children.

Mrs. Patterson told Schauperl she had a longstanding relationship with Ken Hulbert and his family. She said Ken's mother died when he was young. After the death of his mother, she had been hired by Roy Hulbert, Ken's father, to keep house and care for the children. Patterson had done this for many years. She said Roy Hulbert was very strict with his sons Dan and Ken, but Ken had not responded well to his direction and continually got into trouble. According to Mrs. Patterson, Roy and Ken did not get along. She told Schauperl that Ken Hulbert had left home and gotten married in 1973, although she never even met his wife. Patterson said the marriage lasted only a short time before they separated, and they never reconciled. She said Ken did not often speak of this marriage.

Ruby Patterson told Leon it was in December of 1973 when

Hulbert first met Mollye Selfies at an elder care center in Anaheim, where both were working. She said that shortly after they got to know each other, Ken and Mollye left the State of California and went to Mississippi. According to Mrs. Patterson, they also lived for a short time in Nebraska during this same period, but she did not know the exact dates.

Ruby Patterson told Schauperl that Ken and Mollye had returned to California sometime in July or August of 1975. She said she had not had much contact with Ken after their return. Patterson did say she noticed a change for the better in Ken after he met Mollye; Ken seemed to be more responsible and more settled than before he left California.

Mrs. Patterson said that on Friday, January 2, 1976 (the evening Gina Tisher was murdered), she had received strange telephone call from Ken Hulbert at about nine o'clock in the evening. She told us that, at first, she could hardly recognize his voice. She asked Hulbert what he wanted. He said he was stranded on the east side of Fullerton and needed a ride home. He told her he had gone out earlier in the day looking for a job and had been kidnapped by four negroes and driven around all day then dropped off on the east side of Fullerton. He also told her he did not have a coat with him and he was freezing. Patterson told Ken she could not pick him up as she was babysitting her granddaughter, but she would call Mollye and have her pick him up. She couldn't remember exactly, but she thought Ken had told her he was on Placentia Avenue and some other street. She did not write the location down. She did attempt to call Mollye at their apartment, but the phone was out of order, and she was unable to get through. She believes Hulbert and Mollye were living in an apartment in Buena Park at that time.

Ruby Patterson said this was the only call like that she had ever received from Ken Hulbert. She also told Schauperl she did not know what his problem was that night, but she had not believed his story.

Mrs. Patterson told Detective Schauperl that on January 8,

1976, she received a telephone call from Ken Hulbert asking her if she would allow their children to spend the night at her house. She agreed to have the children stay with her. She indicated that Ken had loaded up their belongings into a U-Haul trailer and told her they were preparing to move to Utah so he could look for work.

Ruby Patterson then said Ken and Mollye actually left for Utah on January 11, 1976, but, on the fourteenth of January, she received a call from Ken, who said he was in Las Vegas, Nevada. He told her they were experiencing car trouble and were going to return to California. Later the same day they arrived back at her residence and reclaimed the two children.

She related that during the recent times Ken was with her he did not appear paranoid or nervous, which was why it was hard for her to believe he was responsible for these crimes. She said she couldn't understand why he had not acted more "paranoid" given the fact he knew the police would be looking for him.

Ruby Patterson said Hulbert had mentioned the call he made to her on January 2 on several occasions and had said to her, "You didn't believe that story, did you?"

She also said that, on January 28, 1976, she had suffered a stroke and was hospitalized. Patterson told Schauperl she had not spoken with Ken Hulbert since then.

4: 15 p.m. While Schauperl was interviewing Patterson, Detective Collins was able to show the Polaroid photo lineup to the yellow cab driver, Stanley Ginsberg. Ginsberg had previously told Collins that on Friday, January 2, 1976, at approximately eight forty-five in the evening, he had picked up a male white subject at Chapman and State College, on the east side of Fullerton, and dropped him off at Gilbert and Commonwealth, on the west side of town. Ginsberg looked carefully at the photo lineup shown to him by Collins but was unable to make an identification of the photograph of Hulbert. Despite that, his testimony was consistent with the information Hulbert had given to Detectives when he admitted to the crimes in terms of the date and time, where he had first taken the cab, and where he was dropped off.

CHAPTER 10
KENNETH RICHARD HULBERT

THE QUESTION that always begs an answer for many people is what went wrong in someone's life that would cause them to lose their compassion or concern for their fellow human beings and commit violent crimes against another person? What happened in their life to bring them to the point where they become capable of raping and murdering another human being without any observable remorse? What circumstances had they lived through that caused them to become in many ways less than human? Although we will never know the answer for sure, Ken Hulbert's childhood does provide some clues.

Ken Richard Hulbert was born in Huntington Park California on September 16, 1951. He was the oldest of three children. He had a brother who was only eleven months his junior, and a sister who was the youngest of the three. In the 1950s, Huntington Park was a very nice bedroom community made up primarily of young families, many of whom commuted to Los Angeles daily.

Ken's father had gone into the service shortly after he married Ken's mother and before Ken was born. Before leaving for the military, he had insisted his wife become pregnant so she wouldn't run around while he was gone. Despite his best efforts, she didn't get pregnant before it was time for him to report for active duty. When he returned on leave, he again insisted she become pregnant. His mother later told her family he had "raped her" while home on leave, and she had become pregnant with Ken. Family members observed that it was very difficult for her to accept this son, a fact that didn't go unnoticed by Ken as he was growing up.

His was not a happy family and Ken's earliest recollections are of his parents constantly arguing and fighting. He described his childhood by saying, "I had a disturbed family life and my parents never got along well. There was a great deal of fighting in the home."

When he was five years old, his mother and father temporarily separated, and Ken went to live with his paternal grandparents. The two younger children had gone to live with their mother, while he had not been chosen to go with her. Ken saw this as being "given away" and deeply resented it. Family members say that, despite the way she often treated him and her apparent lack of concern for him, he had loved and idolized his mother. His paternal grandmother reported that, on another occasion, when he was quite young, he became hysterical when he thought he had been abandoned during a move. She believed these incidents had had a profound impact on his later life.

Ken started exhibiting behavioral problems and difficulties adjusting at a very early age. He was first caught stealing candy when he was five or six years old. Shortly after that, he began to run away from home frequently. At the age of eight, he forged his father's name to a bank account statement so he could withdraw money to run away. He often made his way to his paternal grandparents' home when he fled from his parents' house.

His parents finally divorced when Ken was 13 years old, and all three children went to live with their mother. This was a very upsetting time for Ken as his mom was constantly moving from place to place, and was, according to family acquaintances, "running around at night." Ken told one family friend he had memories from when he was young of watching his mother get dressed up to go out almost every night. He said they were left alone and unsupervised and that he, as the oldest, was left in charge of his brother and sister. This proved to be too much responsibility for a 13-year- ended up on the streets a lot during the evenings when his mother was not home.

Ken Hulbert would later say that, for about three years following his parents' divorce his mother was sleeping around with about eight different boyfriends. On a rare occasion, she would allow one of them to stay overnight at the home, but usually she would stay with the men at motels, leaving the children alone. Hulbert told one of the psychiatrists interviewing him after his arrest in Fullerton that he enjoyed this time because he could be out during the middle of the night on the streets, and he liked the freedom, which was in sharp contrast to the structure his father had imposed on him. He claimed his mother became drug-dependent during this period and on weekdays she would take large amounts of stimulants to stay awake, most of which she got from various pharmacist boyfriends. On weekends she would take barbiturates and was groggy much of the time.

His mother was, according to Hulbert, often unreasonable with him when she was under the influence. He ran away from home on two different occasions but returned both times. These incidents were apparently not reported to the police.

When he was fourteen, he and some other boys vandalized several vacant apartments near his home, and he was arrested for malicious mischief. A short time after that, he and a group of boys burglarized a home near his neighborhood. While in the house, they "shot it up" with a gun they had found there. Ken Hulbert recalled he was feeling very angry and destructive at that time in his life, given his tumultuous childhood.

When Ken was about 15, his mother met a man she became very interested in, and they planned to get married. Ken and his siblings were excited about that prospect and of being a family again. Ken looked forward to "happy times," but it would never come to pass. Before they could be married, his mother was killed in a skiing accident in Big Bear, California.

The day of the accident, she was brought home by her companions, still alive, and Ken and his siblings thought she was just drunk, a condition that happened all too frequently. The next day, however, she continued to deteriorate, and she subsequently died of what was diagnosed as a brain hemorrhage. Ken Hulbert never knew the facts of what caused her death. He and both of his siblings were devastated by the death of their mother and were once again uprooted and returned to live with their father. His father later told him her death had been the result of drugs.

Ken was now fifteen years old, and by that time, Roy Hulbert had been remarried, again divorced, and was living alone. Because he was dealing with his own serious life issues, including the loss of his first wife, and his experience serving in Korea, he was not able to cope with Ken or help him with his problems, which were numerous.

Ken Hulbert's father was a Fullerton Fire Fighter and has been described by others close to the family as being "very forceful." A friend of the family described him as "a very stern person and a strict disciplinarian, who insisted on military-like order in the home." Family members said Ken was "scared to death" of his father, who was constantly threatening him and subjecting him to frequent physical punishment. According to some people, Ken's father did not hesitate to use his fists on Ken. They said they thought that Ken's father had recently come to believe he shared some of the blame for how Ken turned out. It was noted by many close to the situation that Roy rarely, if ever, showed any love for his son, and it became even worse after the death of Ken's mother. They believed Roy set impossible standards for Ken, and Ken was constantly struggling for approval.

Ken's father's family had never approved of or liked Ken's mother and they made their feelings known to her and the rest of the family. They would frequently refer to her as a whore and accuse her of running around with other men. This was apparently done within the hearing of the children.

According to Ken, his father married again when Ken was 17, to a psychiatric nurse named Beverly. Ken Hulbert related that his father, for some reason, thought Beverly was trying to poison him and lost a lot of weight because he would refuse to eat. According to Ken, Beverly finally left his father after she awakened in the night while he was trying to strangle her.

Shortly after the death of Ken's mother, Ken's father had hired Ruby Patterson as a housekeeper to watch the three children when he was working. She was a kindly older woman who did her best for the three kids. Mr. Hulbert told her on more than one occasion, speaking of Ken, "I'm going to make or break that kid." She also indicated it appeared that Roy blamed Ken for all the problems his siblings experienced, and often referred to him as "that no-good goddamn kid."

One time, while Ruby Patterson was caring for them, Ken took his father's badge, and it was either lost or stolen, she couldn't remember which. Ken's father recovered the badge, but didn't tell Ken, and, to teach him a lesson, constantly made Ken feel guilty for what he had done. Following this incident, Ken stole a hundred dollars from his father's coin collection and ran away from home for the first of what would be many times while living with his father. Later, when he was apprehended, his father refused to allow him to come back, telling authorities he could not have a thief in the house. Roy arranged for him to be placed in a California Youth Authority halfway house. Ken never went back to live with his father, and their relationship was estranged from then on. This really was the end of any family life, such as it was, for Ken Hulbert.

It was during this time Ken began experiencing even more severe problems in school. He ended up in the Orange County Juvenile Hall on several occasions after he was arrested for burglary, auto theft, and a variety of other property crimes. At

16, he had become involved in a string of burglaries, auto thefts and, according to Ken, armed robberies. He was sent to Joplin Ranch, a youth correctional facility, in Orange County. He later told mental health workers he had run away from Joplin but was caught and sent to the Norwalk Treatment facility of the California Youth Authority for ninety days.

Mrs. Patterson told investigators she believed Ken became a problem as a juvenile because it was so hard for him to cope with things at home. Each time he was released he attempted to come back to his father's home, but his father would not let him return. During this time, Ken developed what she would call "a faraway look on his face." Many times, he told her he just "couldn't cope in this wicked world." According to Mrs. Patterson, Ken later suffered a mental breakdown and was admitted to Metropolitan State Hospital in Norwalk for a while. Patterson told us she believed this incident occurred in 1971, when Ken Hulbert was 20.

After his arrest in Fullerton, Hulbert told the court appointed psychiatrist that he was sent to a California Youth Authority halfway house, but \ he ran away from the house a short time later. While he was out, he stole credit cards from a man he met and was attempting to use them when he was caught and returned to the state operated facility.

Ken said that while at the California Youth Authority (CYA) facility, he became heavily involved in racism and gang wars within the prison system. It was there he tattooed a swastika on his own wrist. He says he was involved in many fights with blacks and Mexicans.[1] He also admitted to sniffing glue and Freon on a regular basis while in custody.

Hulbert spent a total of twenty months in the CYA detention center. While there he attended classes and graduated from high school. He was released from custody in 1970 on parole. He only

---

1. The fact Ken Hulbert was right-handed and he did the tattoo himself would explain the location of the tattoo on his left wrist.

lasted a few months on the street before he was again sent to a CYA facility in Tracy, California for violating his parole by writing bad checks. He was subsequently released in March of 1971.

After his release, he traveled to the East Coast where he became involved in using LSD. He claimed he suffered from an LSD overdose and ended up being placed in Ryker's Island Penitentiary prison ward for 30 days. He was charged with assaulting a police officer but told the psychiatrist he had no recollection of having done so.

Hulbert told psychiatrist Dr. John A. Hunter, a court appointed psychiatrist who interviewed him in the Fullerton jail shortly after his arrest, he left home in 1970 and began traveling to "see the world." "I was looking for my place," he told him. His ultimate destination was to make his way to Europe, by way of Canada. It was while he was on the way to Canada he ended up in New York. He told Dr. Hunter about one incident involving some people he had met who had picked him up while he was hitchhiking outside of New York City. They took him to an apartment in the city and he joined them in some drinks. After taking the drinks, he became acutely hallucinated and confused. He remembers someone there told him they made a living "ripping people off." He said he was struck on the head, knocked out, and robbed of the $240 dollars he had earned a short time before the incident. He claimed he woke up out on the street. He also admitted to Dr. Hunter he had tried working the streets around Times Square as a male prostitute during the last two weeks he was in New York but didn't like the activity, and claimed he had stopped in the middle of his first contact. He told Dr. Hunter this was the only homosexual activity he had ever been involved with.

Dr. Hunter believed Hulbert was not revealing the whole truth in this interview and Ken was only telling him what he wanted him to know. Hulbert did tell him he had traveled through Tennessee and most of the southeastern states, except for Florida. He claimed he had stopped in New York while on the way to Nova Scotia, which was to be where he would embark for Europe. He had no money, no passport, and very little chance of ever making that happen, but that was his plan.

When he was released from Ryker's in October of 1971, he returned to California for a new start, but almost immediately admitted himself as a voluntary patient at Metropolitan State Hospital in Norwalk. This is probably the incident referred to by Mrs. Patterson. The records from Metropolitan indicate Hulbert seemed disorganized and told them he wanted to control his impulses to attack people without cause. He signed himself out of the program about one month later, and, according to the staff, he left with an attractive girl.

Only one week later he was back and signed himself into the program again. The "ward" notes indicated he was quite seductive and aggressive with the girls. His initial diagnosis on admission was of schizophrenic reaction, chronic, undifferentiated, with a secondary diagnosis of drug dependency to hallucinogens.

At the time he was discharged, in March of 1972, the diagnosis had been changed to indicate he was suffering from sociopathic personality disturbance. This was almost exactly the diagnosis made by Orange County psychiatrist Dr. Klatte in his testimony at the sanity hearing for Hulbert in 1976, after his arrest for murder in Fullerton.

According to Hulbert, he continued to use hallucinogens and associated with a group who were also deeply involved in using them. At about this time he also apparently became interested in parapsychology and, by his own admission, became "fascinated with the devil."[2] At this time, he became involved with a girl

---

2. Wikipedia defines parapsychology as "a self-engendered discipline that seeks to investigate the existence and causes and conditions of psychic abilities, near-death experiences, out-of-the-body experiences, crisis apparitions, retro-cognitions, reincarnation memories, regression memories, prophecy, astrology, ghosts and life after death."

who also was heavily into the occult. In a later interview with this girl, Debbie Benson, by the Orange County Probation Department, she told them she had observed a very strange look in Hulbert's eyes, and he appeared to be distracted and "possessed" most of the time. Both Ms. Benson and Hulbert described an incident that occurred while they were driving together at night. They both heard a laugh coming out of the back seat of the car and out of the corner of their eyes perceived a dark figure in the back seat, who both thought was the devil. This incident occurred at a time when Ken was heavily into the use of hallucinogenic drugs.

In the fall of 1973, when he was 22, he married a girl named Cheryl, who was briefly interviewed by Orange County District Attorney investigators after Hulbert was arrested for the Fullerton crimes. She said they had only been together for a very short period, and it was a marriage of convenience as she had been pregnant by another man when they married. Hulbert told Dr. Hunter that Cheryl was three months pregnant when he met her and she was about one year younger than he was. He said they were married somewhere around the time she was due to deliver the baby; however, the marriage only lasted four or five months. He claimed, "She wanted a daddy, and I didn't want to be one." He further told Hunter that Cheryl wanted to be a "little girl." According to Hulbert, they had never formally divorced, and he was still legally married to her and she was living somewhere in the Long Beach area.

It was interesting that many of the relatives who had known Ken Hulbert as a child claimed they found it difficult to believe he had been responsible for the terrible things he was charged with. They described him as a "sensitive and gentle kid," and no one could recall his ever having displayed any hostility toward women. This information, however, seems very inconsistent with the information these same people gave about his troubled childhood, numerous arrests, and anti-social behavior.

Mrs. Patterson also told the Probation Department she never

had the impression Ken Hulbert was capable of this type of crime. She said he was very interested in psychology and in the study of witchcraft, and she felt he had a good understanding of human behavior. She said Ken Hulbert had "a life with no love." She believed she was the only person who had ever shown true affection for him, and she further believed she was the only person he would ever fully trust.

She did not want to see Ken Hulbert go to jail, but at the same time was fearful of having him running loose. She said she was fearful for her grandchildren. She believed Ken Hulbert should be placed in a hospital rather than in a prison.

Ken's father, Roy Hulbert, was interviewed by Detectives, including Schauperl, after his arrest. He was reluctant to talk to them, but finally agreed. He described himself as "a dominant, strong-willed conservative hard neck." He said his own attitude was, "I'll tell you once or twice and then I'll knock you on your ass." He cited an incident where Ken had shot at a California Highway Patrol officer after which he threatened to kill his son. He told the investigators, "While serving in Korea, I lived with a lust to kill, because I knew I had to be a wanton killer, but otherwise, I was an excellent soldier." During the interview he showed very little emotion or concern for his son and wasn't much interested in talking about him.

Ken Hulbert's father said the relationship with his son had broken down many years ago and he had given up on him and detested the things he had done, but still cared for him. He told the investigators he had had intermittent contact with Ken until the time of his arrest; however, he had absolutely no indication he was involved in criminal activities of such a serious nature. He said he thought Ken was a schizophrenic and a "radical" and if he was on the jury and the circumstances were true, "I'd hang him, I'd pull the switch myself." But then he added, "I guess I still love him."

Roy Hulbert tried to explain the reasons for his son's actions, telling the investigators about Ken's psychological problems as an adolescent. He also indicated Ken had been deeply involved in the use of various drugs and narcotics, including LSD and other hallucinogens. He said Ken's younger brother had informed him both had been "loaded on grass all the way through school." Mr. Hulbert said he was also aware Ken had begun sniffing Freon while in state custody. One of the things Ken did that just "blew my mind," Roy said, was when he tried to get his younger sister to prostitute herself to make some money, when they were teenagers. This sister had since married and moved to the East Coast, according to some of Ken's relatives, and had no recent contact with the rest of the family.

He also told Schauperl he was very familiar with Ken's relationship with Mollye, and he believed she was heavily into "devil cults" and other fringe beliefs. In addition, it was his opinion Ken was very heavily influenced by her. Mr. Hulbert said none of the family approved of her. They did not think she was good for Ken. It was a strange interview and left investigators disturbed by Roy Hulbert's responses and the detached way he responded to their inquiries.

Both of Ken's paternal grandparents, Richard and Geneva Hulbert, were interviewed by investigators in March of 1976, and asked about Ken and his childhood. Geneva Hulbert told them, "I couldn't see him kicking a dog, let alone a human." Both told investigators that when he was small, he would let other kids run all over him. They also said Ken had been very close to his mother at the time of her death, and they believed that was the turning point for Ken. Soon after that, he was arrested for the burglary of a residence and sent to Joplin Ranch, a youth correctional facility in Orange County. They also confirmed the incident where Ken had stolen a car and, being pursued, "took a shot at a CHP [California Highway Patrol] car." It was for that crime he was sent to one of the California Youth Authority facilities. They also believed this was when Ken's father gave up on him completely.

According to his grandparents, Ken loved and idolized his

mother, and when she was married to his father, he was always fearful she would leave because of the constant fighting between his parents.

Ken's maternal grandmother, Edith Robinson, was also interviewed by the District Attorney's investigators in April of 1976, after Ken's arrest for murder. It was obvious from the interview she and Ken were not close. She expressed concern that the adverse publicity resulting from this case was causing a lot of stress in her life, and it was a problem for other family members. She showed little concern for Ken. She told the investigators she had only infrequent contact with Ken and had only seen him "a few times" in the years preceding his arrest. She believed his "life pattern" was set many years ago. She also said that in her opinion, the death of his mother and then his father having "kicked him out of the house" were situations he was never able to adjust to. She told them Ken's father was extremely cruel to him and to his sister, who also suffered from severe psychological and physical problems as a teenager. She said Ken's father had abandoned his sister when she was extremely sick at the age of eighteen, and she had not forgiven him for doing so. She confirmed the sister no longer had any contact with her immediate family.

She also told the investigators Roy Hulbert had been very cruel sexually to Ken's mother during their marriage. He had admitted to Mrs. Robinson on one occasion that if anyone had abused him the way he had abused his own wife he would have killed them.

Mrs. Robinson said she blamed Roy Hulbert for a lot of the trouble Ken was involved in, and described him as "a very forceful man." She said life became especially unbearable for Ken after his mother died, and everything fell to pieces. She indicated that, during this time, when he was suffering greatly from the loss of his mother, Ken's father showed him no love or concern. She also told investigators Ken was "a very nice young man who was a brilliant child who could quote poetry and was very sensitive." She also said he had the capacity to, "think what you like to hear," meaning he would tell you what he thought you wanted to hear from him.

Ken Hulbert never held a job for very long and worked at several different menial occupations during the times when he was not incarcerated. These efforts included working in a doughnut shop, as a mechanic, in nursing homes, and in two state hospitals as a custodian or ward worker. There was also a brief period of employment at a third state hospital, Fairview State Hospital in Costa Mesa, California. At the time of his arrest, he was working for a temporary agency and had just started a job at a service station in Whittier, California.

CHAPTER 11
MOLLYE

MOLLYE SELFIES HULBERT was born and raised in Heidelberg Mississippi. She is the daughter of Louis and Doris Selfies. At the time she met Ken Hulbert, she had one son, David Lee, who was five years old, and who was the son of William David Lee of New Orleans, one of her ex-husbands. She was, according to Hulbert and others, heavily involved in drugs, particularly marijuana and hallucinogens. According to Orange County Probation Department reports, Mollye had been divorced twice and had moved to California with young David for a fresh start.

Ken Hulbert had gone to work at the Guidance Center Sanitarium in Anaheim in 1973. While at the Center he had a relationship with a thirty-year-old female employee. The relationship, according to Ken Hulbert, lasted for "one or two months" before they broke up. He met Mollye Selfies in the winter of 1973 after she had come to work at the Sanitarium, and they began to live together after only a couple of weeks into the relationship, probably in January of 1974. Hulbert told court-appointed psychiatrist Dr. Hunter that since living with Mollye, he had not had any desire for other females. However, he did admit he had threatened her with the suggestion he might start to look for other women. He also told Dr. Hunter that she had suspected him of seeing other women, even accused him of doing so, particularly when they were living in Nebraska, and they were experiencing difficulties in their relationship.

Mollye Selfies (Hulbert), young David and baby Unity

Hulbert told interviewers that Mollye was very much into hallucinogens and the occult, and she got him interested in the occult too. On one occasion, she told him she was a "white witch." She also told Hulbert about astrological experiences she'd supposedly had and said she was there to serve as his spiritual guide. According to Hulbert, she also told him he would never know any true realities until he experienced the "magic mushrooms" that grew in Mississippi. She encouraged him to read books by Carlos Castaneda and other "alternative reality" writers. Castaneda, in his works, described the use of psychoactive drugs such as peyote, the active ingredient in the "magic mushrooms" Mollye had encouraged Ken to use.

According to Hulbert, he tired of Mollye at one point, and attempted to get away from her by taking a job as a custodian at Camarillo State Hospital in Camarillo, California. He said her influence in his life made him very anxious. He had gotten the job at Camarillo with the help of his stepmother, Beverly Hulbert, who was married to his father at that time.

He was apparently doing well on the job until Mollye came to Camarillo and moved in with him. Hulbert said Mollye continued to use drugs and he started to use again along with her. Mollye started bringing other people into the apartment, and they all began to use hallucinogens.

As a result of the drug use, Ken's performance at Camarillo suffered, and he was fired. It was at that time he and Mollye moved to Heidelberg, Mississippi, to live with her parents, Louis and Doris Selfies. Her father did not want to let Hulbert live in their home. Hulbert later told Dr. Hunter that Mollye had informed her father he would never see his grandson if he didn't take Hulbert in with them.

Hulbert told interviewers that, while in Mississippi, he was introduced to the "magic mushrooms" by Mollye's grandmother, and he said he had taken many hallucinogenic trips using magic mushrooms over a period of about six weeks.

The living arrangement did not work out for the couple, and Ken ended up stealing Mollye's father's 1972 Toyota station wagon and a .308 caliber rifle and attempting to flee the area but was arrested in a neighboring state and returned to Mississippi to stand trial for grand theft and grand theft auto in the First Judicial District, Jasper County, Mississippi, in August of 1974.

A copy of an indictment obtained from Jones County, Mississippi shows Hulbert was charged on July 8, 1974, as follows: "Ken Hulbert did then and there take, steal and carry away one

1972 model Toyota station wagon automobile and a .308 Remington automatic rifle with a four-power scope from Louis L. and Doris Selfies," Mollye's parents. As expected, the relationship between Mollye's parents and Ken Hulbert were never very good after this incident.

Hulbert told the Jasper County Court he had planned to stay in Mississippi if he could find a job and a place to live, but if he couldn't, he planned to return to California. He also told the court he had worked as a "technician" in the state hospital in California before leaving for Mississippi. What he failed to mention was he had been terminated before he ever completed the training program and he had been a custodian, not a technician.

When he was first arraigned in Jones County, Ken Hulbert pled "not guilty," but after the court appointed an attorney to represent him, he changed his plea to guilty. The judge sentenced him to three years in the State Penitentiary at Parkman, but, because of his age—twenty-two at the time, and the fact he was not from the area—the judge suspended the sentence and gave him one year as a "working prisoner" at the Mississippi State Hospital in Whitfield. He would have been eligible for release after nine months. As a condition of his sentencing, he was also told to have no visits from Molly Selfies, the daughter of the victims. Even though Hulbert had stolen her father's car and tried to leave the area without her and David, she continued to stand by him. They both ignored the order forbidding Hulbert to see her while at Whitfield, and Mollye would sneak in to see him whenever she could. On one occasion they were caught, and Hulbert was told he was going to go to the penitentiary, so he and Mollye fled the area, along with her young son, David Lee, and traveled to Nebraska. There was an active warrant from Mississippi for escape at the time we arrested Hulbert in Fullerton, in 1976. He was never sent back to Mississippi to stand trial for this.

After his arrest for the Fullerton cases, and during evaluations by various mental health professionals, Ken Hulbert would say the longest relationship he ever had with a woman was with Mollye, whom he lived with from approximately January of 1974 until the time of his arrest. According to reports, Hulbert expressed "much ambivalence" about the relationship. She was five years older than he was, and it always seemed to him she was more experienced and sophisticated than he was. In one interview Hulbert said that during the time he was with Mollye he never went out with another woman, except for the rapes, although he thought about it. He told the therapists that while under the influence of hallucinogens he often had questions in his mind about their relationship. At one point, he wondered whether his attraction to her was just "a woman and her guiles," or whether it was something more, such as her having control over him.

Also, after the Fullerton homicide arrest, Hulbert would later tell others "Mollye represented the devil, and perhaps the one he had really wanted to kill had been Mollye, but he could not."

It was while they were living in Nebraska that Hulbert purchased the Titan semi-automatic pistol he used in the kidnappings in California. He bought the weapon from a firearms dealer on July 18, 1975, by lying about his criminal record on the Federal firearms application form. Had he told the truth, he would not have legally been able to purchase a handgun.

Before he fled Nebraska he also wrote two hundred and forty dollars' worth of "nonsufficient fund checks." - He was arrested in California and extradited to Nebraska to stand trial on the check charges where he was found guilty. Because he was living in California at the time, he was allowed to return to California, where he would be on probation for the Nebraska charges. This probation was minimal at best, and he rarely saw a probation officer. There was no active supervision involved we could ever verify. Had he been sentenced to jail in Nebraska he would not have been in California to commit the crimes he was involved in there.

During this time, fall of 1975, he told Mollye he was going to get money by ripping off women, because they were easier to victimize than men. Mollye told Dr. Klatte, one of the courts' appointed psychiatrists, after Hulbert's arrest for murder, she knew he was carrying a gun specifically for this purpose, but said she was not aware he was raping and kidnapping. From this report from Dr. Klatte, she absolutely knew he was involved in illegal activities involving women and the gun.

Mollye told Klatte that, during that time, Ken was becoming more and more disturbed, and although she did not think he was possessed by the devil, she became fearful of him and had visions of him possibly killing her.

Mollye admitted to Klatte that the night preceding his arrest, Ken Hulbert had fully confessed his guilt to her regarding the rapes he had been committing. At minimum, from that point on she was clearly aware of his crimes. In addition, he had been bringing home women's purses, watches, and jewelry for some time, all taken in the kidnapping and rapes of his young victims. She had to have known they were the result of criminal activity on his part.

Mollye also confessed to Dr. Klatte that, even before his admission of guilt to her, she had concluded he was guilty of the rapes and murder. That is why she had taken the jewelry to their marriage counselor in an envelope, telling him she thought he was the one responsible for these crimes.

After Hulbert was convicted of the Fullerton crimes, Mollye was contacted by Laura Vorie of the Orange County Probation Department and an appointment was set for an interview. Mollye later changed her mind and declined to be interviewed. She told Vorie, "I know Ken better than anyone, but I couldn't incriminate him for anything." She did tell Vorie that if she was able to get her thoughts together, she would submit a letter expressing her opinion. To the best of my knowledge, she never sent such letter.

Between April 22 and the first of August of 1976, Ken Hulbert was interviewed by various therapists who worked as part of the Orange County Jail psychological team. During these sessions, occurring after he was arrested for the Fullerton crimes, he told the therapists he was glad he had been caught, because he knew if he was released, he would immediately go back to what he was doing before. He speculated he may have wanted to be caught but had never admitted it to himself.

He told them he "knew when it was time to do one," referring to the rapes of the young women, as he would become very dissatisfied, anxious, and uptight. He described it as "being like having a fit, only it wasn't on the floor." He told them he would become agitated, restless, and unable to sleep, but when he made up his mind to go to a parking lot or supermarket and attack a woman, he would begin to feel calm, with an "air of expectancy." Hulbert told them that, when he found a potential victim, he would experience a feeling of being refreshed, fulfilled, and satisfied.

He said he felt no remorse, nor did he ever think about what he had done. He speculated that perhaps he had been trying to repress the incidents from his mind. In discussing his "modus operandi," he said he would usually walk up and down the parking lots for many hours and observe many different women in the area. Then, suddenly, he would see one particular woman, and something would tell him "this is the one." He would then make his approach, almost always in a public parking lot, usually telling the victim she had a flat tire on her car. After engaging her in conversation he would bring out his gun and force her back into her car, usually into the passenger seat or into the back floorboard area.

According to Hulbert, he would then proceed in three steps. First, he would assault the female materially, robbing her of all her effects and money. Second, he would assault her pride, by having her strip, and last, he would assault her body. He said he believed the rapes "had to happen, that he was born to be a rapist and, conversely, the victims were born to be raped. Even if it meant death, the women had to be straightened out."

After Hulbert's arrest, Mollye stayed in California and helped him defend himself in the criminal proceedings. She acted as his "investigator" and met with him to discuss strategy on several occasions at the Orange County Jail. One inmate testified he was told by Hulbert that he had Mollye flirting with one of the deputies to see if he would get involved with her, as he thought it would benefit his case. This never happened as far as we know.

During the first trial on the issue of sanity, in late January 1977, the prosecutor, Richard Farnell, told the court that Ken Hulbert and Mollye had recently been married, in jail, and she would not have to testify against him. While doing the research for this book, I was not able to find any record of this marriage in Orange County or anywhere in the State of California. In addition, according to information from Hulbert himself, he was still legally married to Cheryl as they had never formally divorced.

Mollye was pregnant with twins at the time Hulbert was arrested in January of 1976. When I spoke with David Lee III, Mollye's eldest son, in 2009, one of the twins was incarcerated in Mississippi for rape; the whereabouts of the other was unknown. The last information on Mollye Selfies I had from David Lee was she was living somewhere in the Mississippi or Louisiana area. He sent me an email he had received from Mollye on March 16, 2009. From the contents of the letter, it was clear she was "homeless" and working her son to try to get him to give her some money to rent a house in the area.

Certificate of No Public Record

This is to certify that a search has been made of the Statewide Index in the Office of Vital Records covering the event shown, and no public record of this event was found based on the information provided.

Name(s):	Mollye Selfies Kenneth Hulbert		
Event:	MARRIAGE		
Period Searched:	**From** July 1905	**Through** Present	

Office of Vital Records

JAN -5 2011

Results of Search of California Records for Marriage of Ken & Mollye

CHAPTER 12
EVIL OR INSANE?

February 2, 1976
Fullerton, California

THE WITNESSES HAD all been interviewed, the evidence was collected, and all the reports had been completed. Now it was time to submit the case to the courts. From here on out, it was pretty much out of our hands. We could gather more evidence if needed, re-interview witnesses if the district attorney representatives thought it was necessary, and do any other follow up work they required. The bottom line was whether we had done our job, if the charges would be filed, and if they would hold up in court.

We filed ten counts in the North Orange County Municipal Court, charging Hulbert with one count of murder, one count of attempted murder, three counts of kidnapping, two counts of rape, two counts of robbery, and one count of sodomy. He was scheduled to be arraigned on February 3, 1976. That arraignment, however, was continued until February 10, on a motion by the Public Defender Glenn Osajina. The request was made so Public Defender Ron Butler, the attorney who would ultimately handle the case, would have time to prepare. Deputy District

Attorney Carl Ilg was handling the case for the prosecution, and he made it plain the charges would include three special allegations. That would allow prosecutors to seek the death penalty should he be convicted of the rape and murder charges.

In the meantime, we had several meetings with the homicide team from the Orange County District Attorneys' Office and discussed the possibility of taking the case to a grand jury, which would eliminate the need for a preliminary hearing in municipal court, and, hopefully, speed up the process of getting the case to an actual trial, which would happen in superior court. With the use of a grand jury the prosecutor presents the case, and the public defender or defense attorney does not have the opportunity to cross examine the witnesses or otherwise participate.

After a lot of consideration, we made the decision to present the case to the Orange County Grand Jury and avoid the preliminary hearing. The decision was based primarily on the fact that many of the municipal court judges had begun holding what amounted to almost a full-blown trial, instead of just a hearing to determine if there was sufficient evidence to bind the suspect over for trial, which was, and still is, the purpose of a preliminary hearing. This practice had caused issues in previous cases where errors were made, allowing the defense to challenge the process.

February 10, 1976
Santa Ana, California

The Orange County Grand Jury heard the evidence and returned an indictment charging Hulbert with fourteen counts including murder, rape, sex perversion, assault, robbery, and kidnapping. The Grand Jury had issued the indictment after listening to what one of the local newspapers call "the chilling testimony of two victims" who described in detail what they went through.

One of these victims was the Fullerton College coed Carmen

Banderas, who testified, "I was thinking I was going to die, but then I thought of my little boy. He will be three in March, and I knew I had to live for him and my husband." The doctor who first examined her at Tustin Community Hospital, Dr. Rettinger, testified, "Well, to be very truthful, I was very surprised she was alive when she came into the emergency room." He described her as being splattered with her own blood.

The second victim to testify was Deborah Hoffman, who was kidnapped at gunpoint in a parking lot and assaulted by Hulbert. After the assault, she said she was forced to call her mother with the demand she turn over her rent money "because I got a gun on your daughter, and you had better listen to her or I am going to kill her." She was released a few hours after he received the couple hundred dollars.

February 11, 1976
Santa Ana, California

Hulbert was arraigned in superior court and all other proceedings were continued until February 26, when he would enter a plea to the Grand Jury charges. The arraignment was quick and uneventful.

February 26, 1976
Santa Ana, California

Once again, the process was delayed when Public Defender Walter Zech asked for another continuance, this time for one week. Zech told Judge William Spears he would file a demurer, a legal process citing constitutional grounds that the charges were not valid, and the case should not go to trial. He also protested the district attorney's action in having the municipal court charges dismissed to avoid a preliminary hearing and taking the case to the grand jury instead. The "prelim" was a process that allowed the defense to cross examine the state's witnesses, and by so doing, they often garnered ammunition they could use against the prosecution's case in the trial. The D.A. objected to the delay, but Judge Spears granted it anyway. He did, however, deny the defense objection to using the grand jury as a way of avoiding the preliminary hearing in a municipal court. All of these were just attempts to delay the actual trial.

Zech also told the judge that Hulbert had been complaining of acute lower abdominal pains since he was jailed, so intense he had doubled over and fallen down. Zech complained that the Orange County Jail was not equipped to handle this illness. The judge told Zech that if he prepared an order to have Hulbert examined at the Orange County Medical Center, he, the judge, would sign it.

March 2, 1976

Santa Ana, California

Hulbert finally entered a plea of "not guilty," but his public defender, Walter Zech, indicated they wanted to "reserve the right to change the plea." (I believe Zech was toying with the idea of an insanity plea as there was little else for them to build a defense on.) Judge Spears set September 13, 1976, for the trial. Zech again indicated he was going to file a motion attacking the "sufficiency of evidence" that led to the Grand Jury's indictment of his client. He also told the court he would meet with Hulbert and his "common-law wife" Mollye in a few days to determine which witnesses to call. In the interim, Zech had gotten Judge Spears to sign the order to have Hulbert examined by doctors at the Orange County Medical Center. The doctors examined him, but they were not able to determine a cause for his pain. It was around this time that the Orange County District Attorney, Cecil Hicks, confirmed his office intended to seek the death penalty for Hulbert.

A hearing had been scheduled for the ninth of April to hear the brief the public defender had prepared in order to attack the grand jury indictment. This, however, was postponed by Judge Jerrold Oliver so he and the prosecutor had more time to study the one-hundred ten page "ten-point brief." The Judge continued the motion until the sixteenth of April.

March 2, 1976
Los Angeles, California

On the same day as Hulbert was pleading not guilty in Orange County, the Los Angeles County Grand Jury indicted him on fourteen counts, charging rape, kidnap, attempted kidnap, robbery, oral copulation, and extortion. The indictment was returned after approximately five hours of testimony was heard, including the testimony of Fullerton Detective Leon Schauperl. The actual prosecution of the Los Angeles County cases would be deferred until the completion of the trial in Orange County.

April 16, 1976
Superior Court
Santa Ana, California

Superior Court Judge Jerold Oliver denied all ten points in the one-hundred-ten-page ten-point brief submitted by the Public Defender's Office. The brief had been prepared by Deputy Public Defender William Kopeny, who argued the motions in front of Judge Oliver. The judge confirmed the trial date as September 13th, 1976.

Members of the National Organization for Women began to attend the hearings, starting with this one. They continued to monitor the case from this point on.

September 13, 1976
Superior Court
Santa Ana, California

We received another surprise when we arrived early the morning of September 13, ready for the trial. Almost immediately, Judge James Walsworth suspended the trial pending a superior court hearing to determine if the defendant was sane and able to stand trial.

While in custody and awaiting trial, Hulbert had been studying law books in the jail library, specifically as to the issue of insanity and the ability to be tried and convicted while insane. At this time, he also started to exhibit bizarre behavior, which had not been in evidence before then. It looked like Hulbert's act was paying off for him, at least for the moment.

October 4, 1976
Superior Court
Santa Ana, California

Jury selection finally began in the sanity hearing in Orange County Superior Court. The purpose of the hearing was to determine whether Hulbert was competent to stand trial at that time. The jury selection was expected to take two or three days and the competency hearing itself could take up to five weeks, according to Judge Murray. Once again, the public defenders' office requested all news media be barred from the courtroom during the hearing on the basis that there was going to be sensitive evidence that could not be made public. This was on the grounds it would breach the attorney-client privilege of confidentiality and would, therefore, be prejudicial. No decision on the motion was made at that time.

JURY SELECTION IN MURDER CASE BEGINS
JEFFREY PERLMAN
Los Angeles Times (1886-Current File); Nov 23, 1976; ProQuest Historical Newspapers Los Angeles Times (1881 - 1986)
pg. OC6

JURY SELECTION IN MURDER CASE BEGINS

BY JEFFREY PERLMAN
Times Staff Writer

SANTA ANA — Jury selection began Monday in Superior Court for a hearing to determine if a Fullerton man accussed of murder and rape is mentally competent to stand trial.

Ken Richard Hulbert, 24, sat silently in Superior Judge William L. Murray's courtroom Monday as prospective jurors were questioned.

Hulbert was arrested Jan. 30 by Fullerton police acting on a tip from a citizen who recognized an artist's sketch of a man who kidnaped a Fullerton College coed on Jan. 6.

The body of Gina Marie Tisher, 19, of Whittier, was found in Fullerton after she had been abducted from the laundry room of her apartment house.

Hulbert has been indicted by the Orange County Grand Jury on 14 counts, including murder, rape, sex perversion, assault, robbery and kidnaping.

He has pleaded innocent to a Los Angeles County Grand Jury indictment charging him with attacks on six other women.

Jury selection is expected to take two or three days. The competency hearing may take five weeks, according to Judge Murray. Should the jury find Hulbert incompetent to stand trial, he would be held at a state mental health facility until he is judged competent. Otherwise, he is slated to be tried soon after the competency hearing.

The public defender representing Hulbert has asked Judge Murray to bar the news media from the courtroom during the competency hearing in order to protect certain evidence relating to Hulbert's competency taken from the defendant himself. It is argued that the sensitive evidence cannot be made public on grounds it would breach the attorney-client privilege of confidentiality and would be prejudicial.

Article on Jury Selection November 1976

October 30, 1976
Superior Court
Los Angeles, California

Hulbert was arraigned on the Los Angeles County Grand

Jury indictment, and he pled not guilty to all the charges. He was held to answer.

December 9, 1976
Superior Court
Santa Ana, California

A new judge, William S. Lee, was assigned to hear the pretrial insanity hearing because Judge Murray was reportedly still recuperating from an undisclosed illness he had suffered during the Thanksgiving holiday. Principal jurors had already been selected; however, no alternates had been chosen at the time Judge Murray became ill.

December 15, 1976
Superior Court
Santa Ana, California

Judge Lee denied the defense motion to close the courtroom to reporters and the public. He then scheduled the hearing to begin on the twentieth of December, but before that could happen, the Public Defender's Office appealed the judge's decision. The San Bernardino District Court of Appeal refused to hear the matter but did "stay" the hearing for ten days to allow the defense to seek California Supreme Court intervention into the issue. The public defender's office did, in fact, appeal the decision to the supreme court.

January 4, 1977
Sacramento, California

The California Supreme Court ordered a delay in the sanity hearing to give the court time to determine if they would hear the appeal, but on January 14, 1977, they denied the appeal and sent the case back down for trial.

January 24, 1977
Superior Court
Santa Ana, California

The actual insanity hearing finally began on January 24, 1977, and the jury was shown the first two of eight tapes that the Defense Psychiatrist Lawrence Stross of Denver, Colorado claimed would prove the defendant was insane. Stross was a well-known psychiatrist who once taught at the Menninger Clinic in Topeka, Kansas. The defense pointed out Hulbert had been a mental patient at Metropolitan State Hospital in Norwalk, California. The tapes were interviews between Stross and Hulbert. Stross would testify that, in his opinion, Hulbert did not understand the charge of murder and the death of one of the victims because of a "delusionary system" in his mind in which women are an extension of Satan and, therefore, couldn't be killed.

In this tape, Hulbert told Dr. Stross, "In true reality there are no women and there is no need for conception" and what is real is a kind of unisex and the "only thing" that makes it (unisex) male is the illusion of female... Satan can't be killed... women are an extension of Satan.... Women fooled us more than any other man because of the ideas of love, of trust and marriage... all the time trying to get deeper into the mind." He said, "The world is an illusion created by Satan to get from him a sort of 'password' into heaven and women are his [Satan's] greatest illusion, tool, and toy..." Hulbert said on tape he remembered that the first time in 1974, in Mississippi, when took drugs he referred to as 'magic mushrooms' (possibly psilocybin, a hallucinogen). He said, "It stimulated that portion of my memory, so I began to see the true reality... my reality." He said his wife was trying to seduce him to continue the illusion so he would drop his guard and "Satan would attack... try and draw the answer out of me..." He said a secondary attempt was for him to have a male child "to bind me to earth…"[1] Hulbert's attorney, Walter Zech, from the Public Defender's Office, told the court Stross was the first of four psychiatrists who would testify Hulbert was insane and therefore incompetent to stand trial.

Stross would testify on the first tape, "I found things hard to understand because things were opposite, and it was irrational thinking. The fact it was a well-ordered system tells me he's had this for a long time. I don't think it started with the magic mushrooms. It probably started right after his mother's death when he was fifteen years old. This would fit the classical nervous breakdown of a teenager and the beginning of mental illness."

On the second tape, Hulbert told Stross that the only time his father paid attention to him was to tell him he had done something wrong. He remembered him as being big and screaming and fighting with his mother a lot. According to Stross, while talking, Hulbert smiled, an action Stross pointed out as "inappropriate feelings… the cardinal, classical signs of schizophrenic illness." Hulbert said, "I wasn't allowed to express bad feelings for a lot of years. I used to feel like a walking bomb." He also told Stross he wanted to strike back at his father but never could because he thought of the consequences, "and because I guess I loved him or something," which Stross explained as "the holding of two opposite feelings for the same person at the same time, a love-hate; one of the cardinal, classical signs used to diagnose the psychotic."

At times during the playing of the tapes, Hulbert said he was "a god visiting here on earth… the world was created by the devil to seduce me and use me to invade heaven." He also told Stross the whole process of interviews by Dr. Stross were an attempt to "get me to believe that I killed somebody." Stross asked him if he did kill someone, and Hulbert replied, "Yes…

---

1. Contrast this with the transcripts of the interviews with Fullerton Detectives and Hulbert that occurred after his arrest in January of 1976, where he did not display any evidence of mental illness.

Gina Marie Tisher. I had to...it was the only way I could survive."

January 26, 1977

Superior Court

Santa Ana, California

During the playing of the fourth tape, Hulbert was heard to say he began thinking he had to kill someone "in October or November of 1975, all I knew was I knew if I killed somebody, I'd be normal... it was the only way." Hulbert said on the tape he thought that, after the death, he would be "greeted by cheering crowds" and "be hailed as a hero."

As we listened to this attempt by Hulbert to appear insane, we couldn't help but contrast his testimony with his actions after the killing of Gina Tisher, where he wiped down the Tisher vehicle with an automotive product, then soaked a rag with the fluid and pushed it into the victim's vagina to try to destroy any sperm evidence. After leaving the scene, he threw her car keys away so he wouldn't be caught with them on his person. Stross said that, under Hulbert's delusionary system, death does not exist, and the souls of women can pass from one body to another, or not at all, by the will of Satan.

It was interesting to note that Dr. Stross, at one point, told the jury Hulbert was very familiar with psychiatric terminology. Stross attributed it to Hulbert's stay at the Metropolitan State Hospital in Norwalk. The more skeptical in the audience, and the law enforcement officers for sure, attributed Hulbert's attempts to appear insane to his studying the subject for months while in custody, as well as the fact he had worked in mental hospitals from time to time.

January 27, 1977
Superior Court
Santa Ana, California

On the next tape, according to an article by Jeffrey Perlman in the *Los Angeles Times*, Hulbert was heard to admit he had killed three people. He was, of course, only charged with killing one in Orange County. Next, the obviously "startled psychiatrist," asked Hulbert to explain who the three murder victims were. "There were no deaths," Hulbert interrupted, according to the article, referring to an earlier statement that death was an illusion in a war between himself and Satan. This was the third day of viewing videotapes for the Superior Court jury of seven women and five men, who would ultimately decide if Hulbert was mentally competent to stand trial.

This reference to "three deaths" came while Hulbert was explaining how he had been able to refrain from telling anyone about his "poem" or "riddle," which he said, involved a "secret password" needed by Satan to invade heaven and destroy it from within.

On the recording, Hulbert expressed fears that if the doctor placed him under hypnosis, which he later did, he could be tricked into revealing the password. "It's been seven months, three deaths," Hulbert repeated. Despite multiple attempts by Stross to pursue the "three deaths" statement, Hulbert refused to come back to the subject. He said he was referring to what somebody told him (about the deaths), but when Stross pursued that, Hulbert said, "You know about it anyway... everybody knows about it." Finally, Stross reassured Hulbert, "I've told you I would limit this [series of interviews] to the three women that I've [previously] named" (Dr. Stross was referring to Gina Tisher, Carmen Banderas, and Deborah Hoffman).

Hulbert's attorney, Walter Zech, told the court, "The D.A. thinks there's something there [more than the single charge he is being accused of], but there isn't."

There had been speculation from the prosecution that Zech's efforts to have the public barred from the hearings were because he did not want the jury to hear Hulbert's taped remarks that he had killed three times, not once. There was, of course, no way to prove that to the satisfaction of the judge.

In other parts of the tape shown to the jury that Wednesday, Hulbert described how he drove around Los Angeles and Orange Counties for eight hours with one of his victims. During this episode, he told Stross on the tape, the woman tried to make him believe he was doing something wrong, and he was having a "head problem." Hulbert described how he argued with the girl, saying this was a battle in the continuing war between Satan and himself. He said he kept telling the girl she was one of Satan's workers. We know from the taped confession from Hulbert and from the statements of this particular victim, Carmen Banderas, that he did drive her around for eight hours, and she did tell him he had mental problems, but at no time did he make the statement that this was a battle in the continuing war between Satan and himself, nor did he tell her she was one of Satan's workers. He made no statement to Banderas she could recall that made any reference to the devil or a bizarre or off-based belief system on his part. Those of us closest to the case believed this was all part of Hulbert's attempts to appear insane. As it turned out, it worked better than we thought it would.

The defense continued showing videotapes, and, at the end, the jury had seen eight hours of taped interviews of with defendant and Dr. Stross.

January 28, 1977
Superior Court
Santa Ana, California

Deputy District Attorney Frank Briseno had his first opportunity to cross-examine the psychiatrist, Lawrence Stross, on January 28. Briseno aggressively questioned the witness about his failure to pursue Hulbert's statements he had killed three times.

Briseno was able to point out to the jury that, in the past, Stross had only testified on behalf of the defense in such cases, and that he was currently being paid five hundred dollars a day for his testimony, for a period of nine days, or a total of $4500. In 1977 that was a lot of money when the average annual income in the United States was $13,570.

Briseno also took on Stross over the fact he had entered into two contracts with Hulbert. He questioned Stross on why he had Hulbert sign a release before the videotaping, giving the doctor permission to use the tapes for teaching purposes. The other was a form that exempted the doctor from liability should Hulbert suffer any ill effects from the hypnosis Stross placed him under. Briseno asked Stross, "Can you contract with a crazy man?" Stross answered, "As I understand the law, no." Briseno then asked Stross who had told him to limit the scope and content of the examination, as he had previously testified he had done. Stross answered he had formulated the limits in his own mind, but later, under further questioning by Briseno, Stross backtracked and said he could not remember if Zech had ever requested him to limit such questioning of Hulbert.[2] (Stross maintained he was unaware of the additional charges that had been filed against Hulbert in Los Angeles County. He would have had to have been completely cut off from any newspapers or television news for that to be true.)

During further questioning of Stross, Briseno was able to let the jury know Hulbert had previously worked at Camarillo State Mental Hospital and Fairview State Mental Hospital as well as at an Anaheim sanitarium. Briseno also brought out the fact

---

2. Law enforcement always believed Hulbert was responsible for several homicides, including the death of Sharon Aldridge, a twenty-three-year-old who was kidnapped from a West Covina shopping center. Her body was later found in her car in the parking lot of a medical center a few blocks from the shopping center where she was abducted.

Hulbert had studied psychology at Fullerton College, had read psychiatric case histories while in custody, and had accessed a reference book of mental illness symptoms. We know from records kept by Orange County that, while in jail there, he studied twenty-four different law books.

Deputy District Attorney Briseno was able to bring out the fact Hulbert had recently married Mollye Selfies, his "common law wife," in jail. (Again, we found no evidence of this marriage, and no evidence he had divorced his first wife.) He also told jurors Mollye was the one who had supplied jewelry from one of Hulbert's victims, through Ronald and Linda Rockenbach, to Fullerton police. Since they were now allegedly married, she could not be asked to testify against him. This action, according to Briseno, was evidence Hulbert was not insane and had full knowledge of what he was doing.

In addition, Briseno had information from interviews with inmates in the Orange County jail, who claimed Hulbert told them he was "putting on an act," trying to fake mental illness as a defense and wanted them to testify he appeared crazy, but not to lay it on too thick.

The testimony of the psychiatrists continued until Thursday, February 10, 1977, after which the District Attorney's Office began to put their case before the jury. Briseno played the tapes of Hulbert confessing to Detective Schauperl, and had the jury read the transcripts as they listened. As the day wore on, Briseno requested one of the psychiatrists, Dr. Seymour Pollack of the University of Southern California, be held over for additional questioning by prosecutors. The request was approved by the judge.

Briseno then introduced the testimony of another psychiatrist, Dr. Seawright Anderson. Dr. Anderson did not deny Hulbert had mental issues; however, he testified, "Hulbert's degree of control of his delusional system is such that he can cooperate with an attorney." He was the first psychiatrist to testify that Hulbert's psychiatric problems didn't necessarily make him incapable of aiding a defense attorney or under-standing court proceedings against him, which were the key criteria involved in the pretrial hearing and whether the actual trial could take place.

March 8, 1977
Superior Court
Santa Ana, California

After almost seven weeks of listening to testimony and after two full days of deliberation, the Santa Ana Superior Court jury of six men and six women rejected the defense claims that Hulbert did not understand the legal proceedings against him and could not aid in his own defense. He was, in their opinion, capable of standing trial on the charges at this time. This would be the longest pretrial sanity hearing in the history of Orange County to date.

Immediately, the defense attorney, Walter Zech, filed a motion for a second hearing. After hearing the motion Judge Lee denied the request for a second hearing on the question of Hulbert's sanity. He set April 4 to hear another defense motion on whether the trial should be moved out of Orange County, and April 18 as the tentative trial date.

March 29, 1977
Superior Court
Santa Ana, California

A week later, in a move that surprised everyone, Judge Lee questioned Hulbert himself in open court then ruled he would grant a new hearing to determine whether Hulbert was mentally competent to stand trial. Judge Lee was quoted as saying, "I concluded that for the defendant to go to trial at this time would be a travesty of justice." Apparently what Hulbert could not accomplish with the jury, he was able to accomplish with Judge

Lee. The judge's action was probably prompted by Hulbert's request to defend himself and the public defender's reluctance to assist Hulbert, should that happen. Statements from Judge Lee seemed to verify this.

The judge said he was influenced by Hulbert's answers to a series of questions designed to help him determine from a legal viewpoint whether the defendant was waiving his right to counsel intelligently (not for determining mental competency). The judge had been expected to rule on Hulbert's request that morning. Both the prosecution and the defense believed Judge Lee would grant the request for Hulbert to defend himself, due to a recent State Supreme Court decision that left the judge with little choice. Under that decision, the issue of the ability to "intelligently" waive the right to counsel was the only issue that could be used to deny a defendant that right.

That same morning, Judge Lee also ruled that a gun and jewelry found by police in the Hulbert home would be suppressed as evidence, as they had been "improperly found by police who entered the home without announcing their intent, and without obtaining a search warrant until later." Judge Lee based this on the initial entry into the residence by Detective Schauperl and Captain Davis when they went to the residence to check on the welfare of Mollye and the children. This decision would be reversed by the California Court of Appeals on October 26, 1977, as well it should have been, and Detective Collins was allowed to testify regarding both items during the actual trial. It was clear to the Supreme Court that the initial entry into the home by Schauperl and Davis was legal under the emergency exemption to the rule, where there was a possibility Mollye was dead or injured in the home, a victim of Hulbert's rage after he found out she had turned over the jewelry to Ronald Rockenbach.

After Judge Lee came to the decision to order a new sanity hearing, the district attorney and the public defender agreed to submit the matter to the judge based on two new court-ordered psychiatric reports. They did this to avoid another two-month jury trial on just the issue of sanity. Judge Lee agreed to this action.

When they got the reports from the two psychiatrists, they were contradictory, as expected. Ernest Klatte, head of the Orange County Mental Health Department, concluded in his report that Hulbert was ready to stand trial, could aid in his own defense, and understood exactly what he was doing. He examined Hulbert in April of 1977. Dr. Klatte pointed out Hulbert had confessed these crimes to the police, and during those confessions, which were quite detailed, he at no time referred to the fact he felt these women were possessed of the devil and his raping, robbing, and degrading them was an effort to force the devil out of their bodies so he could combat it. Neither did he make any references to any of the delusional material he later talked about quite freely. In his report, Dr. Klatte would write the following about Hulbert:

"In summary, this is the case of a twenty-five-year-old young man with a long history of anti-social behavior, who is charged with rape, kidnapping, robbery and in one instance, murder, in incidents regarding three women. Following his arrest, he readily admitted to the crimes after several hours of interrogation, and at no time did he refer to any thought content which would lead one to believe that, at that time or at the time of the incidents, he was overtly psychotic or that his acts were in any way related to a delusional system. Statements made by two of the victims in the case did not indicate that at the time of the incidents there were any references which would lead one to believe that he was operating based on a delusional system."

Dr. Klatte went on to say, "Some months after his arrest, he revealed a complex, delusional system that involved two realities, battles with the devil and the belief that women were temptations placed on earth by the devil and representing the devil. He then revealed that he committed the acts to force the devil to come out of their bodies so that he could combat them, whereas, at the time of the arrest he described the rapes as a compulsion that he had no control over. Once he revealed his delusional system, he maintained that he was completely sane and verbally, to his attorney and to two psychiatrists, resisted any attempts to find him not able to work with his attorney in his own defense or to find him not guilty by reason of insanity. Despite this and a long trial, he was found to be sane, whereupon he fired his attorney, insisted on pro per proceedings, in which he could defend himself and announced that he was not going to plead guilty by reason of insanity, at which time the 1368 proceedings [insanity] were again opened at the instruction of the court."

It was the opinion of Dr. Klatte that Hulbert demonstrated the development of a set of defense mechanisms in which, rather than withdrawing into fantasy life in the face of stress, as is typical of a schizophrenic, he responded by actions that are typical of people with a sociopathic personality disturbance. Based on Hulbert's childhood environment and experiences, Dr. Klatte concluded "the defendant has been and continues to be a basically sociopathic, anti-social individual, with specific problems in his background which predispose him not only to commit anti-social, hedonistic acts, but specifically to have those acts include rape." He also believed that, starting in 1971, the defendant experienced a hallucinogenic drug type of personality disorganization, and the memories of those experiences were very real and could be easily recalled. He believed Hulbert continued to use those to his advantage, to demonstrate - he was currently mentally ill.

Dr. Klatte described Hulbert as extremely clever and manipulative, and a basically suspicious individual who trusted no one. He concluded he believed Hulbert has always been fully aware of the nature of the acts he committed, the quality of those acts, and the possible consequences.

Another psychiatrist who interviewed Hulbert came to a similar conclusion as Dr. Klatte after examining the same circumstances and facts, although his findings were not used in the second sanity hearing.

The second psychiatrist who was allowed to testify in this second hearing was Dr. Seymour Pollock, who had testified in the first sanity hearing. He still maintained Hulbert should not stand trial at that time. He testified that Hulbert continued to flip back and forth between rational and irrational thinking. We had now endured over fourteen months of hearings and motions, and the case had yet to go to trial.

Despite the elaborate delusional system Hulbert described for mental health workers and his public defenders, this behavior apparently did not carry over to his jail relationships. Records of the jail psychiatric team indicate that many inmates in the defendant's cell block were interviewed in 1976. Most of them, along with all the jail deputies, said the defendant appeared to be perfectly sane. They said he would often become restless at night and pace the floor in his cell. They also said he had a quick temper and would get angry easily, even in a friendly game of cards.

One inmate said there were discussions where Hulbert talked about wanting to get a gun for Mollye so she could kill one of the witnesses. Several of the inmates indicated he talked quite openly about the rapes, and they never heard anything indicating a delusional system. Others said he talked openly about his planned defense and discussed his plans with other inmates, and even requested they inform deputies he had "flipped out" in his cell.

Another inmate said Hulbert talked about plans to go to Patton State Hospital. Hulbert told one inmate he wanted to go to Patton rather than Atascadero, because it would be easier to escape from there should he decide to leave. The inmate said Hulbert even described the layout of the hospital and the surrounding streets.

Inmates told authorities Hulbert was planning to use "reverse psychology," and they had heard him say he was going to insist he was sane and competent to stand trial. He also told this inmate he would not cooperate with his public defender for fear the public defender would louse up his case.

Most of the inmates described Hulbert as being very brilliant, and they were impressed he had total recall of everything that had happened to him for a long time back into his personal history.

Ultimately, Judge Lee announced to a shocked courtroom he was going to ignore the decision of the jury that had declared Hulbert as perfectly sane. On his own, he decided Hulbert was mentally unfit to stand trial, and he ordered him sent to Atascadero State Hospital until he was able to properly assist in his own defense.

Judge Lee did this even though he had written reports by several other respected psychiatrists that contradicted the conclusions of Dr. Pollock, not to mention the comments of his fellow inmates and the testimony of Dr. Klatte, all of which completely negated the arguments Dr. Pollock propagated.

This was the end of the road, at least for the foreseeable future. Hulbert was transported to Atascadero State Hospital for an "indefinite period of time."

CHAPTER 13
THE TRIAL

September 1978
Superior Court
Santa Ana, California

HULBERT WOULD REMAIN in Atascadero for sixteen months before the hospital staff declared him mentally competent to stand trial. He was sent back to Orange County for trial in September of 1978.

A written evaluation submitted to the court at the time Hulbert was returned for trial, in September of 1978, indicated that when he was first admitted to Atascadero, he was extremely suspicious and guarded. There were no bizarre behaviors, delusional episodes, or hallucinations noted. His institutional adjustment was viewed as quite good. The hospital psychiatric personnel indicated that the material expressed by Hulbert was based on experience induced by psychedelic drugs which had been ingested heavily on prior occasions. This was exactly the conclusion Dr. Klatte came to and was heard by Judge Lee before his decision to thwart the jury verdict and send Hulbert to Atascadero. They also speculated Hulbert was using these past experiences to his advantage and was incorporating them into his consciousness. They noted he had none of the accompanying symptoms of disordered thinking—such as hallucinations, tangentiality, and looseness of association or inappropriate emotional response. In layman's terms, they thought he was probably faking it. They also indicated that, throughout his stay, he tended to try to manipulate the staff with what he said and appeared to be a person who had difficulty forming trusting relationships with anyone.

October 23, 1978

Superior Court

Santa Ana, California

A hearing was conducted in the superior court room of Judge H. Warren Knight on October 23, 1978, and the trial was scheduled to begin on April 2, 1979. This would be over three years from the time we had arrested Hulbert on Friday, January 30, 1976. Public Defender Zech said he did not see much difference in Hulbert's behavior than he did before he went to Atascadero, and threatened to seek a new sanity trial if he believed Hulbert was still mentally incompetent. Deputy District Attorney Farnell, who had replaced Frank Briseno as the prosecutor in the case, told the press "the jury in the initial case determined that he was faking. That's what the jury found and that's what Atascadero found."

Before the trial could begin, Public Defender Walter Zech made the decision to withdraw from the case because he planned to enter private practice. A young but experienced public defender, Dennis McNerney, was named to replace Zech in the case. No further attempt was ever made by the new defense attorney to resurrect the insanity defense. Hulbert continued to insist he represent himself, despite the advice of both the public defender's office and the district attorney.

July 6, 1979
Superior Court
Santa Ana, California

Hulbert alleged that Superior Court Judge Ted Millard, who was assigned the case for trial, was prejudiced against him. According to the allegation, Millard, while a deputy district attorney, had supposedly told another inmate "Hulbert is as good as convicted. It is only a matter of time." The inmate, Russell Long, had been working as a law enforcement informant at the time. Judge Millard vehemently denied Hulbert's allegation. Hulbert, who was acting as his own attorney, agreed with prosecutor Richard Farnell to let Superior Court Judge Kenneth Lae (not to be confused with Judge Lee) decide the issue of Millard's alleged bias. No date was set for that hearing. Judge Lae later ruled there was no prejudice, and Judge Millard ultimately heard Hulbert's rape and murder case.

September 11, 1979
Superior Court
Santa Ana, California

The actual trial began on September 11, 1979. One of the first people to testify was Deborah Hoffman of Buena Park, the city just west of Fullerton, who nervously identified Hulbert as being the one who had kidnapped and raped her on September 2, 1975, four years earlier.

Hoffman was walked through the attack by prosecutor Richard Farnell. Her testimony was reported by Paul Kelma of the *Fullerton News Tribune*:

She testified that she was shopping at a Buena Park shopping center at about nine o'clock at night and had just put her packages on the trunk of her car and opened the door. "I heard a man's voice come from behind me saying it looked like my tire was flat." She looked and saw it was not, turned and saw the man had a brown package in his hand and was smiling. "He had a gun pointing at me… he said, "Get in the car." I thought about running, but the car door was open. He said, "Do as I say."

Using the gun, he forced her over to the front passenger seat and he sat behind the wheel. She testified that she was ordered to start the car and that he had told Hoffman that he didn't want to touch the keys because of fingerprints.

Ms. Hoffman said that he was nervous… asking me if I had a gun in my purse… said, "Don't look at me." I started being upset and crying. He slapped me… told me to shut up, and to put my head between my knees. He then demanded money and she gave him two or three dollars and some change.

As the man drove, he kept the gun pointed at her and at one point ordered her to perform an unnatural sexual act. When she refused, he said, "Do it or I'll shoot you."

She testified that Hulbert allegedly ordered her to take off her clothes and when she refused, he again threatened to shoot her.

He drove to the deserted parking lot of a church, ordered her into the back, and told her if she did what he said, he would let her live.

She testified that Hulbert raped her twice and "I was telling him 'Please no' because I knew what he wanted me to do…"

She said that Hulbert used his T-shirt to wipe off the seats and sides of the car and said, "I'm not stupid. I don't want my fingerprints on anything."

He then demanded that she contact her mother at her apartment and demand money but before driving to a phone booth and to the area of the apartment to see where he could have the mother leave the money for him, he again forced her to perform an unnatural sexual act (oral copulation).

They went to a gas station phone booth and when she got out of the car Hulbert told her not to run "Because I've shot and killed before, and I'll do it again if I have to."

They drove to the apartment complex where, acting on instructions, her mother put a reported two hundred dollars under a tire of her car in the carport. When her grandmother came out behind her mother into the carport and was locked out of a security gate, Hulbert got upset and ordered her back in.

Hoffman said that when she got out of the car to retrieve the money her mother turned back to look. She said Hulbert reached across her, stuck the gun out the passenger side door and told her mother, "Get your ass back in there lady."

They drove to the Buena Park Shopping Center but before arriving she was again forced to perform an unnatural sexual act.

They left the car to walk to the rear of a store, where she said, he told her she could go.

She drove back to her mother's apartment and her mother suggested she should probably report it and try to catch him, but she really wasn't up to going through such a horrible experience all over again. "I really didn't want to," she said. Her mother told her, "There might be someone else out there you can save," so she agreed to it.[1]

After the trial, Hoffman was interviewed by Laura Vorie of the Orange County Probation Department. She told Vorie that if she had any idea of what she would have to go through these past four years, she never would have contacted the police following the rape. She told Vorie she had also been subpoenaed to testify in the upcoming Los Angeles County trial, which would take place at the conclusion of the Orange County matter.

Despite her reservations, she said she would do anything to assist in getting another life term for the defendant. She told Vorie she would like to forget about Hulbert, but every time she turns around, there are constant reminders. She says she is

---

1. Taken in part from an article by Paul Kelma, News Tribune County Bureau, *Fullerton News Tribune*, September 12, 1979.

continually seeing articles about Hulbert and other rapists in the newspapers and on television. During the past four years her relatives from all over the country have read accounts of what happened to her and are always calling her. It was, she said, impossible for her to get it out of her mind. She pointed out she is a very strong person and has tried very hard not to let this defeat her, but said, "I can never forget it until I die, it has been the most dramatic experience of my life." She also told Vorie she truly believed her strong belief in God is what prevented her from being killed.

Her impression of Hulbert during the incident was that he knew exactly what he was doing, and the whole thing was very well planned and thought out. She definitely felt the defendant was not insane but was an evil person. Hoffman related Hulbert had told her he had killed many times before and he didn't like it but could do it. He told her he couldn't stand women saying no, and he hated all women, and he hated his mother, and his hate would last forever. He told her he had raped before and if she didn't cooperate, he'd kill her, as he had done before to those who did not cooperate.

Hoffman told Vorie that Hulbert had slapped her on several occasions when she had given the wrong response to something he said. She said she had never realized there were human beings with that kind of hatred and evil in their souls as she saw displayed by Hulbert. She still could not believe anyone could be that cruel and hateful.

Hoffman said she was still afraid to go outside at night, and when she heard a noise down the street, she flashed back to her moment of terror. She said she was still plagued by flashbacks of the incident. She believed the crime deeply affected her but thought she had come through it better than most women would have.

Hoffman also told Vorie she strongly believed Hulbert was incapable of any kind of rehabilitation, no matter the amount of time he was incarcerated, and it would be "unthinkable" for him to ever be released back into the community.

September 12, 1979
Superior Court
Orange County, California

Deborah Hoffman's testimony was followed by Carmen Banderas's, the twenty-six-year-old Fullerton College coed who had been kidnapped by Hulbert from the parking lot of the college on January 6, 1976. Her testimony was described in a *Fullerton News Tribune* article dated September 13, 1979, again by Paul Kelma. He wrote:

With a shaky voice and on the verge of tears, a twenty-six-year-old woman testified yesterday about how she was kidnapped, raped and beaten in an attack by murder-rape suspect Kenneth Richard Hulbert.

At one point during her testimony in Superior Court, Carmen Banderas burst into tears as she told how Hulbert, now twenty-seven, forced her to perform sexual acts with him while he drove her car around Orange County.

The dark-haired woman was the second victim to testify in the three-day old trial before a six woman, six-man jury in Judge Ted Millard's courtroom.

She is the second witness to identify Hulbert in court as the man who abducted her.

The young woman testified yesterday that she got out of her car in the college parking lot to attend class when Hulbert threw her back in at gunpoint, took the keys, started the car, and drove off toward the Riverside Freeway.

"He said we were going for a ride and for me to just shut my eyes and relax". He then demanded money and took the twelve dollars she had with her.

"I asked him what he was doing, why he was doing what he

was doing, and he said he was doing it for kicks, and he needed the money, and this was the easy way to get it."

"He told me that he wanted to take me to a Placentia orange grove 'where there is no one around,' and I said, "You have my money, take my car... just leave me alone." He said he needed the money because he was in trouble with the law and was going to Reno or Las Vegas."

"After taking my money, he noticed that I had a checking account and drove to a bank in Anaheim. He wanted me to write a check for one hundred dollars, but I told him I only had ninety dollars. At the drive-up window, the teller took my check and driver's license, but since the branch was different from mine, asked us to come inside to verify the check."

"He told me to act natural, act like nothing was wrong, because the teller might be suspicious... I tried to signal the teller, but he was watching me all the time. He then drove up to the Anaheim Hills area and asked me if my husband would pay $20,000 twenty thousand dollars for my ransom. When I said that we didn't have that kind of money, he took my watch, wedding ring and necklace, saying it was probably worth fifty dollars."

"While he was driving around, he started telling me things about his private life... his wife wasn't satisfying him sexually... his kids... I told him I had a little boy... he means the world to me... [I said,] 'Don't ever hurt me because I don't know what I would ever do, because of my son.'"

"After hitting me several times, he forced me to perform sexual acts with him, and then ordered me to remove my clothing and when I refused, he said, 'I'll kill you."

"Then he started touching me and I begged him to stop. I told him, 'I love my husband, I love my son and I love God and what you're doing isn't right.'"

"He said, 'If you're such a Christian, why not ask him to help you, get you out of this situation and he'll do it'... I prayed out loud... and he got very upset because I was praying out loud."

"Next, he drove around to some orange groves, and he raped me, and then drove back to the shopping center parking lot. He pushed his knee in my back, tied a sash around my neck and pulled until I blacked out. I was gasping for air, I was suffocating... I could feel the car moving... like we were on a bumpy road... I remember calling out for my husband and Hulbert was laughing... he said, 'they'll never hear you'... I was hoping this was all a dream."

"The next thing I knew I was lying down on the bottom of a hole. My whole body was numb. I couldn't see. I tried to get up, but I couldn't. I thought I'm going to die... then I said I'm not going to die... I'm not ready to die... I thought of my little boy... God help me... I don't know how I got out of that ditch."

Testifying next was Mark Paulak who said he and his wife picked Carmen up near the ditch and her clothes were torn, "there was an excessive amount of blood" and she was "rattling [about] things... saying someone was trying to kill her." They drove to a friend's house, and Mark called the sheriff.

"That girl was really in bad shape," Paulak testified.[2]

Prosecutor Richard Farnell said his next witness was to be Dr. Herbert Rettinger, the doctor who examined Carmen after the Paulaks found her along Myford Road and took her to a hospital.

Dr. Rettinger testified he was the on-duty doctor at the time she was first brought into the hospital, and when he first examined her he did not expect her to live because of the extent of her injuries. He described in detail what he observed, and the physical damage done to this young woman. He told the jury her condition so affected him that "I signed off emergency room work. I really hope I never do it again; she had really been gone over."

---

2. Taken in part from an article by Paul Kelma, News Tribune County Bureau, *Fullerton News Tribune*, September 13, 1979.

Even though several years had passed since the incident, it was clear he was still emotionally shaken by what he had seen that night.

In October of 1979, after her assailant had been convicted in court of the assault on her and Deborah Hoffman, and the murder of Gina Tisher, Carmen Banderas was interviewed by Probation Officer Laura Vorie, as part of Hulbert's sentencing process.

Carmen told her that after the attack she had spent a week in intensive care at Tustin Community Hospital. She indicated she had been in very bad shape, and since her entire body was affected, her recovery was slow, and to that day she still had problems with back pain. She also continued to require intermittent treatment from a chiropractor to adjust her neck, which was dislocated when Hulbert smashed her head with a rock. Vorie noted Carmen Banderas still had scars on her forehead. Banderas told her those scars were a constant reminder of what had happened to her. According to Carmen, her initial treatment was covered by medical insurance, but she would require plastic surgery soon, and for that there was no insurance coverage. She also told Vorie her front teeth had been knocked loose during the ordeal, and they continued to be painful to the touch. She indicated she believed she would need extensive dental work in the future. Her nose had also been broken and still gave her trouble from time to time.

Carmen told Vorie she didn't have any recollection of what transpired after being choked into unconsciousness by her attacker. She recalled the suspect as being an extremely intelligent, devious, and cunning individual. She said he was very professional in the way he carried out the crime and it was obvious to her it was premeditated and every move was very calculated. He had admitted to her he had kidnapped numerous other victims, and this became very evident as he knew exactly what to watch for with her. She remembered telling him he would get caught, but he laughed this off, telling her he was so smart, "he could play the game even in prison."

Carmen Banderas said she had no qualms about cooperating with the police department, because she felt someone had to do it. She said she was constantly thinking of other potential victims, and told Vorie her only concern was getting him locked up so he couldn't hurt anyone else. However, this offense, and the subsequent adjudication of the defendant, had changed her whole life, in more ways than she could ever express. She pointed out she could not even hear the word "rape" without cringing, and no longer enjoys watching television, reading, or going to movies, because even the smallest suggestion of violence is disturbing to her now. She cannot bear to be alone in her home and finds it extremely difficult to go shopping or attend any social functions alone. She lives with the constant fear the defendant will someday come back to kill her because there is always the chance of escape. She also indicated to Vorie she knew there were other men just like the person who attacked her still out in the community.

Carmen said she always had perceived of herself as a nice girl raising a family and going to school, but that had changed. Since the rape, she is now plagued by self-recrimination and guilt, and often wonders if she subconsciously asked for it through her dress or demeanor.

Vorie's article indicated Carmen had reported becoming very suspicious of every stranger she encountered. She was still experiencing nightmares about the rape that were "so real it's hard to distinguish from what really happened." She also reported she had difficulty continuing her studies and had since dropped out of school.

Carmen also told Vorie her marriage had suffered, despite her husband's support. For one thing, she could not even bear to be touched and it required six months of counseling before she could resume sexual relations with him. She said both of her parents and her husband had all been overly protective, and if she was gone for more than two hours, they became anxious and worried. Her son was two years old at the time of the attack and had never been separated from her. She believes it was very traumatic for him to have her come home after a week's separation bloodied and bruised, and he had since shown symptoms of being very anxiety-ridden at even the shortest separation.

Carmen pointed out to Vorie that the police, district attorney, and other investigators were extremely supportive and sensitive during the past four years of court appearances and interviews. Despite their support, the assault had greatly impacted her life. Every time she had to go to court and look at the defendant, it was a traumatic experience for her, especially since she gave birth to a second child during that time and was attempting to breast feed him while making court appearances. She said she had never been a hateful person, but it was difficult for her not to be full of hate and loathing for the defendant and for what he had done. She related to Vorie she doubted her life would ever be the same again.

She indicated she had never been in favor of the death penalty, but now believed it would be better for the defendant to be dead than ever have even the slightest chance to do this to somebody again. She believed the assailant was very evil and the type of person who could never change, even with many years of help.

Carmen Banderas said she had read in the newspaper recently about some unsolved rapes and she was quite sure he was responsible for some of them. She indicated she only wished that, somehow, she could be guaranteed her attacker could never get out, but felt that unless he were dead, it would not be possible.

While those of us in law enforcement who were close to the case had certainly recognized how violent the attack was that Hulbert had perpetrated against this innocent young woman, until reading that report in 1979, we were really unable to appreciate how completely and permanently her life had been changed. To this day I am saddened we didn't catch Hulbert before this vicious attack.

September 14, 1979
Superior Court
Santa Ana, California

Several other witnesses were called to testify including Betty Maloney, the mother of Gina Marie Tisher. Her emotional testimony along Tisher's husband, Charles, was powerful in the courtroom. During their testimonies, not another sound could be heard. Once again, *Fullerton News Tribune* Reporter Paul Kelma captured the essence of these testimonies in an article written on September 14, 1979:

"I love you, Mama, I'll see you tomorrow."

Testimony in superior court yesterday showed that these were the last words spoken to the mother of a nineteen-year-old housewife whose body was found January 5, 1976, in the back seat of an auto in a Fullerton apartment complex carport.

The testimony came from Mrs. Betty Mahoney, the mother of Mrs. Gina Marie Tisher, who allegedly was abducted and strangled by Kenneth Richard Hulbert on Jan. 2, 1976.

Mrs. Maloney testified in the trial of Hulbert, 27, who is charged with Mrs. Tisher's murder, and the kidnapping and rapes of two other women in North Orange County in late 1975 and early 1976.

She told a six-woman, six-man jury that her daughter spoke the words before leaving her mother's Anaheim home for a nearby shopping center to pick up her husband's clothes from a cleaner.

Hulbert abducted the Whittier housewife in the parking lot of the shopping center.

Also testifying was Mrs. Tisher's husband Charles, who said

they were married in September of 1975 and that a wedding ring presented as evidence in the trial was his wife's.

Tisher said, "Her death shattered me. She was nineteen years old. She was five foot-two, one hundred pounds and everybody loved her, and someone had taken her and raped her and strangled her to death and left her in a car like garbage. I couldn't accept it."

Tisher added that he has been in and out of mental treatment centers for years since his wife's murder, lost his job at the auto dealership, and takes medication daily.

He said that he launched a search for his wife a short time after she was supposed to pick him up at the dealership. She had driven him to work in a demonstrator auto from the dealership and was supposed to pick him up at about nine o'clock that evening.

Her body was found by a resident of an apartment complex three days after she was slain.[3]

Hulbert sat slumped in his chair, again taking copious notes that would never be used and refusing to look at Mrs. Mahoney or Mr. Tisher while they were testifying.

After the trial, Mrs. Maloney was also interviewed by Laura Vorie, and she told her that even though her daughter was killed four years ago, it still seemed like yesterday. She described her daughter as the "sweetest, dearest girl in the world, who never hurt anyone in her life." She told Vorie that she could not think of a more undeserving person for this type of horrible torture and death. Mrs. Maloney indicated that Gina's father died while she had been pregnant with Gina and therefore, she was always quite special to her. She told Vorie, "She was always my baby."

Mrs. Maloney told Vorie that her daughter had been married just before she had been killed and that she also mourned the loss of grandchildren, who would never be born.

---

3. Taken in part from an article by Paul Kelma, News Tribune County Bureau, *Fullerton News Tribune*, September 13, 1979.

She said that her life and the lives of those who knew Gina closely will never be the same and that there are absolutely no words to explain the grief a mother feels in losing a child in this manner.

She describes Hulbert as being "deranged and devious, but not insane." She was convinced that Hulbert was faking his insanity to avoid the death penalty. Mrs. Maloney told Vorie that Hulbert knew what he was doing and had no respect for human life. She believed that should Hulbert ever be released, it would be "A tragic day for every parent in the world."

Mrs. Maloney told Vorie that Gina's husband, Charles Tisher was totally shattered by his wife's death. They had only been married four months and she says Gina was his doll. He initially responded to her death in a very stoic manner, according to Maloney, however, as time progressed, he suffered a nervous breakdown and had to be hospitalized. She said that he had been in the hospital four separate times in the past four years, but that recently he seemed to be making progress. He is holding a job, but still requires daily medication. He agreed to testify at the sentencing hearing but said "It is just for Gina." She and all who knew Charles said that this was a very moving experience for them as it was indicative of the first step toward total recovery.

Also testifying that day was Detective Leon Schauperl, who identified pictures of Gina Tisher and her vehicle as it was opened in the carport on the date her body was discovered.

Much of the testimony that day revolved around photos of Gina Tisher taken step-by-step as the police officers and coroner deputies removed her body and other evidence from her car. Detective Schauperl described the contents of the photos for jurors. In addition, photos of Mrs. Tisher's autopsy were shown to the jury and explained. Hulbert asked few questions during this graphic testimony, although he was taking notes throughout the day. He did not or would not look at the photos as they were displayed.

Orange County Sheriff's Office homicide detective, Bruce

MacAfee then identified pictures of the culvert from which Carmen Banderas, had staggered, and where she was picked up by a passing motorist. He also identified the softball-sized rock, with which she was beaten over the head, as well as the remains of a blouse that she had been wearing the day of the attack.

Other witnesses also testified and were subjected to little or no cross examination by Hulbert, who continued to act as his own attorney during the trial.

September 19, 1979
Superior Court
Santa Ana, California

Deputy District Attorney Farnell questioned Ronald Rockenbach, the counselor who had brought the items of jewelry to us that subsequently led to Hulbert's arrest in January of 1976. Rockenbach identified three rings and a watch that had been placed in an envelope and given to his wife by Mollye Hulbert for safekeeping.

The rings had already been identified as belonging to Gina Marie Tisher, and the watch to Carmen Banderas. Rockenbach testified he had taken the envelope and the jewelry to the Fullerton Police Department, at the request of Detective Schauperl, when he became suspicious Hulbert was the "Fullerton rapist."

Following Rockenbach's testimony, former Fullerton Detective Charles Collins testified that, on January 30, 1976, the same day Hulbert was arrested, he went to the Hulbert home and served a search warrant and took photographs inside the home. The photos were introduced into evidence and showed other jewelry identified as belonging to some of the rape victims, scattered on the floor and on a headboard in the Hulbert home.

That same day, Joseph Hayes, the senior forensic specialist for the Orange County Sheriff's Office, testified a latent print lifted from a check signed by Carmen Banderas was positively identified as matching Hulbert's right thumb print. This identification had been made previously by Fullerton Police identification technician James Babcock and was confirmed by Hayes.

Late in the afternoon, Judge Millard dismissed the jury to allow a hearing on whether the confession would be admissible during the trial. Hulbert had alleged the confession was not made voluntarily.

During the hearing, Detective Schauperl testified Hulbert had asked for the February 1, 1976, meeting and he was advised of his legal rights and did not ask to have an attorney present. Judge Millard ruled the confession was free and voluntary and it would be admitted into the trial and would be heard by the jury.

Schauperl told the court that, on that Sunday evening, he had received a call from Captain C.D. Davis and was told that Hulbert wanted to talk. Captain Davis told Schauperl he had been contacted by the watch commander at the Fullerton Police Department and advised that Hulbert wanted to speak to the jailer late on the evening of February 1, 1976. Hulbert told the jailer he wanted to talk to investigators. When Schauperl and Captain Davis brought him into the interview room in the jail, Schauperl told Hulbert he had heard from the police jailer that he wished to speak with him. Hulbert responded that he had told the jailer, "It would be worth your while to come to talk to me." Schauperl then again advised Hulbert of his legal rights to remain silent and to have an attorney present during the questioning. He also asked Hulbert if anyone had pressured him into making the statement. Hulbert responded, "No, the pressure is from me to make it." He then proceeded to describe in detail the kidnapping, rape, and attempted murder of Carmen Banderas and the murder of Gina Tisher. Then he listed other equally horrific crimes he was responsible for, but did not go into detail on those. Those other crimes had occurred in jurisdictions outside of Fullerton.

September 21, 1979

Superior Court
Santa Ana, California

The jury heard Hulbert's taped confession to killing Gina Marie Tisher in its entirety. The courtroom was uncannily quiet as the jurors and spectators alike listened in shocked silence to the detailed description of the crime.

September 24, 1979
Superior Court
Santa Ana, California

Hulbert presented his defense, such as it was, calling only one witness, Sheriff's Deputy Michael Curry. Hulbert asked Curry whether he had ever discussed with Hulbert's wife, Mollye, the possibility of assisting her in his execution. Curry shook his head and replied, "The execution of the defendant? No," he said in response to Hulbert's' question. With this one inquiry of one witness, court was adjourned, and closing arguments were set for the following morning.

September 25, 1979
Superior Court
Santa Ana, California

Hulbert made a two-minute statement ending with the words "Iliasu Nogabagundu." He refused to explain what this meant, and his testimony once again left court observers baffled. Later Hulbert would tell the bailiff the phrase could not be translated because it was a "sacred saying" of the Lemurian Society, from the ancient land of Lemuria, which pre-dated the legendary land of Atlantis.

September 26, 1979
Superior Court

Santa Ana, California

In his closing argument the following morning, Farnell told the jury, "There is absolutely no reason why he shouldn't be convicted on each count and each allegation. I'd call him an animal, but animals don't do these things to each other... these horrible, horrible acts," After describing the "humiliation of the sexual attacks" on the three women, Farnell told the jury, "You can't let these people down, ladies and gentlemen. Gina Tisher, just newly married. It reminds me of the song, 'We've Only Just Begun.' Well, it ended for her. What were the last terrifying moments like? Will we ever know?" Farnell said.[4]

About the attack on then twenty-three-year-old Carmen Banderas, Farnell said, "If you have any feeling... any idea of the horrible, horrible terror going through her mind as she lay in that ditch thinking she was going to die..." Then, referring to the attack on Deborah Hoffman, Farnell, in an even voice, emphasized "the terror this man inflicted on innocent people for his own gratification, subjecting her [Hoffman] to the humiliation of sexual attacks. And now, how humiliating for her to come into court and testify."[5]

September 27, 1979
Superior Court
Santa Ana, California

Ken Hulbert rose from his chair and stood in front of the jury box. He told the panel, "Mr. Farnell has broached the subject of what... why. I'm not going to bother to cover any of those subjects. In reference to the defense, there is a very ancient saying that goes back some 5,000 years or so. I ask you to keep

---

4. Article in the *Fullerton News Tribune* by Paul Kelma, *News Tribune* Writer, September 27, 1979.
5. From an article in the Fullerton News Tribune by Paul Kelma, September 27, 1979

that in mind when considering the defense. It may not be familiar to all of you, but hopefully, you have all heard it. It goes 'Iliasu Nogabagundu.' Thank you." That was the extent of his closing argument.[6]

The jury deliberated for only two hours before finding Kenneth Richard Hulbert guilty of all thirteen charges against him, and on sixteen special allegations, including the use of a firearm in the commission of a felony. Sentencing was set for October 23, 1979.

September 28, 1979

Los Angeles, California

After the conviction, *Los Angeles Times* staff writer Jeffrey Perlman was able to get an interview with Hulbert from the jail. Here is what Perlman wrote in his article, quoting what Hulbert had told him:

"I went 'pro per' (defended himself without a lawyer) precisely to keep from being labeled a 'nut' again and
sent back to Atascadero."

"The only thing I had to do to get out of Atascadero was to tell them I understood the charges against me and wouldn't go 'pro per' or talk about my illusions, as we called them once, and which they reclassified for me as religious beliefs."

"I will never say I'm 1368 (mentally incompetent). There's no way I'm going to give up my beliefs. At Atascadero, I just learned not to talk about certain things. Yes, nothing's been changed. I still believe in those things, and nothing can change that."

"I had anticipated putting on several weeks of witnesses, but then I got word that if I proceeded with the kind of defense I

---

6. From an article in the *Fullerton News Tribune* by Paul Kelma, September 27, 1979.

wanted to present, my loved ones would be killed. I still love my wife and my children."

"If I had presented my defense the way I could have presented it, the way I see the facts truthfully, I believe that I should have been found not guilty. That would have required the jury to accept my beliefs as being true for me at the time of the acts I committed. The law, in that case, is clear that it's not a willful, premeditated, and deliberate act. Because, of the law, I was forced to do it, so it wasn't premeditated and deliberate" [his struggle with Satan]. "I'm sure I am going to be executed before I leave this jail."[7]

September 28, 1979
Orange County Jail
Santa Ana, California

Reporter Paul Kelma also interviewed Hulbert after his conviction. Hulbert repeated what he had told Jeffrey Perlman, in that he believed he would be killed before leaving Orange County Jail for prison. He told Kelma he did not willfully commit the acts he was found guilty of doing. He went on to tell Kelma:

"My plans all along were to present a legal defense. The law says a crime is, for example, what a guy did willfully, unlawfully, commit a felonious act. These were not willful acts. I wasn't planning to say I didn't do it. Yeah, I committed them but not willfully, because I was forced to commit them by Satan."

According to Kelma, Hulbert told him this involved him using a riddle, part of which he gave to jurors during the final arguments on September 27, 1979, a day before this interview. The phrase he used was "Iliasu Nogabagundu," and just as he had done during his mental competency hearing in May of 1977,

---

7. From an article by Jeffrey Perlman in the *Los Angeles Times*, September 28, 1979.

he refused to translate it. One juror told Kelma the panel thought "Iliasu" meant "mercy."

Hulbert told Kelma, "I believe that at least one-half of the jury that convicted me knows the meaning of the phrase... I believe the six women knew exactly what I was talking about. The court reporter knows the meaning. The judge and the prosecutor know, because of their involvement with me in the case and a lot of things going on behind the scenes." Kelma asked him to translate it for him, but Hulbert told him, "I'd love to, but I am not allowed to. Otherwise, I would have translated it for the jury."

He also claimed he had received "threats from people associated with my system of beliefs and some in the jail. I personally don't expect to leave the jail alive because of what I said in my closing statement. I wasn't supposed to say that." Hulbert went on to tell Kelma the phrase was part of a ritual of identification, which with the proper responses comprises a kind of poem. Any of the individual exchanges taken by itself or out of context would make no sense at all.

In addition, he told Kelma the phrase dates to 3000 B.C. and was associated with a pre-Atlantis society called Lemuria that still existed but on an astral or spiritual plane. "I wasn't supposed to say what I did as far as a lot of people are concerned, such as the Lemurian Fellowship. They know what it means and I'm sure I upset a lot of people."[8]

Asked whether he considered he might be wrong in his beliefs, Hulbert said, "I've been asked questions like that a lot of times, especially by the police and the public defender. What would I say to Gina Tisher if I found out I am wrong? How could I compensate for what happened as far as her family... if I found out I was wrong, or my beliefs are wrong?"

---

8. A spokesperson for the Lemurian Fellowship near Ramona, California told Kelma they did not know what it meant, and Hulbert was not associated with their group in any way.

Hulbert told Kelma, "I believe Gina Tisher voluntarily participated… she had been presented with a proposition that she
could voluntarily participate in the experience and in return she
would receive compensation, or she could choose not to and
suffer the consequences. I have regrets, but I believe I'm not
guilty." Hulbert also said he had dropped the court-appointed
public defender because he did not want to go through insanity
or other psychiatric defenses.

At the end of the trial, before the jury returned with a verdict,
Deputy District Attorney Richard Farnell and Judge Ted Millard
observed that throughout the case Hulbert had shown no signs
of being anything other than "an able-bodied, normal person."
Hulbert did not object and insisted he wanted to appear
that way.

He told Kelma, "I was upset that the attorneys brought out a
lot of that stuff. The only reason I went pro per [represented
myself], was to keep from getting sent to Atascadero. From the
day I got there until the day I left I never made statements other
than 'I'm competent, I'm not nuts, and I want to get out of this
place… I presented no insanity defense. I fired the public
defender. I'm not insane. I never have been, and I don't want
people striking off my words as nuts."

Hulbert said Judge Millard would not allow him to ask jurors
during jury selection about their religious backgrounds.

"There is a difficulty in overcoming people's biases. I would
be asking the jury to set aside their personal beliefs and relate
this [his beliefs] to the law."

He told Kelma that an opening statement, which he never
made, would have stressed differences in beliefs and the legal
issue of whether he committed the acts willfully.

Hulbert said he had "a couple of dozen witnesses to put on
but that he had heard certain members of my family might be
taken out [killed] if I continued along those lines." He also told
Kelma his beliefs began to form in mid-1974 when he and
Mollye were in Mississippi and they were under the influence of

psilocybin mushrooms ("magic mushrooms," a hallucinogen). He claimed he had been "attacked by a demon… in the sense of a non-physical entity… this red thing with what appeared to be a flaming sword, flying down at me. Testimony by occultists would have served as a 'buffer for jurors' disbelief in the occult, and I could then go into my mental state."

Hulbert claimed "a couple of weeks before the Tisher incident, I was told either become a murderer or be murdered by Satan's followers…"

Hulbert said "it got worse and worse and the women I was convicted of assaulting gave the appearance of innocents, when they were, but in fact, one of the enemies, trying to subvert my values and make me an evil person."

Much of Hulbert's commentary, which according to Kelma was delivered calmly and with an easy manner, reflects what was presented in the mental competency hearing by former Public Defender Walther Zech before a superior court jury found Hulbert mentally competent to stand trial.[9]

It is interesting to note none of this information was related to the police while Hulbert was in custody, even though he had ample opportunity to do so, a fact noted by Dr. Klatte in his summation of his examination of Ken Hulbert.

As was customary in criminal cases, the Orange County Probation Department was asked to evaluate the circumstances and the sentencing in terms of how applicable probation would be for the offender, and to make a recommendation to the court. The report, by Probation Officer Laura Vorie, included interviews with as many of the victims and witnesses as she could locate and with whom she was able to talk. These, as indicated previously, included the mother of murder victim Gina Tisher; Betty Maloney; Carmen Banderas, the victim who had been

---

9. Taken in part from an article by Paul Kelma, in the *Fullerton News Tribune*, September 28, 1979.

kidnapped by Hulbert from the Fullerton College parking lot; and victim Deborah Hoffman of Buena Park, California.

Vorie's final written evaluation of the case is insightful and right to the point in describing the acts committed by Hulbert, the humiliation of the victims, and the impact on the survivors. The emotion she was experiencing is evident from her writing. What follows are excerpts from her report:

"Ken Richard Hulbert has been sentenced to life imprisonment without the possibility of parole, after being convicted of raping three women, one of whom was then murdered. At the present time, he is pending trial in Los Angeles County on rape and kidnapping charges involving numerous victims, and there is much evidence to suggest that the defendant has been responsible for various other unsolved rapes and murders in the Southern California area.

"In each of these cases, the victims were subjected to the most degrading and humiliating of all human experience. They were inflicted with gross psychological terror and fear and endured brutal physical violence at the hands of the defendant. In the instance of Carmen Banderas, the defendant viciously mutilated her face and head with a rock, after assuming she was dead, and then proceeded to stuff her vagina with dirt, leaving her body in a ditch. With victim Gina Tisher, he robbed her dead body of jewelry and stuffed a brake fluid soaked rag in her vagina.

"The depth of this man's contempt, cruelty, malice and evil toward humanity, and especially women is beyond comprehension. It is obvious that he comes with a background of emotional deprivation where he was subjected to extreme physical and mental abuse from his father and neglect from his mother. His heavy involvement with hallucinogenic drugs also has contributed to his emotional instability, which he now attempts to use as a defense for his actions. However, there is nothing that can amount to a defense for the deeds he has done. No amount of remorse, rehabilitation or explanation can ever begin to ameliorate the shattered lives he has left behind or remove the terror and fear he engenders in the lives of everyone in the community, who grow more apprehensive about their fellow man every time this type of crime occurs.

"There appears to be no circumstances under which this defendant should ever even be considered for release from custody. Everyone in the community is entitled to the assurance that he will never again to impart tragedy on the lives of others."[10]

October 23, 1979
Superior Court
Santa Ana, California

Hulbert was sentenced by Judge Ted Millard to multiple, concurrent life terms in state prison, for the strangulation death of Gina Marie Tisher and the vicious attacks on Deborah Hoffman and Carmen Banderas (who had been left for dead). Judge Millard told Hulbert he wished he could make the terms run consecutively but was prohibited from doing so because the law in existence at the time of the attacks failed to allow for such sentencing, although it now did. Afterward, Judge Millard said he would have given Hulbert the death penalty but could not as it was invalid at the time of the crimes, due to a decision by the California Supreme Court in 1972, which resulted in one hundred seven inmates being taken off death row and resentenced. In 1977, the California Legislature re-enacted the death penalty as a possible punishment for first degree murder under certain conditions. Also in 1977, the Penal Code of California was amended to include the sentence of life imprisonment without the possibility of parole. Neither was in effect at the time Hulbert committed his crimes.

---

10. Excerpts from a written report by Orange County Probation Officer Laura Vorie in September of 1979.

May 7, 1981
Superior Court
Los Angeles, California

Almost five-and-a-half years after he committed the crimes, Hulbert was also convicted of multiple counts of kidnapping, rape, and robbery in attacks on five women in Los Angeles County and was sentenced to three concurrent life terms in prison, in addition to his life sentences on the Orange County cases. At the time of his sentencing on the Los Angeles cases, Hulbert was twenty-nine years old.

Ken Hulbert was ultimately sent to Folsom State Prison in Represa, California. While there he continued to study the legal system and even filed a civil suit against Mollye Selfies and David Lee (his stepson) charging that Mollye, David Lee, and others conspired to interfere with his visitation rights with his younger children, in violation of a visitation decree. He sought an injunction to restrain the defendants from further interfering with his visitation rights, as well as asking for compensatory and punitive damages for their past interference. The trial court ruled in Hulbert's favor, but the district court dismissed the complaint before the serving process upon the defendants because it found Hulbert's claim for injunctive relief was barred. He appealed this decision all the way through the Ninth Circuit of the United States Court of Appeals. The Ninth Circuit confirmed part of the findings of the lower court, where it was ruled that the district court erred in dismissing Hulbert's entire complaint. This was based on an earlier case that ruled that in "civil rights cases where the plaintiff appears pro se, the court must construe pleadings liberally and afford the plaintiff the benefit of any doubt. If the plaintiff has an arguable claim, he is entitled to issuance and service of process."[11] Despite the ruling this action did not go any further.

---

11. Case decision reported in **Karim-Panahi v. Los Angeles Police Dept., 839F.2d 621, 623 (9th Cir. 1988).**

CHAPTER 14
KIDNAPPED FOR A CAUSE

I, Lee DeVore, remember being very nervous on that morning of February 8, 1976, knowing this would be the day William David Lee II, young David's father, would take his son home and get him out of the hell he had been living in with Mollye and Ken Hulbert here in California. I was nervous because I had assisted him in executing this plan by giving him information on young David's whereabouts. He was to call me when he had David and was at L.A. International Airport ready to board a plane for Louisiana. I remember wandering around the detective bureau nervously waiting for his phone call. I was finding it difficult to concentrate on what I was doing, not knowing if this was going to work out or not. Right about noon my phone rang. When I answered it was David senior, who said, "Lee, I've got him. We're at the airport and we're out of here. We'll be boarding our plane soon."

When William David Lee II learned his ex-wife's live-in boyfriend, Ken Hulbert, had been arrested for murder in Southern California, he flew to Fullerton from Louisiana to see what he could do for his son, David. He was aware David had been living with Ken Hulbert and Mollye in Fullerton at the time of Hulbert's arrest. Mr. Lee had been anxious about his son for some time and had been trying to get custody of him as he was concerned over the lifestyle of young David's mother and the drug use taking place around his child.

Mr. Lee flew to Southern California and came into the Fullerton Police Department on February 2, 1976, at about three o'clock in the afternoon. He walked in unannounced and told the desk officer who he was. He was interviewed by Detective Chuck Collins, and he told Collins he was there about the murder investigation. He said he had been married to Mollye Selfies for three-and-a-half years and he had information that could possibly assist us in the investigation.

Mr. Lee told Collins that Mollye's maiden name was Selfies, but she also went by the names of Lee, Myers, and Hulbert. He further told Collins that when Mollye and Hulbert had been living in Mississippi, Hulbert had stolen a car from Mollye's parents along with some guns and other items and fled the state. According to Lee, Hulbert was arrested and returned to Mississippi. Lee stated Hulbert was convicted of the theft and sentenced to Whitfield State Hospital in Jackson, Mississippi, for one year. This information was later confirmed.

Lee said that, after Ken had been at Whitfield for about three weeks, Mollye moved from her residence to Jackson, where the hospital was located, to be near him. A short time later he escaped. Mr. Lee believed Mollye had assisted him in the escape, although he could not prove it. He told Collins that, after the escape, Mollye had sold everything she had and left the state with Hulbert and their son David. He had been trying to find them since then.

He thought there was a warrant out for Mollye's arrest for a narcotics violation of some sort under the last name of Myers, in Jones County, Mississippi. He indicated the arrest had occurred in the town of Laurel, Mississippi. He also told Collins that Mollye had at least two prior arrests for marijuana violations. He believed Mollye and Hulbert had been together for approximately a year and nine months at that time, and at some point during that period they had resided in Nebraska.

Detective Collins called Sheriff Green of Jasper County, Mississippi, where the Whitfield State Hospital was located, to determine if Hulbert was an escapee from the facility. The Sheriff confirmed Hulbert had escaped, and he said he would send all pertinent information on the case along with a request for a "hold" to be placed on Hulbert so they could extradite him for prosecution on their charges at some future time, depending on the results of the criminal cases now pending against him in California.

Collins was unable to confirm Mollye had a warrant out for her arrest in Jones County, or anywhere else, and no further information developed on this issue. It may have been the warrant was maintained only in the local area for a short period of time then retracted, as was sometimes the case in those days before completely automated systems were developed.

Mr. Lee left a telephone number with Collins where he could be reached if more information was needed and said he would be returning to Louisiana very soon. Collins gave him my name as the supervisor in charge of the investigation in case he needed to contact the department again.

The following morning, the third of February, I received a telephone call from Mr. Lee. This would be the first of many calls between the two of us over the next twenty-five years. Mr. Lee expressed his fear over the fact his son was living with Hulbert and his concerns for David's mental and physical health, being raised in that atmosphere. He told me that, prior to Hulbert being in Mollye's life, she had taken her son from Mississippi and that, along with her newest husband at the time, a heroin addict, they had hitchhiked across the country to California. Lee said during this trip they had no place to stay and he was very troubled over his son's safety. He had basically been tracking them trying to keep in contact with him. It was through this effort he had learned of the arrest of Hulbert in the City of Fullerton. I felt an almost immediate bond with, and liking for, Mr. Lee during these conversations. It was obvious to me he was acting out of a genuine compassion and concern for his son, which I shared.

Just from the short contact I'd had with young David I could understand Mr. Lee's anxieties over his son's situation, and I knew they were valid. When I first saw David, he was very thin, extremely pale, and appeared to be ill or suffering from lack of nourishment. He was unusually quiet and clearly fearful of something and seemed to be an unhappy child. I shared Mr. Lee's worries over David's condition and his future.

After speaking with Mr. Lee, over the next couple of days, I was able to confirm with authorities in Louisiana that William David Lee II was well known in his community, and he had a good reputation there. I also continued my conversations with William Lee, and, at some point, in one of the conversations we discussed the possibility of young David being taken back to his family and home in Louisiana, away from the unstable environment he was living in. The more we discovered about the depraved situation in which young David had been living, the more an idea began to form in my mind to find a way for David to be returned to Louisiana to be with his family and, perhaps, live a normal life.

By this time in the investigation, a pregnant Mollye had moved out of the house on Paula Avenue in Fullerton and she, David, and her baby, Unity, were living in an apartment in Anaheim. On my own time, I did some surveillance of the apartment area and was able to determine the route young David would take to and from school. Believing this was the only opportunity for David to ever have a normal childhood, I passed this information on to his father. He called me back in just a few minutes after we spoke and told me he would come to California immediately to get his son. He told me he had already made plans with the authorities in his home state. He had arranged to take David to a court in Louisiana as soon as they arrived home, where he would get temporary custody until a permanent custody ruling could be obtained.

So, on February 8, 1976, I watched the clock and worried about whether Lee would be able to locate his son and get him to go with him. About noon, my phone rang. When I anxiously answered, it was David, who told me he had his son and would soon be boarding their plane for Louisiana. By late that afternoon they were both back in Louisiana, and David's mother, Mollye, had been notified by Mr. Lee he had his son, and he had a temporary custody order issued by the State of Louisiana.

A couple days later I was approached by my boss, Captain Davis, and questioned about the sudden disappearance of young David Lee. Davis said, "DeVore, I just got a call from the District Attorney's Office, and they said that Mollye Hulbert had been to see them. She told them that her son had been abducted by the boy's father and taken to Louisiana, and that you helped him do it. Is that so?"

I avoided answering him directly. Instead, I shook my head and told him Mr. Lee had called me and told me he had his son back in Mississippi with him, but I had taken no "active" part in the process, which I hadn't. "C.D.," as he was commonly known, squinted his eyes and gave me that stern, hard look that pretty much said, "I doubt that," but turned and walked out of my office. I never heard another word about it from him or the Orange County D.A.'s Office. I know C.D. knew what really happened, but he cared more about the boy than whether I had given the father any information, and I know he would have done the same thing if he had been in my place.

Given the fact Mr. Lee had a temporary custody order out of Louisiana for his son, the District Attorney's Office refused to investigate the circumstances. Mr. Lee did officially obtain full custody of his son in Louisiana. Later they would move back to Mississippi to be close to family. Over the years I received many calls from Mr. Lee updating me on the progress young David was making, how he was doing in school, his sports activities, and his general health and happiness. I always felt I had made the right decision and never really regretted it. Sometimes doing the right thing is more important than doing things right. This, in my opinion, was one of those times.

The last conversation I had with Mr. Lee, who also went by the name David, was early in 2005. I remember telling him, "David, if we did something like that now we would both be in prison." He laughed and said, "I know it, brother, I know it." We talked about getting together with our families, maybe in Jackson Hole, Wyoming, the following summer, where he had a second home, but it was never to be.

CHAPTER 15
GROWING UP WITH HULBERT

I HAD BEEN TALKING to David Lee III, the son, about doing this book for several years. He agreed it was a story that needed to be told and that he wanted to be involved in the project. I don't think either of us realized what an emotional roller coaster digging up all these memories would create in his life. I know it was a real struggle for him to sit down and write about a childhood that was so dysfunctional. One he could not get away from, even after moving back to Mississippi to live with his father. Going back thirty years opened old wounds and brought back childhood nightmares for him, and I am grateful to David for what he went through to get his story told.

All that I write about David and his family came from the emails he sent to me over a period of several months in 2008 and 2009. I pieced it together as well as I could, and I hope I have done justice to the words I know came from deep within his being. All of it was reviewed by David before I included it.

From correspondence with David Lee 2008-2009:

Life with Mollye was never what could be described as a normal child-hood, but life with Ken Hulbert was a living hell for a young boy who was subjected to physical and psychological abuse on a pretty regular basis. Years later, the little boy, now a man with a family of his own, would write; "If I could get my hands on him at this moment, I would blow his brains out without one ounce of thought or remorse. To think that people of that kind even exist in the world makes my stomach turn and ask God—Why?

David told me, "My mother and father were divorced when I was about two years old. I remember that they went back and forth in a power struggle over me, and there were a number of legal proceedings that involved my custody and visitation. My mom complained that my father didn't pay the court ordered child-support, and my father claimed that he just wanted to see me. And it was a confusing situation for me. Later in my life, my father showed me the cancelled checks that certainly seemed to indicate that he had been paying the support that he was required to pay and had been trying to do the right thing, but it is difficult to tell for sure. In these kinds of situations there are always two sides to every story. Because of the fact that I was very young at that time, a lot of what was going on is not real clear in my mind. I guess it is always this way for the children of a divorce.

I lived with my mother after the divorce, and she dated a few guys during that time. I remember feeling that I was just a kid in the way and that she loved the 'title of mom' and the child-support checks, but really didn't want the responsibility of being a parent. I remember there were a lot of drugs being done in the home and in my presence. Once, I remember my mom laughingly saying that I could roll the best joint she had ever seen by the time I was four years old. Thinking back on it now as the father of a teenager, I realize that her parenting skills were definitely lacking, and that she had questionable intentions at best.

Anyway, she ended up marrying a man from Laurel, Mississippi, named John, who had recently come back from Vietnam and had an addiction to heroin. He was physically abusive to me, and my mom never did anything to interfere with it. I remember that I was afraid to come out of my room when he was around, and that both were arrested in my presence in Laurel, for drug related charges, but I was too young to really understand the charges or the details. I just recall the fear I felt when they were arrested and taken away. After they were released the three of us hitchhiked to California. This was also a frightening time for me. We would often sleep under a bridge on a piece of cardboard or other makeshift bed in the cold, waiting for someone who would pick us up, then wondering who we were riding with and where we were going, and as a child I didn't understand any of this. Why were we leaving Laurel, or my father or my grandparents? We lived in so many sleazy places and towns that I cannot even recollect the names. At one point we lived in a cheap motel, I believe it was in California someplace, and I was in the elevator when a man tried to molest me. I was barely able to get out of that situation by hitting buttons until the door opened, and I ran. I ran into the man upstairs who was my friend in the complex, so I was able to get away.

At some point, before she met Hulbert, my mom took me to Canada, and we stayed with some people there. Some man, I don't even know his name, called my father and my grandparents in Lafayette, Louisiana, and offered to sell me to them. I don't know or remember the details about this and most of what I am relating about this incident was information given to me by my father, many years later. I do remember my mom picking me up and fleeing to Detroit where her aunt lived. We waited there for my mother's parents to drive up from Mississippi and pick us up and bring us back to live with them in their home in Jones County, Mississippi.

When we were living in Anaheim my mother ended up meeting Ken Hulbert at a nursing home where I believe they both worked. They got together and began seeing each other behind her husband's back, and after a while my mother divorced John and moved in with Hulbert. The three of us went back to Mississippi and we ended up moving in with my grandparents. They were against her bringing Hulbert home with her, but my mother told them this was the only way they were going to see me, so eventually they gave in and let us come.

We lived with my grandparents in Jones County, Mississippi, for a while, I don't know exactly how long. During the time we lived there, over the summer of 1974, there was a murder of a young lady named Beverly Ann Moore. It was suspected that she had been raped and strangled, but the absolute cause of death was never confirmed. She had last been seen talking to a man in a Volkswagen, described in court proceedings in August of 1976 as being bright orange in color. The man matched the description of Ken Hulbert. Hulbert, at that time, had been driving a bright yellow Volkswagen that belonged to my mom. Shortly after the incident, her [Beverly Moore's] decomposed body was discovered in a wooded area along the Leaf River. In fact, it was on June 16, 1974.

Hulbert stole several guns and weapons from my grandfather, then stole a car and fled the area. As I recall, he was caught either in Indiana or in Illinois. In any event, he was extradited back to Mississippi and was convicted of the theft crimes but sent to Whitfield Hospital for the insane in Jackson, Mississippi, instead of to prison. I never knew exactly why. He was never formally charged with the Moore murder.

In February 1976, only a month after Hulbert was arrested in California, a Jones County, Mississippi Judicial District grand jury indicted Teddy Andrews for the murder of Beverly Ann Moore. He was tried for her murder, but subsequently acquitted of the crime. After Hulbert was sent to Whitfield, my mother took me and moved to Jackson to be near him. While there, and despite his stealing from her father, she aided him in escaping from custody. After he escaped, we all fled the area, hitchhiking back to California by a very circuitous route that went through Mexico, the State of New Mexico, eventually into Salt Lake City, Utah, and on into California. Along the way we lived in Nebraska for several months, but I don't have any real memories of that time other than what I am telling you. Later, when I was an adult, my mother told me at least three separate times that she believed that Hulbert was responsible for the death of this young woman in Mississippi.[1]

---

1. Investigators from the Jasper County Sheriff's Office came to Fullerton after Hulbert was arrested in January of 1976 and reviewed all the California cases with Detective Schauperl and other investigators. Detective Schauperl recalls that, after hearing the facts of the California cases, the detectives were convinced Hulbert was probably responsible for the death of Beverly Ann Moore. Due to the advanced decomposition of the body, Jones County officials were never able

I don't have any real facts or first-hand information about the crimes that Hulbert was involved in when we were in Orange County. I do remember living in a motel in California and I believe this is when the heat was getting turned up by the police. It was during this time [I was around six years old] that my mom and Hulbert would leave me alone to watch the newborn baby, Unity, sometimes for as long as two days at a time. Hulbert held me totally responsible for her care, including feeding her, bathing her, and changing her diapers. At that time there were no such thing as disposable diapers and all I was provided with were cloth diapers and safety pins. There were times when I had accidentally stuck her with the pins while trying to change her diapers because I just didn't know any better. Hulbert used to beat me with a belt whenever this happened and wouldn't stop until I had soiled myself. Apparently, he would then think that was enough and he would stop. I was terrified during these times they were gone, and I had no idea when they would return or what kind of mood Hulbert would be in when they did. I never knew what they were doing while they were gone. They would usually leave very little food in the apartment, and I would have to eat what I could find.

I was physically and mentally abused by this man daily. I was forced to watch numerous sexual acts between my mother and Hulbert. This happened on many occasions, and he seemed to get some sort of sick satisfaction from it. I remember one of his favorite sayings to me was that he knew I was a 'horny little bastard' and that I wanted to 'f---' my mom and that 'I should watch this, and I will show you how it's done.' My mom did nothing to stop this abuse.

I spent a lot of time alone because we had never lived in any one place long enough to make friends. I can remember many times when I

---

to file the case. We were told they were even able to put Hulbert with Moore at a restaurant in the area, but had no evidence to connect him to the crime. The investigator I talked to in 2005 did not seem to have the background information on the case and didn't seem to know that investigators had come to Fullerton in 1976. They had some latent prints, and copies of these were sent to Fullerton police on August 10, 1976, by Detective Shoemake of Jones County. The prints they had were not those of Ken Hulbert.

used to walk and collect soda bottles in a grocery cart and then turn them in at the 7-Eleven for the two cents deposit that you could get for each bottle. I would use the money so I could have something to eat. Often that consisted of some candy and a soft drink. Sometimes that was the only food I would get for the day. Whenever Hulbert found out I had done this I would get another beating from him.

During this period, I remember a day when I was picked up at school and taken out of class by the police and brought to the police station because my mom was there. The officers were kind to me and even got me some snacks to eat when we got to the Fullerton Police Department. I later found out that that was the day they arrested Hulbert for kidnapping, robbery, rape, and murder. At the time I did not know that.

One day I remember very well, and that was February 8, 1976. Hulbert was in police custody, and we had moved out of the house in Fullerton to an apartment in Anaheim. My mom had just enrolled me in school there, and I would walk to class when I went, which wasn't every school day. When I woke up that morning my mother sent me with two dollars to the store to get quarters for her to wash clothes. As I was walking into the store, I heard someone call my name, and I turned around and it was my father and my grandfather standing there. I was shocked to see them in California. They approached me and my father asked me if I would like to go back to Louisiana with him and my grandfather. I told them that I would, but that I would have to stop and give my mom her money back so she would not be mad. My pop (grandfather) told me not to worry about that because he would give her the money back, so I agreed, and I got into the car with them. The next thing I knew is that I was at the Los Angeles International Airport with my dad and my grandfather. I remember my father making a call at a pay phone at the airport, and I heard him say, 'Lee, I've got him, and we're gone.'

For the first time in my childhood, I began to live a normal life with my father in New Orleans, Louisiana. This new life began on February 8, 1976, the day my father found me in Anaheim, California, and took me with him to New Orleans. [I was still six years old.] We lived there only a short time before we moved to Lafayette, Louisiana, so that while I was still a young person I could be around my grandparents and my uncles and aunts. My father wanted me to have as normal a childhood with my extended family as was possible. My father was my hero, and I really miss him.

We lived for a while with my grandfather and grandmother, Pop and Lou. My dad's sisters, Mary Smith and Diana Gesser and their husbands Dennis Smith and Byron Gesser, lived in the area and played huge parts in raising me both morally and financially.

My dad enrolled me in Woodvale Elementary School in Lafayette in the second grade. Even though I hadn't been to school much when living with my mother, because of our transient lifestyle and a lack of concern for that aspect of my life, I did well in school. I was instructed by my father that in the event my mother showed up at the school, I was to run and hide and tell my teacher what was happening. Two years later I had to do exactly that when my mother showed up at the school with a male companion and wanted me to go with her. I ran and hid and told my teacher what was going on, just as my father had told me to do. My dad was personal friends with the sheriff of Lafayette Parish, Carlo Listi, and the sheriff was notified by my dad of what was occurring. Deputies responded immediately to the school and were able to pick up my mother and her companion. I recall that my mother had been armed at the time, but I don't remember all the details. The two were released, after I was safely at home, and were told not to return to Lafayette Parish or they would be incarcerated.

I ended up transferring to Hamilton Lab School on the campus of the University of Southwestern Louisiana. As I was completing the fifth grade my grandparents (on my dad's side), Bill and Louise Lee built a home out by the country club in Oakburne and when we moved there, I started attending the Catholic School at St. Genevieve and completed the sixth grade there. I attended middle school at Father Teurlings. After I graduated from the eighth grade at Father Teurlings my father built a new home at #12 Pebblestone Drive and I transferred to the newly built Saint Thomas More Catholic High School and began the ninth grade there in the fall of 1982. I played football and golf in high school and was a three-year letterman in both sports. My father had played college ball at the University of Southern Mississippi in Hattiesburg, Mississippi, and then played semi-pro ball in Louisiana. I remember my mother's father telling me one time that my father was one tough customer on the field. I really think my dad wanted the same for me because he was hell on me when I played ball. These were very happy years for me, living with my father and my grandparents in Louisiana.

When I played football I played offensive tackle, and I have some wonderful memories of those times. My best game was as a junior when we played Teurlings. I played against my old buddies from the sixth, seventh and eighth grade. They 'onside' kicked the initial kick-off, a little trick play, but I was able to recover the ball. They scored first, but then we scored in the second quarter to go in at half time tied at seven. I remember that my father, Lou and Pop attended. We got the ball after a stop by our defense with about nine minutes left in the third quarter and then I went to work, and I mean, work! The coaches told us at half time that they were going to run my butt off during the entire second half, and that they did. I was the only underclassman starting on the offensive line. I was playing against two old friends, Kelli Bellot and Steven Lotief, known as the 'tank' because of his size and strength. We drove the ball down their throats and scored at the end of the third to go ahead fourteen to seven. Then we got another stop on defense and took over at our thirty-yard line. We scored again with only four minutes to go, and the score held at twenty-one to seven. This was one of the happiest nights of my life; tired, bleeding and scarred as I was. My Pop told me that this was the most dominant performance he had ever seen by an offensive tackle. Both Kelli and Tank called me the next morning and said they had never been held, leg-whipped, clipped and beat up on at any time in any game more than what I did to them. Kelli called it 'four quarters of pure punishment'. He still talks about it to this day.

The crazy part of all of that was that golf was really my game. I won two club championships as a teen. My father used to bring me into the betting on our team from time to time. One of the biggest *arguments we ever had was during one of these matches. We played like bums on the front half, and we were down four holes in match-play at the turn. My dad told me to 'step it up' because I had only shot 32 on the back... 5 birdies... 3 pars... and 1 bogey. We went to the 18th hole tied, and I hit my tee shot on top of a hill and was stymied. It was here where the argument took place. My dad told me to punch out of the fairway and get up and down for par so we could at least tie. I told him I saw a shot, and he was furious because I told him I wasn't playing for a damn tie and he said, 'it was his money that I was about to blow.' Anyway, here we go: An uphill stance and 170 yards to the pin and a 3-foot window through the trees. I grabbed my 7 iron out of my bag, and he went nuts. When I hit the ball, it cleared the trees and he started yelling, go in the hole, you bitch. I stuck it 2 feet from the cup, tapped in for my birdie, and collected my thousand dollars and went to party with my friends. He just shook his head and laughed. He was a winner, and proud of me, and that is all that mattered to me.*

As you know, Lee, I miss my father terribly. He passed away in August of 2005 from cancer at only sixty-one years of age. That time in my life was the best and made all the others seem like a far-off dream or belonging to someone else. My father was my inspiration, and I can only hope that he knows how much I loved him and miss him each day. I will write more tomorrow. I am having trouble with the tears tonight.

I have four half siblings. The youngest is a good kid and I would like to leave her totally out of this. She is not Hulbert's child. The other three are fair game as much as I hate to say it. The baby that was around at the time of the arrest is Unity. She is autistic and was born out of wedlock. I think she now lives in North Carolina, at least as far as I know. The other two are the twins, Kenneth, and Kati. Kenneth is in prison in North Carolina serving a stretch for rape. He was charged with the crime in Boone, North Carolina. Kati has three children I believe and resides in New Orleans. She has been married and divorced twice. Both girls began stripping when they were young and ended up in New Orleans because, as they put it, 'the money was so good.'

Kenneth is a career criminal, just as I predicted he would be when he was young. I remember that he was stealing when he was seven years old. He stole a handgun from Wal-Mart at around the age of ten in Meridian, Mississippi. I could never figure out how he got it from out of a secure counter and out of the store. My mom had called me on that one and asked me for help and I went to Meridian and made him bring it back into the store and return it to the manager and tell him what he had done. My mom got mad at me because she said that I had embarrassed him in public. He was always her pet and could get away with anything. I believe she felt partial to him because of his dad and always put him ahead of all her other children.

I, on the other hand, was always at the bottom of the totem-pole because I was raised by my father and as she said, 'privileged when the other two were not.' My mother and I are not close at all. The last time I heard from her she was in Asheville, North Carolina, sleeping in a tent and trying to get money. I told her to hit up the Mormon Church because she always received support from them. The bishop called me and asked me for money to help her, but I declined because I have a son to support."

Well, my friend, I can't sleep. It is four-ten in the morning, and I will write some more...[2]

I will get back to Dad a little later, but I wanted to tell you about the biggest mistake I ever made in my life. It was right after graduation from STM [High School]. My friends (Patrick Mouton, Jack Buckner and the mayor's son, Klark Bowen), and I went on our senior trip to Destin, Florida for a week of fun and festivities. We stayed at the Sandestin Resort and had a great time. We partied and did all kinds of things that were trouble and that I should not have participated in, but youngsters will be stupid and ignorant, and we were.

I came back from Florida and did something very stupid, and it altered my life in a bad way. Two things happened. First, I wanted to attend LSU in Baton Rouge, but my dad wanted me to attend USL in Lafayette to adjust to college. He wanted me to do this for just one semester and then if I did well and got good grades, he would send me

---

2. From this footnote to the end of the chapter, everything is taken from the last email I ever received from David Lee.

to LSU. At the time I was also considering "walking on" the football team at the University of Southern Miss, where my dad had played. My dad was not in favor of this as the campus was only forty-five minutes away from my mother's parent's home, and he could not stomach that.

Instead of listening to my dad, I got pissed off about the LSU proposition, which was stupid on my part--to the max. Then about that same time, my dad's mom, Lou, caught me smoking cigarettes and 'threw a fit' and told my dad. My dad said that smoking would not be permitted. I totally over-reacted to these events, and ended up calling my mother's parents in Heidelberg, Mississippi, and asked them to come and pick me up. I couldn't face my father, so I left in the middle of the night with them, like a coward. So it was that I went to Mississippi and lived with my grandparents on my mom's side. My father was very angry, but more than that, was very hurt by what I had done.

About two weeks after I had moved in, my mother came to stay there also. What a nightmare that was. She only came because my grandmother told her to, and I despised her every thought, move, idea and presence. We were never close, not even one little bit, and all I wanted was a mom. She told me that she did not approve of me because I reminded her of my father. Living with her was terrible. One day she got mad at me and tried to assault me on the porch with a pool cue. She swung at me, and I grabbed it, took it away, and informed her that she had made a grave mistake, and that I was going to shove it up her butt.

Part of the reason I went to Mississippi was that my grandmother had 'baited me' with the promise of putting me through college at the University of Southern Mississippi, but this never happened. I ended up at Jones County Junior College in Ellisville, Mississippi. What a dump! It wasn't too bad, but it certainly was not a Division One school like I would have had the chance to attend in Lafayette. I had to have a grant to attend. It was an embarrassing time.

While attending Jones County Junior College I met a girl by the name of Tammy Hays, and she became my first wife when I was nineteen years old. My dad and his family desperately tried to talk me out of this marriage. Obviously, I should have listened to them. The marriage did not last even for one year.

Well, after being married at a young age and divorced at a very young age, I continued to live in Mississippi. I dated lots of different girls. The crazy part of all this is that while I was dating other women I was in love with a young girl from Mississippi. She was 2 years younger than me, and we used to spend lots of time together. There was only one problem... she was married. I knew that she loved me too, and this was brought to light several years later. At the time, I was the 'bad boy of Heidelberg' and her grandmother didn't want her to have anything to do with me. You see, I was different from any person these folks had ever meet. I was young, brash, and cocky and probably the worst thing was that I was a Cajun and to a redneck, that is a total taboo.

It was while I was living in Mississippi that I began receiving threatening letters from [Ken] Hulbert, to which I responded in a very vicious fashion. I probably shouldn't have reacted that way, but what was I supposed to do with a psycho who said, 'he wished I was in jail with him so he could f--- me in the a--s until my eyeballs popped out of my head.' I later reported this to the warden at Soledad Prison in California. The warden told me that it was Hulbert who was being gang-raped repeatedly and that this had been going on since his initial incarceration. I made a point of letting Hulbert know that I was aware of this. If I had been smart, I would never have communicated back to him at all, and I could have achieved an immediate end to all of that, but unfortunately, I responded.

I was also told by the warden that they had caught Hulbert walking out of the front gate of the prison in civilian clothes and that they found out that the clothes had been smuggled in by a visitor. I was advised at this time that if I ever saw him in the area to shoot him dead and ask questions later. I took this advice to heart.

Hulbert had told me several times that he had a buddy who was getting out and he was going to be paying me a visit. I also spoke with the warden about this threat. He told me that occasionally when an inmate is paroled, he will make a promise to another inmate such as

Hulbert was insinuating, but that they rarely carried out the plan. The warden warned me to be as cautious as I could be.

At that point, I had no idea of what Hulbert might be capable of, after being caught walking out of Soledad in civilian clothes. That was a point in my life where I constantly looked over my shoulder. I continued this until you, Mr. DeVore, confirmed his death. Before that I lived many years of uncertainty, not knowing if he might one day show up.

They said his death was suicide, but I doubt it very much. At least he has gone away from this earth. I have often wondered if he ever made peace with the Good Lord himself, and whether he ended up in heaven or was damned to hell for all of eternity. What do you think happened to this 'monster?' This may sound crazy, but I hope that he is in a happy place. Just because he committed those terrible crimes, I hope that he asked for forgiveness as it says in the Bible.

I did not always feel that way, but as I grew older, I realized that if you have no forgiveness in your heart that you yourself can never be forgiven for your sins, mistakes, and shortcomings. Obviously, I do not condone anything he did and never would.

I have often thought it would be 'sweet just ice' for Dad to get a crack at him in heaven. That may sound selfish and sick, but Dad always wanted a piece of him and if he had a shot, he would hurt him badly. I know this. I know that if anyone ever treated my son in the ways he treated me, I would have to settle it once and for all, good, bad, or indifferent. Does that sound wrong, Lee [DeVore]? Am I a bad man, father, son, or person for feeling this way? Sometimes I do not know, so that is why I ask an elder of mine who has always put me first and always told me the truth and provided me with sound advice. How do you feel, Lee? What if it had been your child?

I'm getting tired... will continue soon... next day or so."

Sincerely,

David Lee

I believe it was only normal for him to feel the way he did

about Hulbert after what he had been through. This was the last time I would hear from David.

Final Thoughts

On March 31, 1993, I was informed by prison officials at Folsom that Ken Richard Hulbert had committed suicide a day earlier in his jail cell, by wrapping an electrical cord around his neck and plugging it into a wall socket. He was found by prison guards at approximately twelve-forty in the afternoon and was pronounced dead shortly after that. Hulbert was twenty-seven years old when he was first sentenced to prison on the Fullerton cases. He was forty-one years old at the time of his death. His body was sent to the North Sacramento Funeral Home and the remains were apparently claimed by his daughter, Unity Hulbert, of Mesa, Arizona, on April 10, 1993.

A few days later I received a telephone call from David's father, William David Lee. He wanted to confirm Hulbert was actually dead and the "nightmare" was finally ending for his son. He said David wouldn't believe it until I personally confirmed the death. He told me then his son had always feared Hulbert would get out of prison, somehow, and come back for him. He said Hulbert had written David from prison on several occasions threatening to do just that.

Death Certificate for Hulbert

I last spoke to David Lee, the son, in early October of 2009, to review some of the emails he had sent me. I could tell he was discouraged due to difficulty finding employment in a recessionary economy. I talked to him at length that day and by the time we finished talking, he seemed to be feeling much better. I was saddened to receive a telephone call from his son, William David Lee IV, on Sunday, October 18, 2009, informing me his father had taken his own life on Sunday, October 11, 2009, at the age of forty-one, at his home in Heidelberg, Mississippi. His son told me David had been despondent over a breakup with a girlfriend and his continuing problems finding employment.

I will always remember David as he was when I first met him on January 30, 1976, a scared little boy sitting on the porch of the Police Department in Fullerton California. He had been waiting for his mother, alone, after the arrest of Ken Hulbert for murder. I can't help but wonder how much his childhood with Hulbert and Mollye ultimately impacted his life, and his death at such an early age. It is ironic he died at the age of forty-one, and by his own hand, just as Hulbert had.

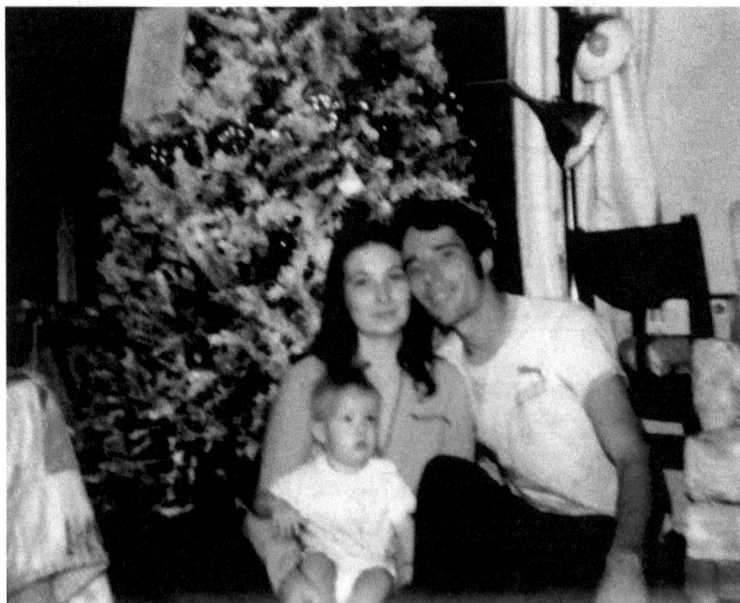

Ken Hulbert, Mollye Selfies, young David before the arrest

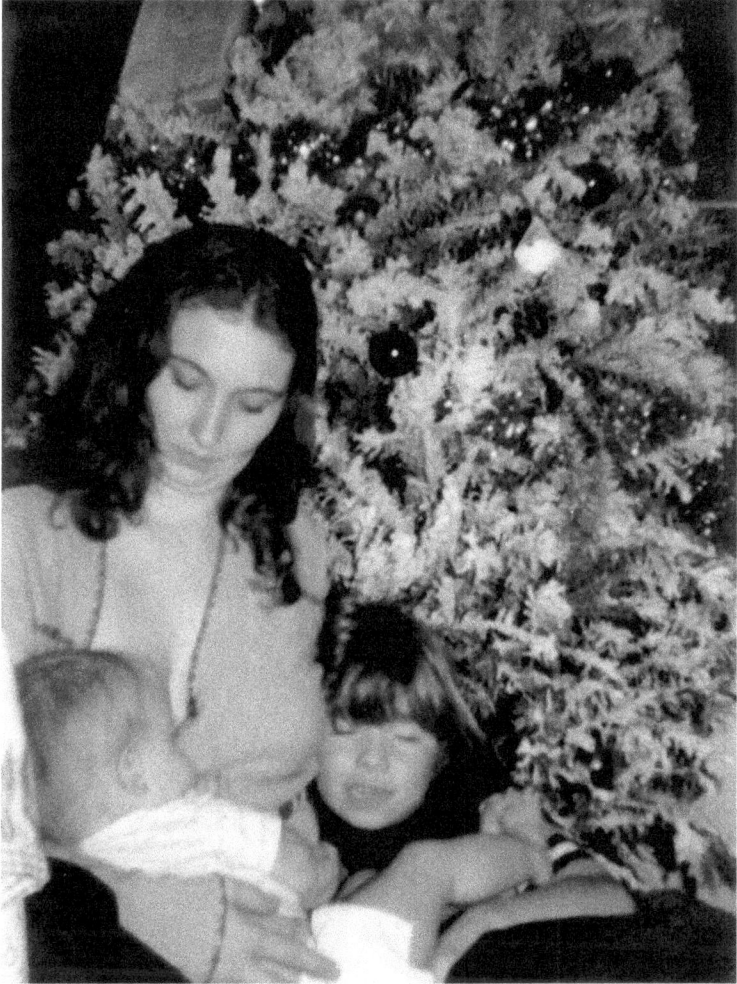

AFTERWORD

Many years ago when I was transferred to the detective bureau to supervise the Crimes Person Detail, which included homicides, I was told by a seasoned homicide investigator that working a homicide was different than working any other crime as the victim could not tell their story, and it therefore became the obligation of the investigator to be the voice of the victim and to find justice for them and their loved ones. I tried never to forget that when working a homicide, and it was certainly the mantra that guided Detective Leon Schauperl and all of us who worked with him on this particular case.

Another thing I learned from that seasoned homicide investigator was that just because it is 5: 00pm and quitting time for the detectives, you don't stop investigating a case. When working a homicide your regular schedule is set aside and you continue to work until there are no more immediate leads to follow. I can remember when we worked 36 hours or more in a row before we took a break from an investigation. Many cases involve being called out in the middle of the night and on weekends, and it didn't matter if it was a family member's birthday, a major holiday, or whatever you had planned for the weekend, you dropped everything and responded to work the case.

The Parking Lot Rapist case was one of those where all the police officers, after finding Gina Marie Tisher murdered and left in an apartment complex garage, were determined to solve the crime, and bring justice for Gina, her family, and friends. Over the course of the investigation, we met the family members and stayed in touch with them when there was anything new on the case. We never forgot how their lives were changed because of this senseless crime.

We were determined to solve this case and try to prevent another victim from being terrorized, raped, and killed as Gina had been. Unfortunately, the next victim came only a few days after Gina Tisher's body was found. This discovery led us to expand the investigation with the help of the media and all the law enforcement agencies in Orange and Los Angeles Counties.

While I have been involved in several murder investigations, this is one I could never forget for the violence and complete disregard for the lives of these young women, the lack of remorse shown by the perpetrator, and for the number of victims and the impact on their families and friends. But, in this case, I also formed an emotional bond with young David Lee, who through no fault of his own had been forced to live with Hulbert. I also formed a close bond with his father, David Lee Senior, who I stayed in touch with for many years until his death from cancer in the late 1990s. As detailed in the book, David Lee Junior never really got over his experiences and the abuse he suffered, and at the age of 41, committed suicide in Louisiana. I deeply regret I did not see the signs from David Junior during the time he was struggling and therefore did nothing to try to prevent it.

I will always be grateful for all the police officers, the many agencies, the media, and the private citizens who were involved in the successful conclusion of this case. I am also grateful for the fact we were able to tell Gina's story for her and in one sense for all those victims of these vicious crimes, including young David Lee Junior.

Lee DeVore
   Twin Falls, Idaho
   June 26, 2023

ACKNOWLEDGMENTS

Detective Leon Schauperl in Uniform Circa 1970

Much of what you have read in this book comes from the actual police reports, newspaper accounts, and court documents that were all maintained by the Fullerton Police Department in the murder book for this case, from the memories and documentation provided by retired Homicide Detective Leon Schauperl, and from my own personal recollections.

In addition to these sources, I received invaluable assistance from Leon's wife Sharon, who edited the complete manuscript, made notes by hand, and mailed it all back to me as she proceeded. Also, Sharon provided information I had forgotten or never knew and sent me photographs, newspaper articles, and other information I used in the writing of this book.

I would also like to acknowledge the help provided by my son, Bryan DeVore, an educator with incredible computer skills. I can't even remember the number of times he had to fix my computer, or maybe I should say, fix what I had messed up on my computer. I know these things are second nature to the younger generations but, in my day, the ultimate in word processing was an IBM Selectric Typewriter. For the first 25 years of my police experience, my reports were either dictated to some very amazing secretaries, put on tape recorders, and given to them to work on later, or handwritten. Without Bryan I might still be looking for missing stuff.

I am also very grateful to my daughter, Wendy DeVore Taylor, who holds a master's degree in fine art, for her hard work editing this manuscript over many months and making sure my use of the English language, sentence structure, and the organization of the material all made sense. I was amazed at how much better it all looked after her detailed work. This book would not have been completed without her help.

I would also like to thank the Fullerton Police Department for graciously allowing me access to their files, allocating the time to interview some of the officers involved in the case, and for the 30 years plus I was allowed to work for this honorable and professional law enforcement organization.

Finally, I want to thank my beautiful wife, Barbara, for all her encouragement, reading of manuscript drafts, suggestions, and in helping me recall various aspects of the case. I also want to thank her for staying with me through all the years of being gone for days at a time working cases and leaving the important job of running our family to her during these times.

This book is dedicated to the memory of David Lee III, who lived with Hulbert during most of the events in this book. It is difficult to imagine what horrors he went through. And to Detective Leon Schauperl, an outstanding and dedicated homicide investigator with an amazing ability to interview, investigate, and solve major cases, who passed away on August 21, 2019.

Lee DeVore
Twin Falls, Idaho
February 2024

ABOUT THE AUTHOR

Lee DeVore was hired by the Fullerton Police Department as a police officer in October of 1963. During his tenure for 30-plus years, Lee worked in all areas of the Department, but most of his career was spent in the Detective Division as an investigator, a supervisor, Detective Lieutenant, then the captain of the division. During his career at Fullerton, the author was instrumental, along with others, in writing and administering a program known as "Operation Cleanup," which launched "community based" rather than "incident-driven" policing. This program was active in Fullerton for many years. It was recognized by the State of California and honored as the Community Policing Program of the year in the 1990s. Lee wrote several articles for law enforcement magazines and publications on this program and other police-related subjects. Lee DeVore is a graduate of the California State University in Long Beach with a Bachelor's degree in public administration and has a Master of Arts degree from Redlands University in Redlands, California.

Lee retired from the Fullerton Police Department in December of 1994 and accepted a position as the Chief of Police with the Police Department in Twin Falls, Idaho in August of 1995. Lee spent the next 10 years as the Chief of Police in Twin Falls, and retired in August of 2005. During his tenure in Twin Falls, Lee was the President of the Idaho Chiefs of Police Association, the Chairman of the Idaho Peace Officers Standards and Training Commission, and an Executive Council member for the Western Regional Institute for Community Oriented Public Safety out of Washington state.

Lee and his wife Barbara live in Twin Falls, Idaho and enjoy spending time with their children, grandchildren, and five great grandchildren, and being active in their community.

www.ingramcontent.com/pod-product-compliance
Lightning Source LLC
Chambersburg PA
CBHW062121020426
42335CB00013B/1046